Accession no.
36132372

D1578863

Harmony for Computer Musicians

Michael Hewitt

Course Technology PTR

A part of Cengage Learning

LIS - LIBRARY

Date	Fund
24.5.2011	781.34 pt HEW

Order No.
0 2217727

University of Chester

COURSE TECHNOLOGY
CENGAGE Learning· 36132372

Australia • Brazil • Japan • Korea • Mexico • Singapore • Spain • United Kingdom • United States

COURSE TECHNOLOGY
CENGAGE Learning

Harmony for Computer Musicians

Michael Hewitt

Publisher and General Manager, Course
  Technology PTR: Stacy L. Hiquet

Associate Director of Marketing: Sarah Panella

Manager of Editorial Services: Heather Talbot

Marketing Manager: Mark Hughes

Executive Editor: Mark Garvey

Project Editor/Copy Editor: Cathleen D. Small

Interior Layout Tech: MPS Limited,
  A Macmillan Company

Cover Designer: Luke Fletcher

CD-ROM Producer: Brandon Penticuff

Indexer: Sharon Hilgenberg

Proofreader: Geary Yelton

© 2011 Michael Hewitt.

ALL RIGHTS RESERVED. No part of this work covered by the copyright herein may be reproduced, transmitted, stored, or used in any form or by any means graphic, electronic, or mechanical, including but not limited to photocopying, recording, scanning, digitizing, taping, Web distribution, information networks, or information storage and retrieval systems, except as permitted under Section 107 or 108 of the 1976 United States Copyright Act, without the prior written permission of the publisher.

For product information and technology assistance, contact us at
Cengage Learning Customer & Sales Support, 1-800-354-9706

For permission to use material from this text or product,
submit all requests online at **cengage.com/permissions**

Further permissions questions can be emailed to
permissionrequest@cengage.com

All trademarks are the property of their respective owners.

All images © Michael Hewitt unless otherwise noted.

Library of Congress Control Number: 2010922090

ISBN-13: 978-1-4354-5672-3
ISBN-10: 1-4354-5672-6

Course Technology, a part of Cengage Learning
20 Channel Center Street
Boston, MA 02210
USA

Cengage Learning is a leading provider of customized learning solutions with office locations around the globe, including Singapore, the United Kingdom, Australia, Mexico, Brazil, and Japan. Locate your local office at: **international.cengage.com/region**

Cengage Learning products are represented in
Canada by Nelson Education, Ltd.

For your lifelong learning solutions, visit **courseptr.com**

Visit our corporate website at **cengage.com**

www.cengage.co.uk

Printed in the United States of America
1 2 3 4 5 6 7 12 11 10

This book is dedicated to Coleg Harlech WEA—may it long continue to provide vital adult education.

Acknowledgments

Thanks are due to Mark Garvey for commissioning this book and to Cathleen Small for her excellent development editing.

About the Author

Dr. Michael Hewitt was born in South Wales in the United Kingdom. He earned his bachelor of music degree at London University and a master's degree and doctorate at the University of North Wales, Bangor, where he specialized in musical composition. He is a classically trained musician, composer, lecturer, and author on musical subjects. He also writes classical scores as well as soundtracks for various television productions both at home and abroad. He is currently working as a music technology tutor at Coleg Harlech in North Wales.

Contents

Chapter 5
Voicing the Common Triad and Its Inversions   49

Chapter 6
Tonic and Dominant Harmony   59

Chapter 7
The Three Primary Triads   71

Chapter 8
Secondary Triads   89

Chapter 9
Repetition, Arpeggiation, and Melodic Decoration   109

Chapter 10
The Chord of the Dominant Seventh   129

Chapter 11
Secondary Seventh Chords   137

Chapter 12
Seventh Chord Harmony in the Major Key   147

Chapter 13
Seventh Chord Harmony in the Minor Key   161

Chapter 14
Modulation   173

Chapter 15
Suspended and Added Note Chords   189

Chapter 16
Chords of the Ninth

203

Chapter 17
Chords of the Eleventh

215

Chapter 18
Thirteenth Chords

225

Chapter 19
Modal Interchange

231

Chapter 20
Secondary Dominant Chords

239

Introduction

The rapid development of musical technology over the latter part of the last century led to significant changes in the musical production environment. Some of the main changes were largely due to the increased accessibility of the means of musical production. The development of affordable hardware synthesizers and samplers gave many aspiring music producers and composers immediate access to an infinite variety of both realistic and highly imaginative electronic sounds. The spectrum of available sounds included different types of drum kit and percussion sounds; orchestral sounds, such as string, brass, and woodwind instruments; and a whole host of original and often very colorful electronic timbres. And this comparatively new resource has proved itself over the years to be an invaluable and exciting facility for those engaged in the occupation of composing and producing their own music.

Yet this is not all. Over the last 10 years or so, there has been an increasing trend toward the development of software emulations of such hardware devices, many of which could be obtained at a fraction of the cost of the original device. Taking advantage of Steinberg's Virtual Studio Technology (VST) interface, a good example is the Korg Legacy collection, which features software versions of Korg's classic Wavestation and M1 Synthesizers. Other notable examples are the availability of software emulations of Roland's TB-303 and TB-808 and Sequential Circuit's Prophet-5. Add to this the advancing development of VST effects plug-ins, such as compressors, reverb, delay, and so on, and it means that home music producers can now gain access to a large rack of synthesizers, samplers, and FX devices on their computer that had previously only been available in expensive hardware forms.

One of the remarkable features of all of this is the relative affordability of the setup. Due to this affordability, the means of producing high-quality and professional-sounding music tracks has now been placed into the price range of the ordinary person. So it perhaps comes as no surprise to see that as a result of this, the number of people involved in the music production community has surged considerably. Indeed, there are now many thousands of people worldwide who are producing their own music on their home computer. As a direct result of this, there is now a new type of musician in the world—a type of musician that may even outnumber all other types of musicians. This is the *computer musician*—that is to say, a person who uses his own home computer as a musical instrument and production device.

The computer musician is a rather unique animal. I teach such musicians in a full-time music production course. And in my experience, although computer musicians often show a high degree of skill and expertise in terms of the technology they use to produce their music, many mistakenly assume that this is all they need to be able to produce the kinds of tracks they hear on the radio or dubbed on films or television programs. And in some ways this assumption may bear out. The computer musician does indeed have all of the tools necessary to create beautiful and professional-sounding tracks. Yet there is often a vital ingredient missing: a working knowledge of the way in which music as a language actually works—what its ingredients are, how it is put together, and what scales, chords, modes, keys, the principles of arrangement, melody, harmony, and so on are. In other words, computer musicians may have learned how to use their instruments, but this does not necessarily mean that they know how to properly create professional-sounding music using those instruments. To create effectively using those instruments, computer musicians also require an in-depth knowledge of the musical language.

However, there is a basic problem here. Because the computer musician is relatively new on the music scene, there is a distinct lack of materials that provide the vital musical learning that computer musicians so desperately need. Instead, it is generally assumed that computer musicians should adapt to those classical methods of musical training ordinarily used in our schools and universities. And because such courses of study often take many years to accomplish and are often preceded by a good few years of specialized musical training in childhood, this means that computer musicians are thus faced with a huge hurdle to overcome in order to acquire the essential musical learning and training that they need.

It is for this very reason that I began writing a series of books for computer musicians, of which this particular volume is the third. Rather than assuming that computer musicians should adapt themselves to classical methods of musical training, the premise of these books is that the musical training should be adapted for computer musicians. This means that the materials need to be presented in formats that are familiar to them. So rather than presenting the learning in a conventional score format, most of the materials are presented in the familiar piano roll format of computer music sequencing programs.

So what types of musical training do computer musicians need? First of all, they must be thoroughly familiar with rhythm, tempo, meter, time signatures, keys, intervals, scales, and modes, for the simple reason that these are the basic ABCs of the musical language through which computer musicians are trying to communicate.[1] Computer musicians also need to learn how to use these materials in order to put their tracks together. This necessitates the learning of particular skills, such as writing drum tracks, composing

---

[1] To provide for this need, I produced the first book of this series, *Music Theory for Computer Musicians* (Course Technology PTR, 2008).

effective bass lines, creating beautiful melodic leads, and putting music into a clear and effective structural format.[2]

As composers of their own music, computer musicians also need to learn how to write for what is in effect an ensemble of many different instruments working together. This includes bass instruments, lead instruments, vocals, properly tuned samples, harmony instruments, pads, strings, and so on. To be able to do this effectively, computer musicians require a good working knowledge of musical harmony. That is the knowledge that enables musicians to write their parts in a harmonious and effective fashion. And this again is where a problem lies. To be able to write effectively for, say, a symphony orchestra, classical composers will spend a good few years studying the principles of musical harmony. And as a result of this study, they will then be able to put together their music with fluency and ease. Yet for computer musicians who do not read music in a conventional sense, there are scant materials available to them through which they can learn these arts of musical harmony. And because these arts are an indispensible part of the tools of professional composers, computer musicians are once again operating at a disadvantage in the marketplace.

I wrote this book to help further computer musicians' knowledge of musical harmony—knowledge that is absolutely essential for the skilled creation of complex musical works. However, although this book provides the essential learning that is required, it is not enough to simply read this book or indeed any other book on musical harmony. To properly learn the skills of musical harmony, computer musicians must spend time away from the composition of their own tracks and must practice the arts of harmony as an independent pursuit. This, I suppose, is rather like the way in which runners will spend time away from the track doing weight training in order to increase their muscle power! The result is a massive improvement in their performances on the track.

Similarly, computer musicians need to practice numerous exercises that not only will help teach them the principles of musical harmony, but also will enable them to acquire the skills necessary to apply them to their own tracks. For computer musicians to be able to do this, I have provided a PDF file on the CD that contains numerous short exercises. Successfully completing these will considerably improve computer musicians' skills with regard to the art of musical harmony. Each exercise is also provided in the form of a MIDI file that may be imported conveniently into whatever sequencing program the computer musician uses. In this way, computer musicians can then complete the exercises and hear firsthand the results of their efforts. To open the exercises, follow these instructions:

1.   Open your sequencer (Logic, Reason, Cubase, SONAR, Ableton Live, or whatever).

---

[2] To provide for these needs, I wrote the second book of this series, *Composition for Computer Musicians* (Course Technology PTR, 2009).

2.   Go to File > Import > MIDI file.

3.   Select the CD drive into which the CD has been placed. There you will see a list of all of the MIDI files. Select the required exercise number.

4.   Once the MIDI file has been loaded into your sequencer, bear in mind that you will not get any sound until you associate the file with a sound-producing device. To do so, you need to select a suitable instrument patch for that channel in order to be able to play the file. Unless otherwise indicated, an acoustic piano patch will be ideal for completing the harmony exercises.

5.   Press Play, and you should hear the MIDI file being played.

Work through these exercise files, in the order in which they are presented on the PDF, at your own time and pace. And above all, do not try to rush them. You will not make much progress if you speed through them, hoping to learn the arts of harmony in a hurried fashion. And because you might need to go back to a particular exercise and rework it, save each exercise that you complete in a dedicated folder on your computer. Some exercises do require you to rework previous exercises. Having all of your harmony exercises available within a single folder will therefore be advantageous to you.

The CD also contains numerous work files that are MIDI files pertaining to particular areas of harmony covered by each of the chapters. You can also import these into your sequencer and use them for the purposes of study and illustration of the features indicated by their general title.

Having said this, let us now take a general approach toward the main topic of this text: the art of musical harmony. Initially, we will concern ourselves with the place that musical harmony has as a part of the musical language. Having looked at and understood that place, we will then approach the study of musical harmony in a methodical and progressive fashion. This approach will begin with a prior consideration of the elements of music that count as universals. What I mean by universal is those ingredients of music that are used everywhere, regardless of the age, style, culture, or place of origin of the music concerned. This study will begin with the chapter that follows. In the meantime, I wish you every success with your journey through the fascinating world of musical harmony.

CD-ROM Downloads

If you purchased an ebook version of this book, and the book had a companion CD-ROM, we will mail you a copy of the disc. Please send ptrsupplements@cengage.com the title of the book, the ISBN, your name, address, and phone number. Thank you.

1 An Introduction to Musical Harmony

Whatever type or style of music you are interested in producing, in doing so you will no doubt come across what are in effect the universals of the musical language. Now, what do I mean by the term *universal*? Well, generally it can be observed that music—of whatever kind—has three main ingredients. These ingredients are simply rhythm, melody, and harmony. All three could be described as being *universal* for the simple reason that wherever in the world music is produced and played, these three ingredients will somehow be involved. It therefore seems logical to conclude that any person wishing to create his or her own music will spend a considerable amount of time exploring, studying, and understanding these three universal ingredients, especially as they apply to that person's own particular favored styles of music. In fact, not to do so is to fail to take advantage of the incredible amount of knowledge that is actually out there—knowledge that can propel the computer musician toward ever greater heights of composition and musical skill. Now notice that one of these three universals is harmony—the topic of this particular book. To be able to see where harmony fits into the picture, we will therefore briefly consider these three universals.

Rhythm

The first and perhaps most important of these three ingredients is, of course, the rhythm, which concerns the patterns of beats and note lengths that are used in a piece of music. As a part of the language of music, it is the rhythm that gives music its sense of forward motion, speed, drive, and vitality. This feeling of forward motion is imparted through the beat—that regular pulse that flows through the music. As such, the beat is rather like a motor—it drives the music forward. A sense of beat seems to be innate to our species. Echoing the natural rhythms of our own heartbeat and motor activities, the presence of a beat is something we all instinctively respond to. This response finds a natural expression in movement in the form of dance.

The presence of a beat in music allows us to mark and measure musical time. This process of marking and measuring musical time is so important to our music generally that all of the computer programs with which we create music have particular windows in which these marks and measures are clearly visible to us. These can be seen clearly at the top of the Piano Roll view of any sequencer and in the vertical grid in which regular divisions of

1

the beat are clearly marked. In Figure 1.1, this grid is clearly visible, where each bar of four beats is clearly marked by a bold vertical line, each of the four beats by a fainter line, and the subdivision of those beats into sixteenth notes by even fainter lines.

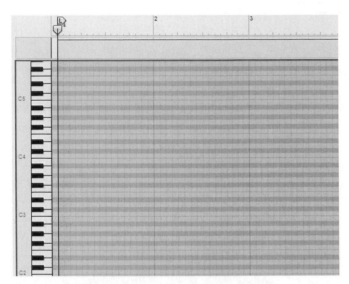

Figure 1.1   Piano Roll view of sequencer.

The length of the beat will determine the tempo or felt speed of the music, while the way beats are counted and accented will give rise to different types or kinds of musical time. These are called *meter*. Therefore, a regular count of one, two, three, four will give rise to one kind of meter (see Figure 1.1). This is called *common time* or *four beats to the bar*. A count of one, two, three will give rise to another kind of meter called *triple* or *waltz time*. However, whatever the count of beats, you will notice that it is the regular beat itself that gives music its particular sense of flow and motion.

But music needs far more than simply the sense of a beat. While the beat gives drive to our music, the vitality of the rhythm is imparted through the particular pattern or patterns of note lengths that a composer uses. In this light, you will notice that if the same note lengths are used all of the time, the result is a mechanical rhythm that has very little interest for the listener. However, when motives that use a variety of note lengths are used, it creates more interesting and varied rhythms, which are notable for their sense of energy and vitality—which, of course, is where the rhythm becomes a direct field of interest for the composer and music producer. To be able to produce music that has energy and vitality, you must give considerable attention to the rhythms used.

The universal ingredient of rhythm finds its most obvious and powerful platform in modern music in the form of the rhythm track—the main part of which is often provided by the drums. Except for Western classical music, perhaps, music the world over makes great use of drums to impart an essential sense of rhythmic life and vitality to the music. It is therefore hardly surprising that many computer musicians spend a great amount of their time learning how to write and produce effective and realistic sounding drum tracks.[1]

Melody

While rhythm provides the essential heartbeat and lifeblood of the musical language, it is melody that provides our music with a sense of meaning and emotional power of expression. The emotionally suggestive power of melody is quite remarkable considering that all melody really is nothing more than a succession of musical notes. From this, it becomes apparent that there exists a whole art surrounding this choice of the succession of notes in order to be able to create a powerful and moving melody.[2] For this very reason, a random tone generator is generally incapable of producing an emotionally satisfying and artistic-sounding melodic line.

The melodic ingredient of our music is perhaps just as important as the rhythmic. In recognition of this, we can see that on the left of the Piano Roll view of any sequencer, there is a vertical keyboard that enables the composer to record and identify that sequence of different pitches whereby a melodic line is created. In contrast to the rhythmic aspect, which is signified by vertical lines, the melodic aspect arising from the succession of notes of different pitches is represented by horizontal lines on the Piano Roll view, thereby giving rise to a simple two-dimensional XY axis scheme (see Figure 1.2).

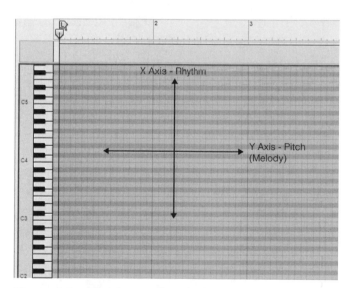

Figure 1.2   Rhythm and melody as XY axis.

Within modern music the main platform for melody occurs in the form of the lead. Whether vocal or instrumental, the lead is clearly the most important melodic part of

---

[1] It is for this reason that in the previous book of this series—*Composition for Computer Musicians* (Course Technology PTR, 2009)—some three full chapters were devoted to the topic of writing for drums.
[2] See *Composition for Computer Musicians*, Chapter 8, "Writing Melodic Leads," pp. 99–111.

the music—and thus it is often the ingredient by which we chiefly remember the music itself. Some music is all lead—that is, the melodic lead *is* the music. Examples of this are plaintive bamboo pipe solos evocative of the Himalayan foothills, the continually modulating melodies of the didgeridoo, or those examples from our own Western musical traditions, such as the reel or jig, which are often played on the pipe or fiddle. While often possessing a sense of great beauty and expressive intensity, within modern music this type of lone instrumental solo is perhaps comparatively rare for the simple reason that we all tend to enjoy and appreciate much more the sound that comes from a complete ensemble of instruments all playing together. Whether a rock band, a choir, or an orchestra, the full sound of an ensemble is unbeatable for creating a sense of emotional power and excitement. Within this context, therefore, solo melody (when it does occur) is used simply as a means of creating contrast and interest in a work that is essentially written or played with a group of musicians or instruments in mind.

Harmony

This sense of power and excitement that can be generated when lots of musicians play together is mainly due to the presence of a third universal ingredient of music—an ingredient that in its way is just as important as the rhythm or the melody. This third ingredient is the harmony of sound created when different instruments are playing at the same time. Here it is interesting to note that while rhythm and melody between them create a two-dimensional fabric of expression (referring back to that XY axis shown in Figure 1.2), harmony gives to our music an all-important third dimension. Therefore, if rhythm were considered analogous to, say, the dimension of length and melody to the height of an object, harmony would thus be analogous to the depth of that object. As such, like the technique of perspective in painting, which also creates an impression of depth, harmony represents an ingredient that raises the possibility of the language of music to an entirely new dimensional and expressive level.

The ingredient of harmony is present in one way or another wherever musicians get together and play at the same time. And the evidence is that musicians have been doing this for many thousands of years. Even as far back as ancient Egypt, we find wall paintings that depict various ensembles and groups of musicians playing together. When musicians do play together like this, harmony is the inevitable result. The importance of the ingredient of harmony for music therefore cannot be underestimated. This becomes apparent if you think about what would happen if you got all of the members of a band to play anything at random at the same time. The result would be a total chaos of sound. And for our ears this sound would soon become intolerable, owing to the random clashes between different notes all being heard at the same time. From this simple example, you can see that the sense of power and emotional expression that comes from a band or ensemble all playing together lies precisely in the harmony of their parts—a harmony that in itself is one of the great arts of the musical language. By learning about this art, it becomes possible for us to create tracks that use the full power of an ensemble in such a way that everything blends and harmonizes together to create that sense of power and excitement that we all enjoy so much.

It therefore stands to reason that any person who is interested in composing and producing his or her own music—of whatever type—will spend some time becoming familiar with the principles underlying musical harmony. Of course, this is not as easy as it might sound. For many computer musicians, the art and principles of harmony tend to remain very much a mystery for the simple reason that knowledge of harmony is often written about and presented in such a way that it is only really accessible to those who have received the privilege of some type of classical music training—which means that it is only really available to those who are well-versed in reading and writing music in a conventional classical sense. This book breaks down that barrier and presents to you the core knowledge and techniques of musical harmony through the more accessible medium of the Piano Roll view of any sequencer. In order to supplement this, Score Edit views, jazz notation chord symbols, and guitar chord shapes are also used where appropriate.

Knowledge of harmony is essential for anybody wishing to write his or her own music, because it enables us to create music in such a way that everything fits together nicely. The bass complements the lead, and the inner parts harmonize nicely with both bass and lead. And the music itself is guided and led by a chord progression that makes the music sound like it is going somewhere, leading the listener on an exciting and imaginative journey.

As an ingredient of music, harmony occurs when more than one note is being played at the same time. Naturally, this can happen in a number of different contexts. It can happen when, say, a guitarist plays as an accompaniment to a voice or when a melody on piano is supported by a soft background of pads or strings. At any given moment, the sound of one instrument will be heard against the sound of another. And for our ears, the audible relationship between them is a vitally important part of the listening experience. Indeed, this is so vital that classically trained composers spend years studying and learning the art of harmony. And through doing so, they become able to compose music that has a degree and depth of musical and emotional expression that is literally awe-inspiring.

This audible relationship that occurs between different instruments or tracks that are playing simultaneously is called their *harmony*. Another way in which harmony can occur is when different notes are played simultaneously on a polyphonic instrument. The piano represents a good example of this: an instrument that—unlike the flute, which is essentially monophonic and therefore only capable of producing one note at a time—allows us to play such simultaneous combinations of notes. These simultaneous note combinations, as you probably know, are called *chords*. It is a fact that some combinations of notes sound great together—they harmonize. Others clash and create an impression of disagreement. Knowledge of the art of harmony allows us to use these forces to our own advantage and create musical works of great emotional power and expressiveness.

The art of harmony has behind it a definite body of learnable knowledge that has been built up over a considerable period of time. This body of knowledge represents the natural inheritance of every musician—computer or otherwise—passed on to us by other musicians and composers who have spent their lives perfecting their own particular craft. By learning this knowledge, you can obtain considerable skill in the use of the element of harmony within your own music. To the listener, this music will then have about it a beauty and a power that has the capacity to both reach and move them emotionally. And although it might seem to the listener that the composer has a great talent as far as music is concerned, a very large part of this apparent talent will be simply knowledge. The composer has an acquired knowledge of harmony, and this knowledge expertly guides his or her choice of which notes to combine with others.

Chords

The first question to arise, therefore, is where this knowledge begins. Generally, knowledge of the art of harmony begins with the consideration of chords—a chord being a result of the simultaneous sounding of different notes. Not surprisingly, there are a huge number of chords that can be used in music. The musical scale we use in the West has 12 notes to the octave. For the purposes of harmony, any of these notes may be combined with any of the others. In terms of simple two-note chords, there are more than 100 possibilities to begin with. When a third note is brought into the picture, we can multiply that number even further. The result is over a thousand possible three-note chords! The number of permutations that is mathematically possible for a single chord of, say, four notes is therefore absolutely enormous.

One way of looking at and classifying these chords is according to how many notes they contain. Naturally, the more notes in a chord, the more complex the resultant sonority—the term *sonority* signifying the particular sound a chord makes. This method of classification therefore looks at chords in terms of their relative complexity for our ear. A chord of few notes is less complex than, say, a chord of seven notes. On this basis each chord can be given a name that is determined by how many notes it has. Chords of only two notes are called *dyads,* while a chord of three notes is called a *triad*. Chords of four notes are called *tetrads,* while chords of five notes are called *pentads*. An extremely complex chord consisting of 10 different notes would thus be called a *decad*.

Figure 1.3 shows some examples of well-known chords, starting with the simplest chords of all (dyads) on the left, becoming gradually more complex as the number of notes in the chord increases, moving from left to right in the illustration.

Starting off on the left with a dyad, which takes the form of a simple open fifth, the triad adds a third to the fifth in order to create a C major chord. In the tetrad the interval of a seventh has been added to the original triad to create a C major seventh chord. For the

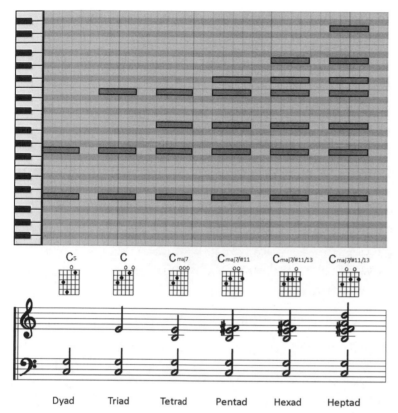

Figure 1.3 Chords of increasing complexity.

pentad an augmented eleventh has been added to enrich the basic sonority of the seventh. This enrichment continues with the hexad, where a thirteenth has been added, and finally ends with the heptad created by adding a major ninth to the original hexad. The final result is an extremely complex sonority that consists of seven different notes sounding at the same time.

Naturally, to be able to handle and use such chordal sonorities with any skill, a considerable degree of knowledge in the art of harmony is required. Yet this knowledge cannot be acquired all at once; it is knowledge that needs to be graduated in some way. If not, students of harmony will simply find themselves getting out of their depth. For this reason, study of the art of harmony generally begins with the use of the simpler chords, and then, as students progress, the use of increasingly complex chords is brought into the picture.

Yet even this process can present certain difficulties. Observe, for example, that the language used to describe and explain such chords (for example, ninth, thirteenth, augmented eleventh) depends upon a clear understanding of musical intervals and the particular terms and symbols used to describe and represent them. This knowledge of intervals is an absolutely vital prerequisite for the study of harmony for the simple reason that ultimately, as the next chapter will show, all harmonies consist of a combination of different intervals. Without knowing what these are, computer musicians will quickly find themselves becoming lost in their studies. For this reason, before you can make any real progress with the study of harmony, it is recommended that you first acquire knowledge of the theory behind intervals, what they are, how they are named, and what their different aural qualities are.

Conveniently, this theory has already been dealt with in the first book of this series, *Music Theory for Computer Musicians* (Course Technology PTR, 2008), particularly in Chapter 6, "Intervals," and Chapter 8, "Chords." Having already covered this knowledge in a previous book, it is pointless for me to repeat the same material here. Therefore, in the case of this particular book, no more than a brief summary will be offered. If this summary is not sufficient, then I recommend that you obtain a copy of *Music Theory for Computer Musicians* in order to learn this important prerequisite knowledge.

The prerequisite knowledge required is:

- The ability to name and identify any interval

- An understanding of the difference between simple and compound intervals

- The ability to recognize and identify perfect, major, minor, augmented, and diminished intervals

Now that I have pointed out the prerequisite knowledge, let us consider the world of musical intervals in more detail, paying special attention to the important part that they play within the general sphere of musical harmony.

2 The Interval

The study of harmony really begins with the interval. The reason for this is that if I play two notes simultaneously on the keyboard, it is obvious that one note will automatically be the lowest in pitch, and the other will be the highest. This difference in pitch between them is called an *interval*. When the two notes belonging to an interval are played in this fashion, the ear recognizes not only the upper and lower notes, but also the harmonic relationship between the two notes. This relationship will have a particular quality to the ear for the simple reason that the two notes will be heard as either agreeing or clashing, as the case may be. In this quality of agreement/disagreement, therefore, we can see the basic forces that form the very foundation for musical harmony.

Combinations of two notes that sound agreeable together give rise to intervals, which are described as being *concords* or *consonances,* while combinations of two notes that seem to clash or disagree with one another are described as being *discords* or *dissonances*. The reasons why some intervals are consonant and others are dissonant are complex and are intricately bound up with issues of acoustics, the harmonic series, and the mathematical ratios between the frequencies of the two notes. But in basic terms, we can observe that notes whose frequencies are in simple ratios to one another, such as 2:1 (the octave), 3:2 (the perfect fifth), or 5:4 (the major third) are heard by the ear as being a pleasing or concordant combination of notes. On the other hand, notes whose frequencies are in more complex ratios with one another, such as 15:8 (major seventh) or 45:32 (augmented fourth) are heard by the ear as being a more tense and discordant combination of notes. So it would seem that the simpler the ratio of the two frequencies, the more concordant the interval.

Musical harmony begins, therefore, with the unit of the interval. This means that the interval thereby represents the foundation for all more complex types of harmony. This becomes obvious when we realize that no matter how complex the chord being considered, it will ultimately boil down to being nothing more than a combination of musical intervals. This fact can be easily demonstrated by considering the case of the chord of the C major triad. This triad has three notes, which are C, E, and G. As a chord, therefore, it represents a sum of three particular intervals: the perfect fifth between notes C and G, the major third between notes C and E, and the minor third between notes E and G. These three intervals are represented diagrammatically in Figure 2.1.

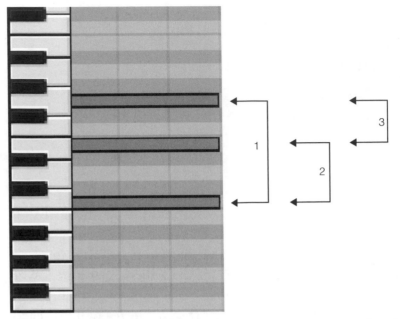

Figure 2.1   Major triad as a sum of three intervals (1: perfect fifth; 2: major third; 3: minor third).

Given that we begin with note C, it will become apparent that any of the 12 notes of the chromatic scale available on the MIDI keyboard will form a particular interval with it. This means that in this context, there are 13 possible intervals that may be used as harmonies in their own right or may be incorporated into more complex chords. These are shown in Figure 2.2, as taken from note C.

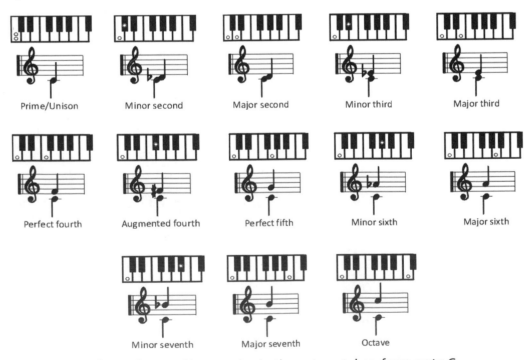

Figure 2.2   The 13 interval harmonies in the octave taken from note C.

In this case, note C is only a convenient starting point. We could equally start from any note and generate the same set of intervals.

As harmony begins with the interval, and there are 13 simple intervals, this means that the array of intervals shown in Figure 2.2 provides the core foundation upon which musical harmony is based. For this reason, the computer musician who is interested in mastering the arts of harmony should spend a considerable amount of time getting to know these intervals. And this does not mean just being able to name and recognize intervals, but also getting to know their particular aural qualities. Every musical interval has a particular aural quality, and when that interval is present in a chord, it will contribute that quality to the overall sound of the chord itself.

It is also important that you are able to recognize and name each interval in order for you to be able to learn how to properly interpret chord symbols. To assist you, the figures underneath the intervals as represented on the staff of Figure 2.3 are how these intervals would be portrayed or represented within the unique language of chord symbolism. They have been placed here for you to become accustomed to the particular way in which chords and intervals are usually represented in modern music. You will note that some intervals are given two sets of symbols. This is due to the fact that in complex chords, the second, fourth, and sixth often appear as extensions of seventh chord harmonies in which they appear in their compound forms as the ninth, eleventh, and thirteenth of the chord, respectively. However, do not let this trouble you at this stage. As you work through this book, you will soon begin to understand what I mean by this.

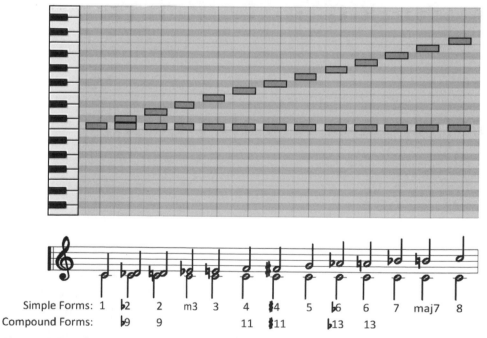

Figure 2.3 The 13 intervals of harmony.

Simple and Compound Intervals

When looking at intervals as harmonies in their own right, it is important to realize that simple and compound intervals have the same essential chordal values. To explain this, we can observe that intervals are conveniently measured by the number of alphabetic scale steps that separate the two notes. Those intervals that span eight scale steps or fewer are called *simple intervals*, while those intervals that span more than eight steps are called *compound intervals*. See Figure 2.4.

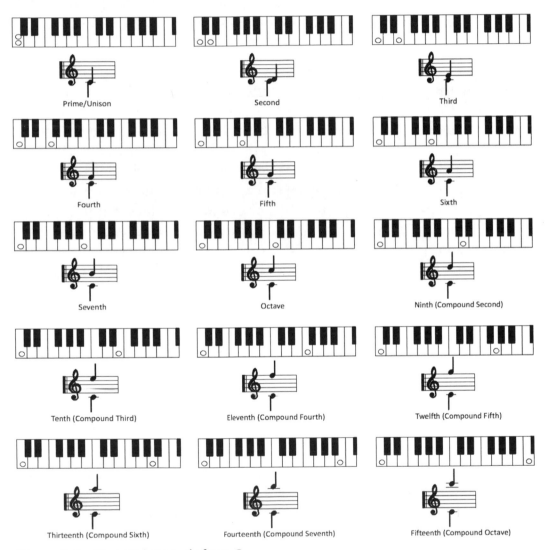

Figure 2.4   First 15 intervals from C.

For the study of musical harmony, it is important to recognize that, consisting of an octave plus a simple interval, a compound interval represents nothing more than a simple interval that has been more widely spaced. The importance of this lies in the observation that as a chord of two notes—the interval of a ninth, for example—is equivalent to a second. Both intervals, after all, represent a combination of the same two notes: C and D. Figure 2.5 clearly shows this. As harmonies in their own right, the second and ninth differ only in terms of their spacing. In the case of the interval of a second, the interval is closely spaced, while in the case of the ninth, the spacing is wider. But involving the same two notes, they have an equivalent value as musical harmonies. This means that really, they are the same two-note chord, the difference lying in the particular spacing of their individual sonority. For this reason, as shown with reference to Figure 2.3, a second can appear as a ninth in a chord, a fourth as an eleventh, and a sixth as a thirteenth. In Figure 2.5, you can see an illustration of how the ninth as a harmony is actually equivalent to a second and vice versa.

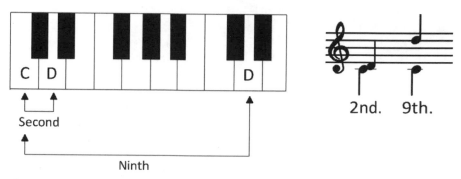

Figure 2.5   Comparison of the interval of a second with the interval of a ninth.

Drone and Melody as a Simple Type of Harmony

Some types of music take great advantage of musical intervals as simple harmonies. A good example of this is Hindustani classical music, with which we often associate the sound of the sitar. The sitar has numerous drone strings that continually sound while the melody is being played. This means that each melody note is heard as an interval in relation to the main drone note. And this is where the harmonic interest of this type of music lies—in the particular harmonies that the melody notes make with the drone.

This use of a drone bass, however, is not just confined to Hindustani music. It is also found in many types of Western music. The music of bagpipes is a good example in which each note of the melody is heard as an interval with the drone pipes, which sound along with the melody itself. And for both classical and film music composers, the use of a drone bass over which a melody or melodies is played is still a very atmospheric and powerful technique. Representing a very basic type of musical harmony, it is a harmony that completely depends upon the aural qualities of particular intervals. In Figure 2.6 you will see the notes of a scale slowly rising upward. Observe the way each note of the scale forms a particular interval with the drone bass and that while some of the scale notes will form dissonant and tense harmonies with the drone bass, others will form relaxed and peaceful harmonies.

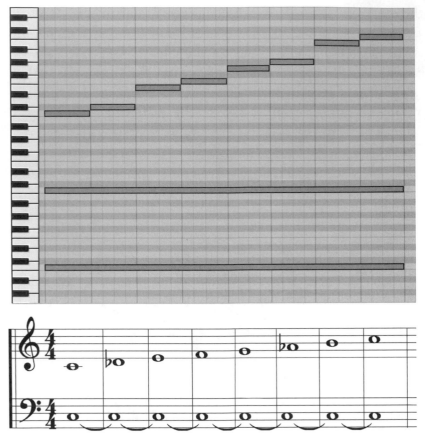

Figure 2.6   Notes of a scale rising upward against a drone bass.

Aural Qualities of Intervals: Consonance and Dissonance

The aural qualities of intervals invite comparisons with other spheres. For example, intervals can be considered very much like the relationships we form with other people. Some people we get along with and we feel a sense of harmony and agreement with them. With others we tend to clash, and there is a sense of disagreement or discord. The relationships between different notes are exactly the same. There are different degrees of harmony or tension present between them. Depending upon the degree of harmony or tension, each interval contributes its own particular quality to the overall range or spectrum of such harmonic qualities available to the composer.

The best known way of appreciating and grading these qualities is in terms of consonance and dissonance. In some intervals, the notes seem to blend together in a way that is very harmonious and sweet. These intervals are called *consonances*. Ordinarily, these are considered to be the unison, octave, perfect fifth, and fourth (which are classified as the perfect consonances) and the major and minor third and sixth (which are the imperfect consonances). Figure 2.7 shows the array of consonances.

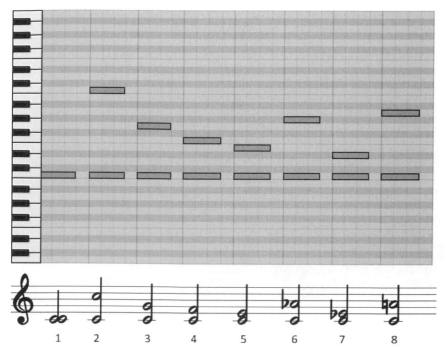

Figure 2.7   Prefect and imperfect consonances.

These interval names are (with reference to the number given underneath each interval):

1.   Unison

2.   Octave

3.   Perfect fifth

4.   Perfcct fourth

5.   Major third

6.   Minor sixth

7.   Minor third

8.   Major sixth

In all other simple intervals not listed here, the notes seem to disagree in some way. For this reason, they are called *dissonances*. Here it is notable that there are two basic degrees or levels of disagreement. Major seconds and minor sevenths have a relatively mild degree of dissonance, while major sevenths, minor seconds, and augmented fourths have a much sharper or increased level of dissonance.

The names of these intervals (with reference to the numbers given below each interval in Figure 2.8) are:

1.   Major second

2.   Minor seventh

3. Minor second

4. Major seventh

5. Augmented fourth

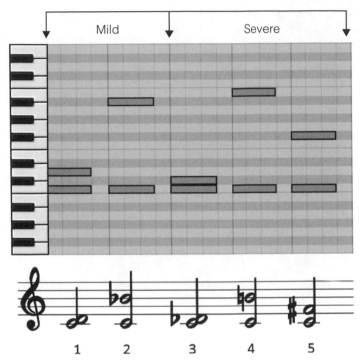

Figure 2.8 Dissonant intervals.

Given the presence of these different aural qualities in musical intervals, it becomes possible to arrange intervals in a graduated spectrum, which, beginning with the most concordant interval, gradually progresses on toward the most discordant. This spectrum—first formulated by the German composer Paul Hindemith (1895–1963)—can be represented as in Figure 2.9, in which the most consonant interval is on the left while the most dissonant interval is on the right.

The names of these intervals (with reference to the numbers given below each interval) are:

1. Prime or unison

2. Octave

3. Perfect fifth

4. Perfect fourth

5. Major third

6. Minor sixth

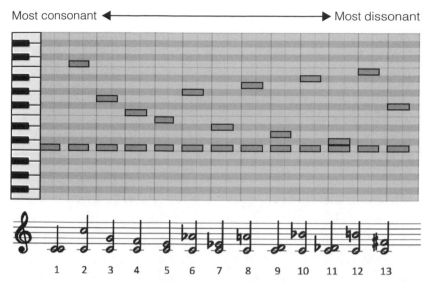

Figure 2.9 Graduated spectrum of consonant and dissonant intervals.

7.   Minor third

8.   Major sixth

9.   Major second

10.   Minor seventh

11.   Minor second

12.   Major seventh

13.   Augmented fourth/diminished fifth

The intervals portrayed here begin with the unison and the octave on the left as the most concordant intervals and ends with the interval of the augmented fourth, widely considered to be the most dissonant interval. In between there is a nice gradation of increasing tension from the octave onward.

Enharmonically Equivalent Intervals

Many intervals have enharmonic equivalents. A good example of this is the minor third between notes C and E[b] and the augmented second between the notes C and D#. Although of different types, both of these intervals are played using the same notes on the keyboard. For this reason, they are classed as being *enharmonically equivalent*.

So how do we know which is which? This is all to do with the context in which the intervals are used. Therefore, the minor third between the notes C and E[b] could occur in the context of being the root and third of a C minor triad. Yet in the key of E minor, the same interval—but this time spelled as C/D#—could also occur as the augmented second between the sixth and seventh degrees of the harmonic scale belonging to that key. Therefore, the context in which the interval is placed determines how an interval would be spelled. For you to progress in the art of harmony, it is worthwhile to learn what the various enharmonic equivalents of intervals are. This will help you to complete some of the exercises in the "Practical Harmony Exercises" section. There is an appendix of intervals in the Appendix section in which you can locate these enharmonically equivalent intervals located.

Intervals and Emotions

For many composers the degree of tension expressed by particular intervals has offered a great vehicle for the expression of various feelings and mind states. The reasoning behind this is fairly easy to appreciate. Peaceful and pleasant states of mind are free of internal conflict. As such, they offer a direct parallel to the more consonant intervals where the two notes seem to agree with one another. At the other end of the scale, agitated and angry states of mind are those resulting from a state of internal conflict within a person, which means that they have more in common with those musical intervals in which the two tones seem to conflict with one another. The intervals shown in Figure 2.9 thus offer a nice gradation of qualities between the two extremes of peaceful harmony on the one hand and tense states of inner conflict on the other.

Another factor that runs across this is the observation that minor intervals tend to suggest to us sad and melancholic frames of mind, while major intervals suggest quite the opposite. The exact reasons for this have never been satisfactorily explained, yet the fact of it is undeniable. Therefore, in looking at musical intervals as vehicles for emotional expression, this issue of major/bright or minor/dark also needs to be considered. It shows us that the perceived emotional character of intervals tends to operate simultaneously along two poles: the pole of consonance and dissonance on the one hand and the pole of major and minor on the other. Figure 2.10 shows these two poles.

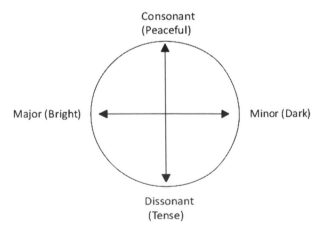

Figure 2.10   Two poles of expression of musical intervals.

Applying this, you can see that a major third, for example, is a consonant interval and it is major. This means that it therefore speaks of a bright or happy state of contentment.

A minor third, although also consonant, is minor, which means that it has an element of sadness to it. Therefore, rather than speaking to us of contentment or peace, it speaks more of a state of passive acceptance—as in the case, for example, of a person who has come to terms with a difficult situation.

To a large extent this implied emotional spectrum has a subjective value in that a particular interval may suggest one emotion to one person and another emotion to another. For this reason, rather than endeavoring here to precisely define the emotional suggestions of an interval, I recommend that you think about your own emotional correlations with particular intervals. You can do this by playing an interval on its own and seeing what kind of feelings it evokes in you. The correlations thus obtained can then provide a useful starting point for creating music—that is, the type of intervals to be used for, say, angry, peaceful, or sinister music. Table 2.1 might prove a useful starting point for this process. The emotions listed are those independently suggested for each interval by the music producer Alex Carlin.

Table 2.1 Perceived Correlation between Emotions and Interval Harmonies

Interval	Notes	Emotion
Unison	C/C	Pleasing, peace
Octave	C/C	Pleasing, peace
Perfect fifth	C/G	Joy, triumph, courage
Perfect fourth	C/F	Excitement, contentment
Major third	C/E	Harmony, peace, joy
Minor sixth	C/Ab	Harshness, meanness, confusion
Minor third	C/Eb	Sadness, sorrow, annoyance, gloominess
Major sixth	C/A	Sweet, enjoyable, pleasing
Major second	C/D	Sadness, strangeness, tension
Minor seventh	C/Bb	Sadness, dismay, sorrow
Minor second	C/Db	Harshness, sinister, confusion, shock
Major seventh	C/B	Surprise, suspicion
Augmented fourth	C/F#	Suspense, shock, sorrow

Looking at this table, you can see that this array of intervals offers for Alex a rich and varied spectrum of emotional expression. And although this emotional spectrum clearly has a personal subjective element, there are nonetheless examples of common interpretations that most composers would tend to agree with. The augmented fourth interval, for example, has always been notable for the sense of sinister suspense it can create. Hence its peculiar name of Devil's fourth—an appellation that goes back to Medieval times! Similarly, the minor second forms a sharp, stabbing discord that is used universally by composers to create a sense of hostility and fear. And the sense of triumph linked to the perfect fifth proves a notable feature of many famous triumphant Hollywood theme tunes, with the theme music to *Star Wars* being a good example.

Naturally, this is a vast area of study, and no more than a brief mention can be made of it here. The important point to grasp is that the interval represents the very foundations of musical harmony, both in terms of the important place that the interval has in the makeup and constitution of chords and also the emotional effects and psychological implications of particular chords. For these reasons alone, you would be wise to spend a considerable amount of time familiarizing yourself with all of the members of the family of musical intervals, which means playing them, studying them, and getting to know them as thoroughly as possible.

Conclusion

This chapter stressed the importance of developing a sound understanding of musical intervals as a foundation for the study of musical harmony. We have shown that all chords, no matter how complex, are essentially the result of a combination of intervals. It has also shown that intervals themselves are basic units of harmony, a feature that is especially prevalent in those types of music that employ a melody played over a drone bass. We considered the total spectrum of intervals that are used in music, together with the particular aural qualities of each interval as a chordal sonority in its own right. Additionally, we discussed the emotional implications of these interval sonorities, and we learned that this works along two poles or axes: the pole of consonance and dissonance and the pole of major and minor intervals. In addition, we discussed the emotional affiliations of particular intervals based on their aural qualities.

Although the subject of intervals is a very basic one for harmony, you would be wise to spend as much of your spare time as possible studying intervals and getting to thoroughly know how they are named and described. Having done so, you will then find yourself in the fortunate position of having a firm foundation from which to properly begin the study of musical harmony. This study will commence with the next chapter, which concerns itself with the musical territory or field in which the principles of musical harmony are generally applied.

3 Tonality and the Key System

The music of today is notable for the different types of musical harmony that are and can be used. For example, there is functional harmony, associated with the common inheritance that is classical music. Composers such as Bach, Beethoven, Mozart, and Brahms thus wrote their music using this system of functional harmony. Then there is modal harmony, which looks beyond the major and minor key system of classical music and uses other musical scales and modes, such as the system of church modes that preceded the adaption of our major and minor scales. There is also jazz harmony, which, as well as possessing its own idiosyncratic approach to harmony, has now reached a high level of complexity and sophistication. Another type of harmony is quartal, quintal, and secundal harmony, which is based on chord shapes and structures that were not commonly used by classical composers. Then there is pandiatonic harmony, which represents a free use of chordal materials within the seven-note diatonic scale without reference to traditional harmonic functions. Another type of harmony is free chromatic or atonal harmony—that is, harmony that does not base itself or organize itself around tonal centers. An offshoot of this is serial harmony, in which the notes of the chromatic scale are arranged in a particular order. The chords to be used are then selected from this predetermined order and its derivatives.

Naturally, viewing these different types of approach to harmony can be both confusing and bewildering. And to make matters worse, today there is not one single theory or system that covers and explains all possible types of harmony. Bearing this in mind, where does a person who wishes to learn the arts of harmony begin? For a computer musician wishing to learn the arts of harmony, probably the best place to start is with functional harmony—that is, the system of harmony originally used and developed by classical composers such as Bach, Mozart, Beethoven, and Mendelssohn. Despite the fact that this may imply that functional harmony is therefore an old or outdated type of harmony, most popular music that we hear on the radio today uses or makes reference to the common inheritance that is functional harmony. Probably the main reason for this is that functional harmony is essentially simple, very musical, and pleasing to the human ear; it is also relatively easy to learn. For this reason alone, all computer musicians and songwriters wishing to write their own music should really waste no time in learning at least the principles of functional harmony, because it still represents the very root and foundation from which most modern and popular music springs. Having learned those principles, you can then progress on to the study of more advanced or different types of harmony, such as modal or jazz harmony.

This book will give you a good grounding in the principles of functional harmony. It will also, where useful or appropriate, make reference to some of these other types of harmony, so that you have the option to investigate these further, should you wish. Although elements of theory are necessary to be able to learn functional harmony, the primary concern will always be toward the practical use of harmony. Therefore, modern theories that try to explain how harmony works are not our concern here. Neither is a lengthy analysis of the use of harmony in a given body of music. Our concern is simply the practical musical use of the materials of harmony.

The main purpose of this chapter is to review and indicate those key elements of musical theory you'll need to know to make any progress with the study of functional harmony. Nearly all of the elements of theory that are reviewed here were already well covered in the book *Music Theory for Computer Musicians* (Course Technology PTR, 2008). Therefore, wherever possible I will avoid full and lengthy explanations of theory matters that have already been covered in that book. If nothing else, this chapter will offer a clear reminder of the basic elements of musical knowledge, which are prerequisites for the proper study and understanding of musical harmony.

This chapter also represents a repository for ideas and information, which, as you progress through this book, you will then return to with greater understanding and clarity. In some ways, the content of this chapter might be quite daunting. Yet do not let yourself get put off by that. As you progress through the book, you will acquire firsthand experience and knowledge of the ideas and information given in this chapter. This experience and knowledge will provide a clear foundation for you to be able to appreciate the ideas and concepts in this chapter, at which point you will grasp what is being written here with total clarity and lucidity.

The Classical Key System

The type of harmony called *functional harmony* is based on the classical key system with its characteristic set of scales—the major and the minor scales, both of which are depicted in Figure 3.1. In this case they are both presented as they appear in the key of C. Both major and minor scales are built using a characteristic pattern of tones and semitones. This pattern of tones and semitones is always preserved, no matter which keynote is taken to be the starting point. Figure 3.1 reminds you of these patterns. In the figure, T stands for tone and S for semitone.

Each such scale is built upon a principle note, which is called the *tonic* or *keynote*. The tonic is the first degree of the scale, which, in the case of the major and minor scales depicted in Figure 3.1, is therefore note C. Both the major and the minor scales of a given key take the notes that they need from a foundation scale, which is called the *twelve-tone chromatic scale*. This scale is represented by the five black and seven white

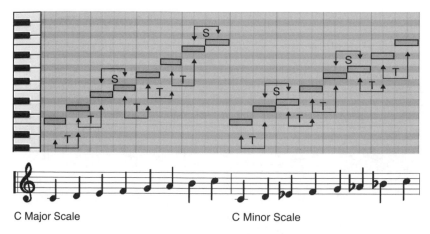

Figure 3.1   The scales of C major and C minor.

keys visible within a single octave of the keyboard. Figure 3.2 illustrates both the chromatic scale, whose notes have been labeled on the keyboard, and the particular notes selected from that scale for the major and minor scales of the key of C.

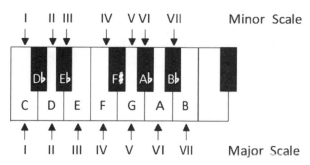

Figure 3.2   The major and minor scales as selections of notes from the chromatic scale.

Because there are 12 possible notes in the chromatic scale—as represented by the black and white keys of the keyboard—this means that there are also 12 possible keys or keynotes. Upon each of these keynotes, a particular scale—major or minor—may be built. Each such scale would take the given keynote as the first degree of that scale. Because there are 12 possible keynotes and two basic scales, major or minor, this means that there are 24 basic keys belonging to the key system. Each key is named by the note that is taken to be the tonic or first degree of the scale in conjunction with the type of scale used—major or minor. Therefore, the key of F♯ major is the key that takes note F♯ as the tonic of a major scale, while the key of D minor is the key that takes note D as the tonic of a minor scale.

For each key, a certain number of sharps or flats is required to properly preserve the pattern of tones and semitones that belongs to each of the scales—major or minor. In written music, these sharps or flats are portrayed at the beginning of each system of music. And they are known as the characteristic key signature by which a particular key is identified. In Figure 3.3, you will see an illustration of the 24 keys together with their names and key signatures.

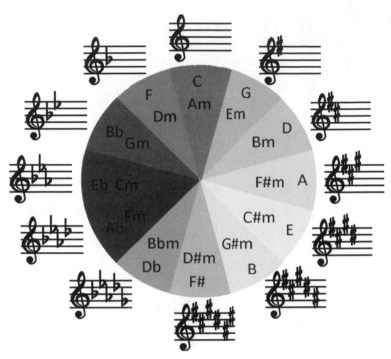

Figure 3.3   Keys used in functional harmony.

Both scales of C major and A minor, therefore, have key signatures without any flats or sharps, while the keys of A major and F♯ minor both use three sharps. To get the best from this book, you would be wise to get to know all of these keys and ensure that you are comfortable working in any key required. A good way to get to know these keys in the first instance is by learning how to play all of the relevant scales upon the keyboard.[1]

I have often been asked the question, "Why learn key signatures when these are not actually used in the Piano Roll views of computer music sequencers?" This is a very good question, and the answer to it is that, excluding C major and A minor, each key requires a certain number of sharps or flats. Unless these are known to begin with, you will not know which notes to use for which key. If you are writing in, say, A major, you need to know that the key of A major has three sharps and that those three sharps affect the notes C, F, and G. So learning the key signatures for each key is far from being redundant. On the contrary, it is vital knowledge without which you will be restricted to writing music within the limited range of those one or two keys with which you are familiar. And this itself is a limitation that is not really to your advantage, because it means that you will be operating within a very narrow territory, which in the end will have a stifling effect upon your own creativity.

---

[1] A list of these scales, together with information on how to play them within each and every key, is given in Appendix A of *Music Theory for Computer Musicians*.

The Spectrum of Expression from a Range of Keys

Each key is a complete scale system—whether major or minor—together with the various chords that can be derived from the notes of that particular scale. The fact that there are different keys is of great advantage to you, because a given song or composition can in theory be played in any of 12 keys, depending upon whether it is in a major or a minor key. As but one example of the usefulness of this, sometimes a vocalist will object that a particular song is in a key that is too high or low for him to sing comfortably. In this situation, rather than force the vocalist to strain his voice, it can be relatively easy using MIDI technology to adjust the key of the song in order to adapt to the vocalist's own particular voice register. This process of changing the key in which a piece of music is written is called *transposition*, which means that the whole song is literally raised or lowered in pitch by so many semitones.

The use of different keys also offers a wide range of expressive and coloristic possibilities. These possibilities have been gradually built up through the history of the use of the key system to the degree that they are now a part of our basic music programming. Keys with lots of sharps are usually regarded by musicians as being bright, sunny keys, while keys with lots of flats are regarded as being darker and more pensive. And many musicians and composers have spoken of particular emotional and coloristic associations with particular keys. Therefore, the key of C major is often associated with purity, D major with feelings of triumph, while the key of F major speaks of the pastoral world of nature. Similarly, B♭ minor is often described as being a key filled with darkness and despair, while C♯ minor is often linked to intimate religious feelings.[2] Again, as in the case of musical intervals, there is a great element of subjectivity here. What cannot be avoided, though, is the conclusion that the entire range of keys as a whole offers great scope for atmospheric and colorful emotional suggestions. Therefore, to limit your knowledge to only a few keys is to severely limit the potential for your musical expression. That full potential can only be fully realized by developing an all-round knowledge of all of the keys of the key system.

Key Relationships

It would be a great mistake to view musical keys in isolation from one another. This is because a vital part of our music is changes of key—called *modulation*. Through modulation, a song can suddenly enter into new tonal territory, and with that can come a sense of excitement, renewed interest, and the sense of new vistas opening up. Through use of modulation, one section of the music might be in one key—say, the verse section—and another section might be in another key. A good example that everybody will likely be familiar with is John Lennon's "Happy Xmas (War Is Over)," in which the verses are in the key of A, and the chorus is in the key of D—a keynote that lies a fifth

---

[2] For more information on the connection between keys and emotion/color, see Rita Steblin's *A History of Key Characteristics in the Eighteenth and Early Nineteenth Centuries* (University of Rochester Press, 2005).

below the original tonic. In this way, as demonstrated by this particular song, the use of modulation not only serves to underpin the structure of the music as a whole, but it also offers a nice tool for contrast in the music and therefore a means for bringing to the music a sense of interest, atmosphere, and progression. In simple terms, the change of key brings a new energy to the music.

The more notes that two keys share in common, the closer the felt relationship between them. Therefore, because C major uses the same set of notes as A minor, the two keys are related in the closest possible way. The key of A minor is thus termed the *relative minor* of C major, while C major is termed the relative major of A minor. The closest connection between keys of the same kind—in other words, all major or all minor—lies in the key that is a perfect fifth above or below a given key. This is because the scales belonging to keys a fifth up or down from a given keynote only involve one change of note—an extra flat, as in the case of a key a fifth down, or an extra sharp in the case of a key a fifth up. This means that these keys all share six notes in common. Therefore, the most closely related keys to C major are G major, whose key signature has one sharp, and F major, whose key signature has only one flat.[3]

Keys whose tonic notes are a fifth apart (for example, C major and G or F major) form one link in the continuous cycle of keys that is known as the *circle of fifths*. This circular arrangement of all of the keys of the key system is portrayed in Figure 3.4. The circle of fifths interlinks all keys within the combined system that is known to us as the key system. As such, the key system represents a complete world in its own right, of which individual keys are but the parts. And it is the circle of fifths that connects all these keys as a whole.

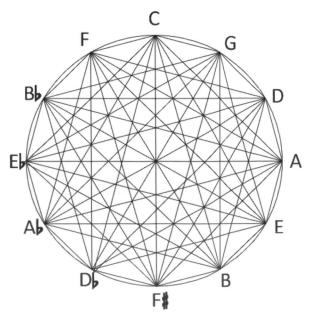

Figure 3.4   Relationships between keys in the circle of fifths.

[3] See *Music Theory for Computer Musicians*, Chapter 15, "Expanding Your Knowledge of Keys."

Naturally, a composition can begin at any point on the circle of fifths—that is, it can base itself initially on any key. When and if the key of the music changes—a process called *modulation*—this will always be from one point on the circle of fifths to another point. For the listener, this represents itself as going on a musical journey through different territories. As such, the circle of fifths represents a precise map of the entire territory of the key system as a whole. This can be more readily appreciated if we draw in the various relationships between keys within that closed circle. The result is a complex geometric diagram that visually reveals a precise map of key relationships.

Major and Minor Scales

As a part of this network of key relationships, each key of the key system has its own particular scale. Each note of this scale is called a *scale degree,* and each scale degree is ascribed a Roman numeral indicating its place relative to the tonic or keynote. The tonic note—in other words, the keynote itself—is designated as the first degree of the scale. Other degrees are so numbered as they rise upwards from the tonic. In Table 3.1, you will see this applied to the scales of four separate keys: C major, F♯ minor, G major, and D minor.

Table 3.1 The Numbering of Scale Degrees

Key	Degree of the Scale							
	I	II	III	IV	V	VI	VII	I
C major	C	D	E	F	G	A	B	C
F♯ minor (harmonic)	F♯	G♯	A	B	C♯	D	E♯	F♯
G Major	G	A	B	C	D	E	F♯	G
D minor (natural)	D	E	F	G	A	B♭	C	D

Each degree is numbered because a triad can be built upon each degree of the scale. Each triad can then be identified by the degree of the scale that is its root note. Because there are different kinds of triad—major, minor, augmented, and diminished—it has become customary to identify:

- Minor and diminished triads by a Roman numeral in lowercase—for example, ii

- Major and augmented triads by a Roman numeral in uppercase—for example, II

You can see the application of this to the triads of the major scale in Figure 3.5.

The usefulness of giving each chord a Roman numeral lies in the fact that it is a system that remains true no matter what they key is. Therefore, chord I refers to the chord built on the first degree of all major scales regardless of their keynote. Similarly, chord ii

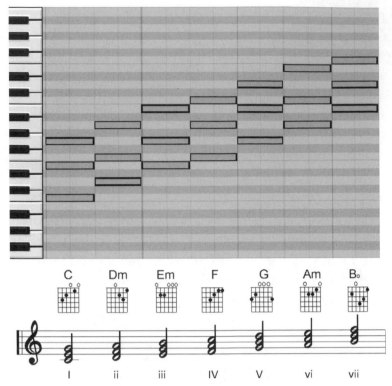

Figure 3.5 The seven triads of C major.

refers to the chord built on the second degree of all major scales. And it works in exactly the same way with the minor scales, as you can see in Figure 3.6.

Each triad can be used in a number of different positions, called *inversions*. Inversions are determined by which note of the triad is in the bass. When the root of the triad is in the bass, the chord is said to be in *root position*. This position is considered to be the default position, so it is represented simply by the numerals as you see them above. When the third of the triad is in the bass, the chord is said to be in *first inversion*. This is represented by the numeral that indicates the chordal root, after which is placed a letter b. When the fifth of the triad is in the bass, the triad is said to be in *second inversion*. Second inversion triads are represented by the numeral that signifies the chordal root, after which is placed a small letter c. Therefore, I in the key of C Major signifies the tonic triad in root position, Ib signifies the tonic triad in first inversion, and finally, Ic signifies the tonic triad in second inversion. Figure 3.7 demonstrates this principle as it applies to two chords in the key of C major: chord I and chord ii.

Where more complex chords are concerned—in other words, chords of the seventh, ninth, eleventh, or thirteenth—a letter is also used to describe the inversions. Figure 3.8 demonstrates this principle with reference to a ninth chord built on the first degree of the C major scale. Here you can see that the ninth in root position uses simply the figure describing the root, added to which is the number 9 to signify what type of chord it is.

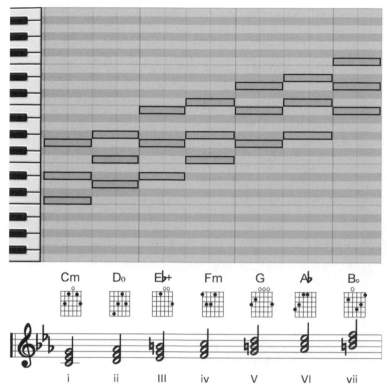

Figure 3.6   The seven triads of C (harmonic) minor.

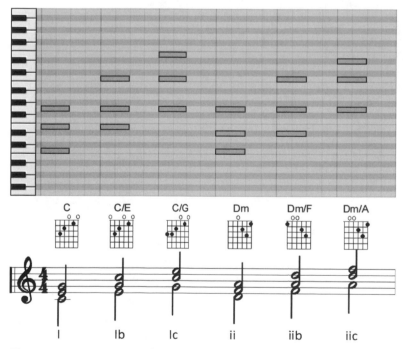

Figure 3.7   Figuring of chords in inversions.

The first inversion uses the same symbols to which has been added a letter b, the second inversion a letter c, and so on.

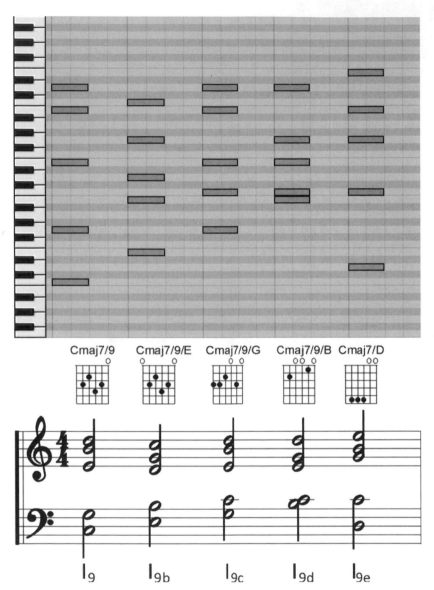

Figure 3.8   Figuring of the inversions of a ninth chord.

Popular Music Harmony Notation

Above each chord you will see both guitar chord shapes and the jazz/popular music notation symbols for each chord. Both the traditional figurative and the popular music notation methods of indicating chords will be used in this book wherever possible or appropriate. The usefulness of jazz/popular music notation lies in its ready comprehension to today's songwriters and the fact that it offers another, often more flexible, way of depicting chords and harmonies in general. It also enables progressions of very complex chords that sometimes seem to defy the principles of functional harmony to be notated in a relatively simple fashion. The advantages of this will become increasingly apparent as you progress through this book. In jazz/popular music notation, each chord is identified on up to four levels.

- The root of the chord is identified by the note symbol itself. Therefore, a chord with a root of C is notated as chord of C, while a chord with a root of F♯ is notated as a chord of F♯.

- The type of chord—major, minor, augmented, or diminished—is indicated by a second set of symbols. Unfortunately, these can vary. So for clarity's sake, we will adapt one such system here. If a chord is major, no other symbol is needed bar the note symbol. Therefore, C would automatically signify a C major triad. A minor chord is signified by m. Therefore, Cm signifies a C minor chord. An augmented chord is indicated by a plus sign after the chordal root. Therefore, C+ is an augmented triad built upon the root note C. Similarly, a diminished chord is identified by a small circle. Therefore, Co would signify a diminished chord built on note C. Figure 3.9 offers an illustration of those chords just mentioned.

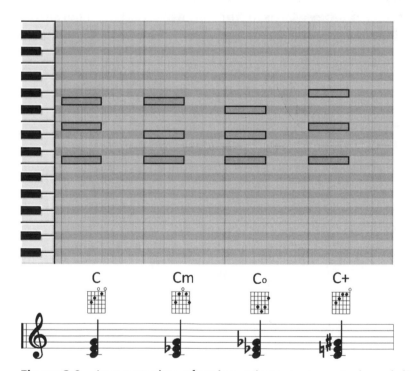

Figure 3.9   Jazz notation of major, minor, augmented, and diminished chords.

- Inversions of these triads—where a note other than the root is in the bass—are represented by a slash, after which the bass note is indicated. These are called *slash chords*. Therefore C/E signifies the first inversion of a C major chord—in other words, with the third (note E) in the bass—while C/G represents a second inversion chord—in other words, with the G in the bass.

■ In jazz and many other types of popular music, extensions that enrich the chord and give it a greater complexity are often added to the basic triads. These extensions are signified by a numeral, where a seventh is represented as 7, a ninth as 9, an eleventh as 11, and a thirteenth as 13. As seventh chords are so common in jazz and popular music, these have their own peculiar notation. Because this can also vary, we'll adopt a consistent method here. A minor seventh will be signified by 7, a major seventh by maj7, and a diminished seventh by dim7. Therefore, Cmaj7 signifies a major chord to which has been added a major seventh. Here it is important to realize that the notation *maj* refers not to the type of chord, but to the type of seventh—in other words, it is a major seventh rather than a minor seventh. Figure 3.10 shows some examples so that you can see what I mean.

■ Alterations to those extensions are indicated by a sharp or flat sign that precedes the figure. Therefore, 9 indicates an ordinary ninth, which is considered to be major (in other words, C/D), while ♯9 indicates that the ninth has been augmented by a semitone (in other words, an augmented ninth C/D), while ♭9 signifies that the ninth has been made smaller by a semitone (in other words, a minor ninth of C/D♭). Therefore, the chord symbol Cmaj7/♯9 signifies a major seventh chord built on note C to which has been added an augmented ninth. The notes involved are therefore C E G B D♯. Figure 3.11 shows some examples of chordal alterations so you can see how they are notated in practice.

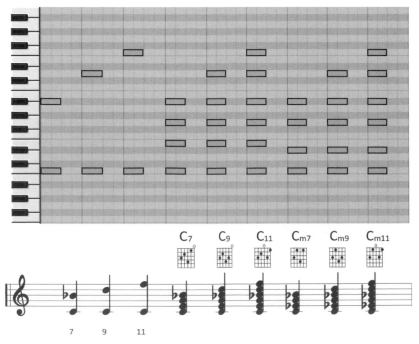

Figure 3.10   Common chordal extensions (bars 40–57 MIDI file 03).

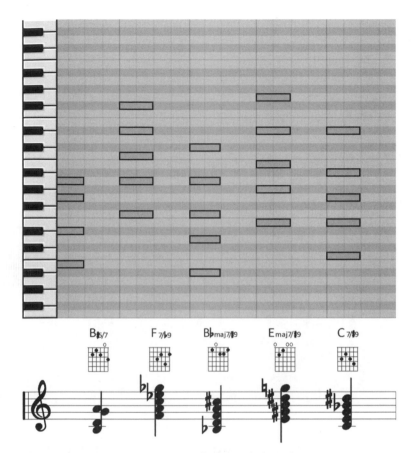

Figure 3.11   Jazz notation of altered chords.

The Functions of the Seven Triads

The key system of tonal music depends in the first place upon being able to establish a particular point on the circle of fifths as being a stable tonal center. This tonal center is the keynote by which the key is named. The chord that takes that keynote as the root is aptly named the *tonic chord,* which means that the tonic chord itself represents and supports that tonal center or keynote. Within any chord progression in that key, the tonic chord will represent the central chord around which the other chords of the key will revolve. And this is where the idea of functional harmony comes in. Each chord performs a role in establishing and maintaining the tonic chord as the tonal center of the music. Figure 3.12 shows the seven chords of the major key and the way in which six of those chords revolve around the central tonic chord—rather in a similar way to which the planets of the solar system revolve around the central sun. In this diagram, the outer circle represents the key itself, while the inner circle at the center represents the tonal center of that key. The other six chords are aptly portrayed as revolving around it.

Music that uses the key system in this way is called *tonal music* in that it is music that is built up and organized around a particular tonal center. Most of our popular music still has its roots in the traditions of tonal music, which means that virtually every song that

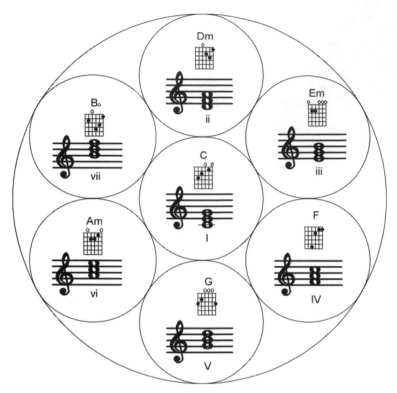

Figure 3.12 Central function of the tonic triad.

we hear on the radio is composed and organized using this tonal system. When we study such songs, therefore, we will soon discover the familiar signs that inform us that the music is tonal.

One such familiar sign is continual reference to and return to a central tonic triad. Take for example Bob Dylan's song "Blowin' in the Wind." Basically, this is a three-chord song based on the chords of D, G, and A Major—that is, the chords built on the first, fourth, and fifth degrees of the D major scale. Looking at the way these chords are used in the first verse, for example, we can clearly see how the chord progression revolves around the tonic triad D. Notice that the chord progression both begins and ends with the tonic triad of D major, and in between these points of the chord progression the tonic triad represents a constant point of reference.

Table 3.2 Chord Progression in Bob Dylan's "Blowin' in the Wind"

Intro:	D	D						
Line 1:	D	G	D	D	D	G	D	D
Line 2:	D	G	D	D	D	G	A	A
Line 3:	D	G	D	D	D	G	D	D
Line 4:	G	A	D	D	G	A	D	D

The chords other than the tonic that Dylan uses in this song—the major triads of G and A—are also very important chords for the key, G being called the subdominant chord and A the dominant chord. The terms *dominant* and *subdominant* relate to the particular function of the chord as a part of that key. Within the system of functional harmony, each and every chord has its own particular job to do. If you are new to musical harmony, you might find these functions difficult to understand or appreciate. However, don't worry. This information is here for you when you need it. When you have made some progress through this book, you will soon begin to acquire a clear appreciation of these functions. The functions of the chords are generally defined as follows:

Chord	Function
Chord I	Tonic
Chord II	Supertonic
Chord III	Mediant
Chord IV	Subdominant
Chord V	Dominant
Chord VI	Submediant
Chord VII	Leading tone triad

Of these seven chords, three chords are considered to perform primary functions. These are the tonic, the chord built on the first degree of the scale, the dominant built on the fifth degree of the scale, and the subdominant built on the fourth degree of the scale. Figure 3.13 demonstrates their close relationship to one another.

Figure 3.13   Relationship between the three primary chords.

Notice that between them, these three chords define all seven notes of the scale. This is an important observation for the simple reason that by using these three chords, it is therefore possible to put a harmony to every note of the scale. This means that, feasibly, every melody could be harmonized using these three chords alone—not that it would be wise to do so. Although some musicians and songwriters are content with limiting themselves to these three chords, doing so puts an unnecessary limitation on the creative process. A three-chord song should be written because one chooses to, not because this is one's only option.

As a group, the tonic, subdominant, and dominant triads are called the three *primary chords*. Lying between the dominant and subdominant, the tonic chord represents the seat of tonality, while the dominant chord—whose root lies a perfect fifth above the tonic—acts as the principal supporter of the tonic. The subdominant—whose root lies a fifth below the root of the tonic chord—similarly performs a supporting role to the tonic. In this way, both dominant and subdominant help to stabilize and support the tonic chord. This means that the function of the primary chords as a group is to preserve and maintain a stable sense of tonality throughout the chord progression.

All other chords perform a secondary function within the key, which means that they are chords that usually act as intermediaries between the three primary chords or are used as temporary substitutes for them. This, in turn, gives chord progressions the possibility of greater interest, diversity, and the expression of a wide range of emotions depending upon the particular chords chosen for use in the chord progression.

The mediant is the chord whose root lies halfway between the tonic and the dominant. As such, the mediant can provide a nice alternative to either tonic or dominant in chord progressions. The submediant is similarly the chord whose root lies halfway between the tonic and the subdominant. The submediant can also provide a nice alternative to either the tonic or the subdominant. The supertonic, as its name suggests, is the chord whose root lies one step above the tonic. The supertonic represents a very important substitute or alternative to the subdominant. Finally, the leading tone triad is the chord whose root lies a semitone below the tonic. Lying a semitone below the tonic, the leading tone triad performs a specialized secondary role as an assistant to the dominant triad. If this sounds confusing, it will all become clear once you start using this triad in chord progressions of your own making.

Conclusion

This chapter began by discussing different types of musical harmony that can be used by composers in their music. Although in total, these offer a bewildering and confusing picture of harmony, a person should first learn the principles of functional harmony inherited from the music of our classical composers, especially in view of the fact that this system of functional harmony still has a powerful influence and place in modern popular music. From there, we went on to discuss the importance of the key system and the necessity for those who wish to study harmony in any depth to have knowledge of all of the major and minor keys belonging to that system. We learned that this system of keys offers a wide and varied spectrum of emotional and coloristic expression, a spectrum that every person wishing to compose and produce his or her own music should have the full use of. From there, we went on to discuss key relationships and showed the way in which, as a result of those relationships, the key system itself represents an integral whole. From there, we discussed the nature of an individual key and how a key itself is made up of a particular scale system—major or minor—together with the various chords that can be built upon and used within that scale. I also mentioned methods of representing and signifying those chords. Finally, we went on to discuss the concept of tonality and how each of the chords belonging to a particular key performs a particular function within that key—a function that itself derives from the necessity for maintaining a clear tonal center within the music. I then briefly explained each individual function.

Having put forward these foundational ideas, it is now time to begin to put them into practice. How can you learn to use these materials to your advantage? What can you do to increase your skills with respect to musical harmony? With these questions in mind, the next chapter will look at the important principles of part writing, for it is through the practice of part writing that you can learn how to connect one chord to another within an overall chord progression.

4 The Principles of Part Writing

Under ordinary circumstances, a given chord that is used in a musical composition will itself form a part of chain of connected chords called a *chord progression*. In Figure 4.1 you will see an illustration of such a typical chord progression.

C	Em	F	Dm7	G7	C

Figure 4.1 Typical major key chord progression.

Looking more closely at this chord progression, it becomes apparent that the F major chord both follows the E minor chord and precedes the D minor seventh chord. As such, the F major chord is playing its part in a chain of connected events. For this chord to play that part satisfactorily, the ear needs to be persuaded that there is a logical connection both with the chord it follows and with the chord it leads into. Now, what establishes that logical connection? One of the main factors involved are the melodic connections that link the succession of chords together. Examples of this are the top note of each harmony, which is heard by the ear as being the lead, and the lowermost notes of each chord, which are being heard as the bass line. Both lead and bass are melodic forces that, for the ear, help to connect the successive chords together. If these do not have a clear melodic logic to them, then no matter how good the chord progression, the music simply will not sound right.

Voice Leading

As such, a chord progression can be viewed in two different ways. On one hand it can be viewed as a succession of vertical chords, while on the other it can be viewed as a combination of separate melodic parts—in other words, melody, bass, inner parts, and so on. This observation is very important for the study of harmony, because it means that when writing a harmony, we need to consider not only the chord progression itself, but also the melodic movement of each of the individual parts, which serve to connect the chords logically together. This feature—the melodic movement of individual parts within a chord progression—is called *voice leading*.

The aim of good voice leading is to ensure that each individual part forms a logical and self-sufficient melody in its own right. For example, the upper part of the harmony is usually heard by the ear as being the lead. Now, it is obvious that the lead—in addition to providing the upper notes of the harmony—needs to have its own distinctive melodic character. The lower part of the harmony, on the other hand, is heard by the ear as being the bass line. Although not as prominent as the lead, a good bass line also merits from having its own logical, melodic quality. Now, provided that the lead and the bass have their own strong melodic character, it is perhaps possible to get away with giving less attention to the inner parts because the ear will tend to focus on the lead and bass. Yet for a smooth and balanced musical texture, ideally all of the separate parts of the harmony should have their own strong melodic identity. For this very reason, generally harmony is written with a specific number of parts in mind. By parts, I mean the number of melodic voices involved. The reason for writing harmony in a certain number of parts is so that attention can be paid to the melodic movement and character of each individual part. If the melodic character of the parts is illogical, erratic, or awkward, the harmony itself will suffer.

In *Composition for Computer Musicians,* I talked about the principles of melodic writing as they apply to the writing of good leads.[1] These principles also apply to good voice leading. Ideally, each melodic part of the harmony needs to be a natural and free-flowing melodic line. In practical terms, this means plenty of stepwise movement to give the melody a smooth, flowing quality, together with the use of leaps here and there to give it energy and character. A good test here is whether the melodic part is easy to sing. If it falls naturally to the voice, then it will probably work well as a melodic part in a harmony. A productive area of study in this respect is to look at the voice leading of traditional part songs—that is, songs written in a certain number of parts, each part of which (ideally) has its own melodic character.

Studying Part Song Writing

A good example of a traditional part song is "In the Bleak Midwinter"—which, in the case of Figure 4.2, has been voiced for four vocal parts: soprano, alto, tenor, and bass. Look closely at the treatment of each individual melodic part. You can tell these apart because the soprano and alto are on the treble stave, with the tails of the notes of the soprano part pointing upward and the tails of the alto part pointing downward. Similarly, the tenor and the bass are on the bass stave, with the tails of the notes of the tenor part pointing upward and the bass part downward. Notice that while in all cases the harmony for each chord required is complete, the individual voices themselves each have a smooth, flowing, and natural-sounding melodic part. This in turn gives a natural, free-flowing quality to the chord progression.

Observe as well the way in which the harmony makes good use of notes that are common to two successive chords, such as the E in the Em chord of bar 2 and the Am chord of bar 3. Being common to both chords, the E as it occurs in the alto part is held over, and in this way provides a valuable link between the two chords for the ear. This in turn

---

[1] Chapter 8, "Writing Melodic Leads," pp. 99–112.

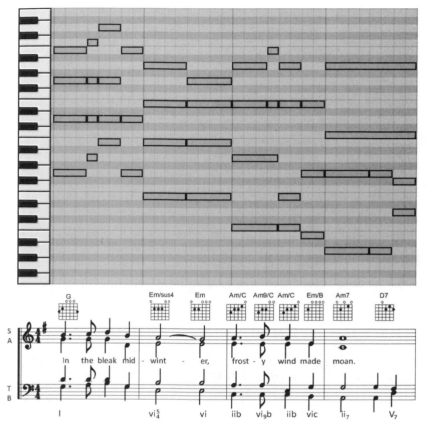

Figure 4.2   Excerpt from traditional part song "In the Bleak Midwinter."

helps to knit the chords together, enhances the smoothness of the harmony, and gives it a sense of continuity.

Three Kinds of Part Motion

When creating or adding a harmony to a lead or bass line, therefore, it is not just a matter of finding the right chords; it is also a matter of voicing these chords in such a way that the individual parts or voices that connect the harmonies together have a smooth, distinctive, and natural melodic character of their own. Toward this end, it is useful to bear in mind that when writing more than one melodic part at the same time, there are three possible types of part motion. These are similar, oblique, and contrary motion. Similar motion is where both parts move in the same direction at the same time, either up or down. Oblique motion is where one part remains static while the other rises or falls. And finally, contrary motion is where the parts move in opposite directions. See Figure 4.3.

Through the course of a chord progression, it is very likely that all three types of motion will be used. And generally, a nice mixture of all three leads to a varied and interesting texture. Have a look again at Figure 4.2. Try to pick out the three types of movement as they appear in this passage. You will see that there is a varied mix of all three. And

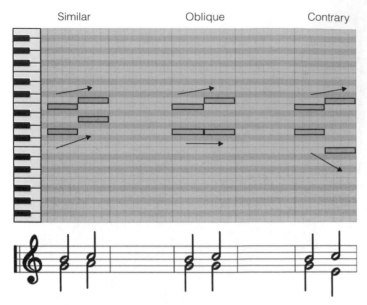

Figure 4.3   Three types of part motion.

although at a given moment, one or the other type of movement might dominate for a while, a general mix of all three is what you would normally expect from a suitable harmony.

The main type of movement that can often tend to undermine good part writing is similar motion. For example, it is obvious that too much similar motion can lead to the impression that the parts are just following one another around. Figure 4.4 shows an example of this.

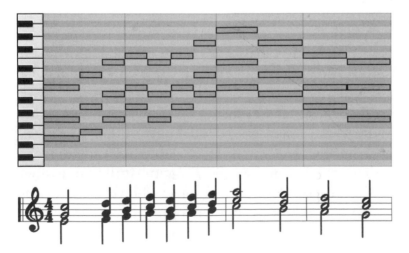

Figure 4.4   Chords in similar motion.

The two lower parts in this example simply follow the lead a fourth and a sixth below. As such, the harmony works in the sense that it is using the chords properly and effectively; but as a general technique, this is not often the best solution to providing a satisfactory harmony. This is because the ear hears this as being a single melodic line that has been thickened up with chords. If that is what is required at a given moment in a track, then that's fine. But bear in mind that for the ear, the parts are no longer melodically independent, which makes a very mechanical and predictable method of providing a harmony. Suffice it to say that for the individual parts of the harmony to have their own melodic independence, in most contexts the use of contrary and/or oblique motion is also necessary.

Consecutive Octaves and Fifths

The use of similar motion also carries the risk of introducing consecutive unisons, octaves, and/or fifths. This brings us to what is perhaps the famous rule encountered in the study of musical harmony. This rule is that consecutive unisons, fifths, and octaves between the same two parts are not allowed. In Figure 4.5, you can see what is meant by consecutive fifths and octaves. The lead and the bass are moving in the same direction at the interval of the octave. Similarly, the bass and the lower inner part are moving in the same direction at the interval of a fifth.

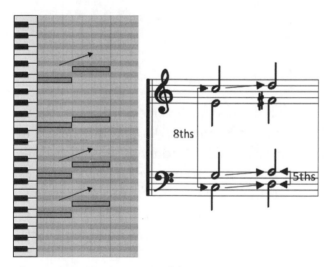

Figure 4.5   Consecutive fifths and octaves.

Consecutives therefore occur when two given parts move in similar motion to one another at the interval of the unison, fifth, or octave. The rule regarding the unison is pretty easy to understand. If you are writing a harmony in four parts, to have two or more of those parts simply duplicating one another is to fail to take advantage of the opportunity to create a full harmony. The rule prohibiting consecutive octaves and fifths needs further explanation, though.

When consecutive octaves and fifths occur, this causes the two parts that carry them to suddenly jump out from the rest of the harmony. And this just doesn't sound good. Ideally, a harmony needs to come across as a balanced and even sound in which all of

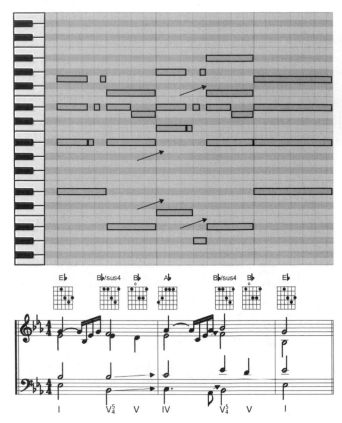

Figure 4.6 Consecutive octaves.

the voices are nicely blended together. To get this balanced and even sound, consecutive fifths and octaves need to be avoided like the plague. If not avoided, then they should at least be used consistently, as was done in the harmony of the Middle Ages and as is done in power chords in rock music. As a consistent feature, they sound great. But when they creep in unannounced and cause two voices to suddenly stand out from the harmony, they are definitely not wanted. In Figure 4.6, you can see two examples of consecutive octaves unobtrusively hidden away in the harmony. These have been highlighted with arrows.

In the first case (reading from the left), the consecutive octaves occur between the bass and the lower inner part, while in the second case they occur between the bass and the lead. In both cases, the octave stands out like a sore thumb. And this is where the weakness lies. Although I would not suggest that you stick to this rule when you are writing and producing your own music, I do suggest that while practicing harmony exercises, you avoid them altogether.

Looking back at the example given in Figure 4.6, it becomes apparent that the two occurrences of consecutives can be eliminated, and by doing so, the harmony of this passage can be greatly strengthened. Figure 4.7 shows one such solution to this problem.

UNIVERSITY OF CHESTER, WARRINGTON CAMPUS

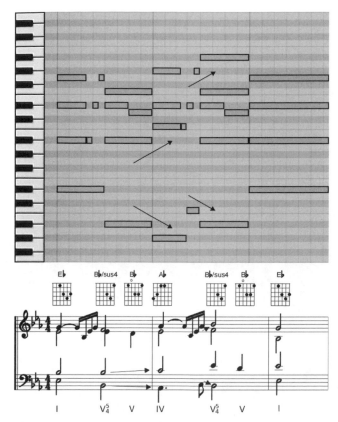

Figure 4.7 Harmony of Figure 4.6 corrected to eliminate unnecessary consecutives.

If you compare Figure 4.7 to Figure 4.6, you will see that the solution to this problem was simply to swap the notes A flat and C in the bass. Looking at the positions of the arrows, you can see that the offending parts now move in contrary motion to one another, and the harmony, as a result, is much stronger.

It is inevitable that when writing a harmony in, say, four parts, octaves and fifths will occur when the voices move in similar motion. These are okay and are to be expected. It is when they occur between the same melodic parts—especially between the bass and the lead—that they tend to stand out and intrude upon the harmony. So this is a possible eventuality that you always need to watch out for.

Consecutive fifths pose a similar problem. In Figure 4.8, the harmony has been re-written to include as many offending consecutive fifths as possible. If you listen to this, you will soon hear the obvious defects in this type of treatment. The harmony sounds bare, awkward, and crude. It's a far cry from a nice, balanced harmony where all of the voices blend together as equals.

Disjointed Voice Leading

Another thing to watch out for is disjointed and awkward voice leading. This usually occurs where there are leaps in one or more voices. It can give rise to what were in

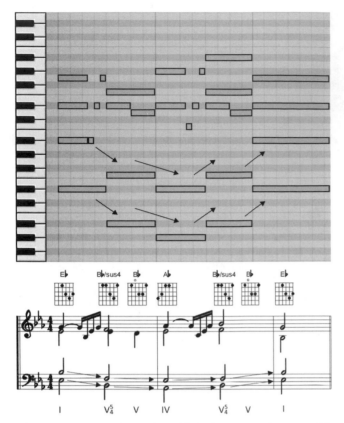

Figure 4.8 Consecutive fifths between bass and lower inner part.

classical times recognized as being various weaknesses in the harmony. Examples of this are so-called hidden octaves and fifths. These occur when two voices moving in similar motion land on the interval of a fifth or octave, as you can see in Figure 4.9.

The weakness of hidden octaves and fifths is due to the fact that, as both octave and fifth are such strong and distinctive intervals, when they are approached by similar motion in this way, they tend to receive such emphasis that they then stand out from the harmony. Thus standing out, they tend to have an intrusive effect upon the balanced blending of the parts. And it is for this reason that—in traditional harmony, at least—hidden octaves and fifths tend to be avoided between the outer parts.

Another eventuality to watch out for is where two or more voices overlap. This occurs when two voices leap in similar motion in a manner that you can see in Figure 4.10.

In this case the overlap occurs between the two upper voices. This involves the lower part moving to a note that is higher than the note previously sounded by the upper part. If this sounds confusing, just look at the example, and you will see what I mean. On the treble staff, the upper note of the first chord is G, while the lower note of the second chord is A—a tone above the G. The result of this is a disjointed connection between the two chords owing to the sudden shift of register between the two voices. This in turn can

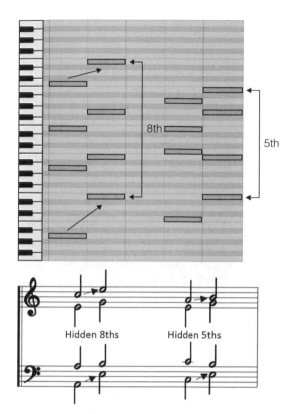

Figure 4.9   Hidden octaves and fifths.

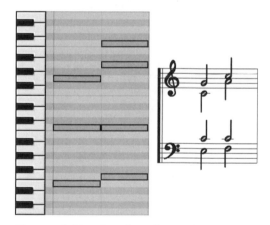

Figure 4.10   Overlapping voices.

undermine that valued sense of continuity in the harmony—a smooth and easy flow between one chord and the next.

Conclusion

This chapter looked at the importance of the principles of part writing in the study of harmony. It showed that most chords in music occur in transit between one chord and another and that, therefore, you must obtain a smooth, logical connection between chords. It also showed that this connection is secured through the use of the melodic forces that knit the successive chords of a chord progression together. The topic that arises from these concerns is called *voice leading*, a topic that primarily looks at chord progressions as a combination of separate melodic parts, such as bass and lead.

We discussed the necessity for giving these melodic parts their own strong melodic character. So that due attention might be given to this, I suggested that the study of harmony is best made through an approach that creates harmonies from a certain fixed number of melodic parts or voices. I offered an example of melodic part writing in order to demonstrate this important idea. We then went on to look at the different types of motion that can occur when writing harmony in parts, and I pointed out the necessity of using a nice mix of these different types. Finally, we looked at the various weaknesses that can occur in harmony, especially in terms of the use of similar motion. This included the famous prohibition of consecutive fifths and octaves, hidden fifths and octaves, and the unnecessary use of overlap between voices. Having duly considered these principles, we will now consider the different ways in which chords can be effectively scored and voiced.

5 Voicing the Common Triad and Its Inversions

The common triad is a chord of three notes that has provided the mainstay of musical harmony for many hundreds of years. This is for the simple reason that the common triad represents what is perhaps the most perfect and harmonious combination of more than two notes as it is possible to get. For this reason, composers and songwriters throughout the ages have continued to find in the common triad a resource for their music that has—and probably always will have—a perpetual appeal to the human ear. Indeed, it does not matter what kind of music you write, in one form or another you will be using common triads. Because of this, one of the first jobs of the student of musical harmony is to study the common triad in all of its forms and guises and learn how to voice common triads in the most effective way possible.

The Major Common Triad

Common triads are called common for the simple reason that they form the majority of the chords used in music. There are two kinds of common triads—the major triad and the minor triad. A good example of a common triad is the chord of C major, which is perhaps the first chord that any music student learns to play. This chord is composed of three notes—C, E, and G—which are respectively termed the root, third, and fifth. You can see this chord illustrated on the keyboard in Figure 5.1.

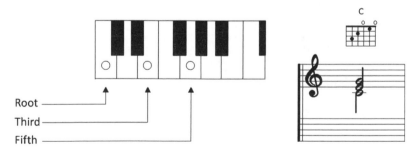

Figure 5.1 Example of a common triad—the chord of C major.

This type of common triad is called a *major triad* for the simple reason that the interval between root and third—notes C to E—is a major third (as opposed to a minor third, which would be notes C and E flat). Being a major third, the major common triad suggests a feeling of brightness, optimism, and contentment. For this reason, it can often be the prevalent harmony used in happy, optimistic, and upbeat music.

The most important note of a common triad is the root note. The root note is the note upon which a chord has its foundation. This note is rather like the foundation of a house: It gives the chord a sense of being firmly anchored. For this reason, a chord is always named by its root note. Any chord that has a root note of C, as in this example, is thus a chord of C. If you play the C major chord on your MIDI keyboard, you will discover how brilliantly the three notes blend together. This is due to the aural qualities of the intervals present in the chord. The fifth of the chord—note G—provides a very strong harmony with the root note. If you play this fifth—C and G—on your keyboard without including the third, you will hear this for yourself (see Figure 5.2 (a)). The harmony that they produce is very powerful, and it is characterized by a great strength and firmness. The third of the chord—note E—also beautifully harmonizes with the root note. Try playing the root and third on their own without the fifth (see Figure 5.2 (b)). You will also hear how beautifully the two notes blend together. Although lacking the strength of the fifth, the harmony of the third has a richness and beauty to it. Finally, try playing the third and fifth together—note E and G (see Figure 5.2 (c)). You will hear that these two notes also give rise to a pleasant-sounding harmony. Because all three of the intervals present in this chord create a consonant harmony in their own right, this means that when combined together as in Figure 5.2 (d), they give rise an even more powerful three-note harmony that is the major triad.

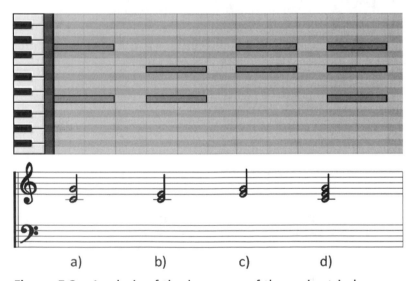

Figure 5.2   Analysis of the harmony of the major triad.

The Minor Common Triad

Another chord that also counts as a common triad is the minor chord. The minor chord differs from the major in one respect: The third of the chord is a minor rather than a major third. Having a minor third in this fashion, the minor common triad has a darker emotional quality. For this reason, the minor chord is usually the prevalent harmony in sad, moody, or blue music. To turn a major chord into a minor chord, all that is necessary is to flatten the third by a semitone. See Figure 5.3.

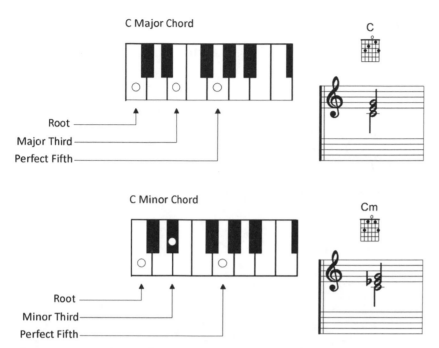

Figure 5.3   Major and minor common triads for comparison.

Along with the major chord, the minor chord is the only other example of a chord of three notes in which all of the intervals form beautiful consonant harmonies in their own right. In fact, looking at the minor chord, we can see that it has the same three intervals as the major chord but occurring in a slightly different way. In common with the major chord, the minor chord also has a perfect fifth, which means that the perfect fifth is the common backbone to both major and minor common triads. The way in which the two chords differ is in the placing of the thirds. In the major chord the lowermost third is major, which gives the chord a bright, sunny quality, while in the minor chord the lowermost third is minor, which gives it a darker, moodier, and sadder quality.

Voicing Major and Minor Common Triads

If you want to bring a sense of harmony into your music, the major and minor common chords represent powerful harmonies to use. However, to use them effectively, you need to know the different ways in which they can be used in a composition. This is to do with the fact that there are numerous ways in which a chord can be treated in a composition. This difference in the way a single chord can be used is known as *voicing*. Each chord can be voiced in a number of different ways, and each of these different ways of voicing a chord will give that chord a different profile. This profile is distinguished from the chord itself using the term *sonority*. Each chord may give rise to numerous different sonorities, some of which are effective and others of which are less so.

To be able to write really good harmonies, it is necessary to study these different ways of voicing chords and to learn to use the most appropriate voicing for the particular musical situation in which the chord occurs. These different ways of voicing a chord have to do with three different yet related factors: chordal doubling, chordal spacing, and chordal inversion.

Chordal Doubling

If to the three notes of the C major chord illustrated in Figure 5.3 I add another note an octave above the root, the resulting chord will have four notes, as shown in Figure 5.4.

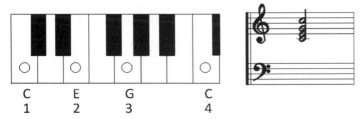

Figure 5.4   C major chord as chord of four notes.

Although the chord now has four notes, it is not a new chord simply because all we have done is doubled the root note. Instead of there being one note C, there are now two note Cs. This is called *doubling*. If you play this chord on your MIDI keyboard, you will hear that the addition of another note C an octave above the root gives the chord a quality of greater strength and resonance. Somehow the chord stands out more, and it has a greater brilliance. This is for the simple reason that the root note has been reinforced by another note C an octave above it.

From this it becomes apparent that no matter how many note Cs are present in the chord, the addition of these extra notes does not change the identity of the chord simply because we are only duplicating and thereby reinforcing notes that are already present in it. It also becomes apparent that it is feasible to double any of the notes in the C major chord. As well as doubling the root note C, it is also possible to double the fifth note G or the third note E.

The issue of doubling arises from the need to have many instruments playing the same chord. Say, for example, you are voicing a chord for a string orchestra patch. A complete string orchestra is composed of double basses, cellos, violas, and first and second violins. To score the chord for the entire orchestra in a balanced and effective way, it will clearly be necessary to double numerous notes of the chord at different registers. Figure 5.5 shows an example so you can see what I mean.

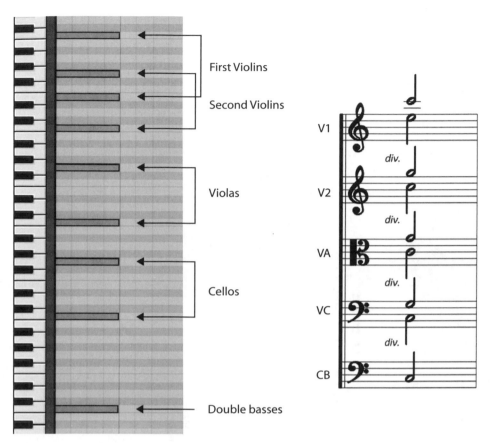

Figure 5.5   C major chord scored for string orchestra.

Here the C major triad is scored over a range of four octaves in which the root has been doubled four times and the fifth doubled twice. The result is a powerful chordal sonority in which all of the different notes blend together in an even and balanced way.

This example goes to show that generally, when using a common triad in a particular situation, you will often need to double certain notes. Indeed, for the chord to have a wide spread over the register, the necessity for doubling is unavoidable. However, bear in mind that some notes of a chord will double well, whereas others, when doubled, seem to detract from the quality of the resultant sonority. A good example in terms of the major chord is the doubling of the third. When the third of a major triad is doubled, the third seems to stand out and imbalance the sonority. For this reason, within the study of functional harmony, a rule is often introduced that prohibits the doubling of the third of a major triad. But of course it has often been said that rules are made to be broken, and in terms of music this could not be more true. Music as a language has often progressed as a result of composers breaking established rules and conventions. So my advice for the person studying musical harmony is to be aware of the rules but not necessarily be bound by them. Rather than relying on rules, trust your own ear. Because music is there to be listened to, the best arbiter is always the human ear. Consequently, if your ear tells you that a given doubling sounds good, then go ahead and use it.

Personally, I avoid doubling the third of a major triad if possible, because I don't feel it adds anything to the sonority. When the root or fifth is doubled, it gives the sonority greater strength and brilliance. When the third is doubled, the sonority sounds unbalanced, and the third tends to stand out too much. On the other hand, for some reason the third of a minor triad, when doubled, is not so obtrusive. So I am less likely to avoid doubling the third of a minor triad.

Figure 5.6 shows the voicing of a major triad, which is prohibited in classical music harmony because the third has been doubled.

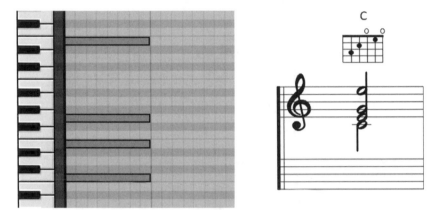

Figure 5.6   Voicing of a C major triad in which the third has been doubled.

Chordal Spacing

Another important consideration when using a chord is the way in which the different notes of the chord are spaced relative to one another. This consideration arises from the fact that the available range of notes for composition purposes is over seven full octaves of sound. Because of this, the notes of a chord can be distributed all over the pitch register, leading to different kinds and types of chordal spacing. This represents an important consideration for the simple reason that not all of the different ways of spacing a particular chord are that effective. For a chord used in a particular musical situation to sound balanced, it must be spaced properly. If not, the chord will sound dull, unclear, or unbalanced. The ideal is a chord that sounds complete, full, and balanced throughout the whole range in which it is being used. For this reason, one of the first areas of practice for the student of musical harmony is to learn to space chords in an effective way.

There are two kinds of chordal spacing. When the notes of a chord are crowded together as closely as possible, this is called *closed position*. Figures 5.1 and 5.3 are both examples of closed spacing. Then there is *open position,* in which the notes are spread out over one or more octaves of the pitch register. Figure 5.7 presents some examples of different ways of openly spacing a C major common triad.

The factors that make the aforementioned effective ways of voicing the chord are the balanced and as even as possible arrangement of the intervals between the lead note and

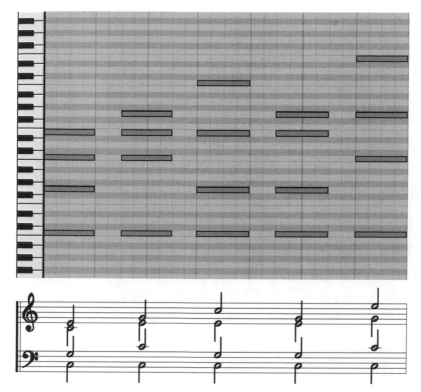

Figure 5.7   Different ways of spacing a C major common triad in four parts.

the bass note. This gives the notes of each chord a fair spread over the register in which it spans. The result is a chord in which all of the notes play a more or less equal role in the creation of a balanced chordal sonority, in which no one note stands out from the rest. Observe also that the widest spaces are usually between the bass and the next note up. This is for the simple reason that the bass note is so rich in harmonics that it is able to offer a secure foundation for chords whose notes are quite a distance above it. For this reason, wide intervals of an octave or even more can often be used between the bass note and the upper three parts.

In contrast to these examples of effective spacing, Figure 5.8 gives some examples of ineffectual chordal spacing. Each of these has been enumerated so that I can explain why it is ineffective.

In Example (a), the gap between the two inner parts is just too big. This means that the harmony is split off into two bands of sound—a strong and powerful fifth in the lower parts with a weak third too high up to balance the power of the fifth below. In Example (b), the chord is also split between the three lower parts, which crowd together to give a chord that is just too bassy and a fourth part that, to the ear, does not sound like it is even a part of the chord. In Example (c), you can see a reoccurrence of the same problem that affects Example (a). The gap between the two upper and two lower parts is just too big. So rather than coming across as a balanced sonority, the chord comes across as being split across different frequency bands. In Example (d), the spacing

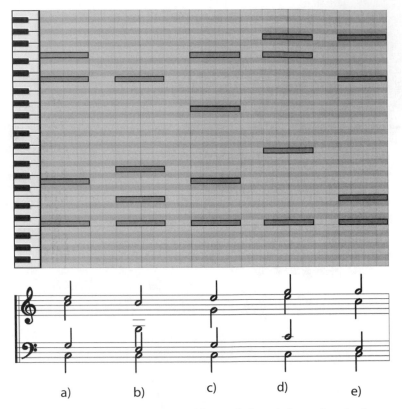

Figure 5.8   Examples of ineffectual chordal spacing in four parts.

is just as about as ineffectual as it could get, because it offers a powerful octave in the lower parts with a weak third too high up to sound as if it is part of the same chord. Finally, with Example (e), the third right down with the bass gives a cloudy and muddy harmony, while the root and fifth are alone in the upper register. So again, rather than coming across to the ear as a balanced sonority, this voicing splits the chord up over separate frequency bands. To come across as a balanced and powerful sonority, the chord needs to be voiced in such a way that it has a balanced and even representation throughout the chord's span.

Chordal Inversion

Another powerful consideration that affects the voicing of chords is the particular inversion that is being used. A chord has three notes, which means that it is possible that any of the three notes can be used to provide the bass note. When the root is in the bass, the chord is said to be in *root position;* when the third is in the bass, the chord is said to be in *first inversion;* when the fifth is in the bass, the chord is said to be in *second inversion.* Figure 5.9 shows the three inversions of both a major and a minor common chord.

The particular inversion being used is therefore always determined by the note of the chord that is in the bass. Acting as a support for the upper parts, the particular note chosen will strongly affect the aural quality of the chord. When the root is in the bass,

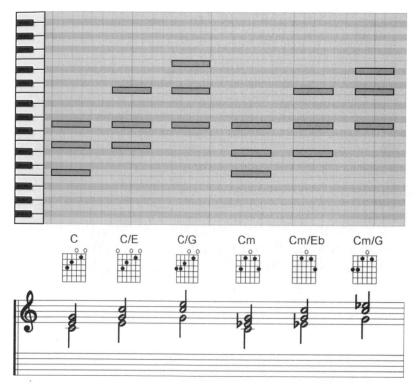

Figure 5.9 Root position, first inversion, and second inversion of major and minor common triads.

the chord is well anchored and strong sounding; whereas when the third is in the bass, the chord is not so stable, although it still has a nice, rich sound. When the fifth is in the bass, the chord has the least stability. For this reason, functional harmony triads in second inversion are often only used in certain contexts.

To become familiar with the three positions of each triad, I suggest that you spend some time playing through both major and minor common triads in their three positions to accustom your ear to the qualities of their particular sonorities.

Conclusion

This chapter looked closely at the two kinds of common triad: the major triad and the minor triad. Because these are probably the types of triad you will use most often in your music, it makes great sense to acquire an all-around knowledge of these two types of chords, together with an ability to voice these chords effectively within a particular musical work. We also looked at the intervals within the major and minor common triads, and we saw that, consisting of nothing but consonants, the harmonies of the major and minor triads are themselves completely consonant and therefore very pleasing to the human ear.

Having studied the two types of common triad, we went on to look at the issue of voicing and how a given chord can be voiced in numerous ways—some being effective ways of voicing a chord, and others being less so. We discussed three important factors when voicing common triads: doubling, spacing, and chordal inversion. Doubling concerns the necessity for duplicating certain notes of a triad when writing in more than three parts. Here we saw that while all notes of a triad can feasibly be doubled, it is not necessarily advantageous to double the third of a major triad because it can make the third of the chord stand out too much.

Spacing concerns the distribution of the notes of the chord over the register in which it is being used. Here we noted that there is close position spacing, where the notes of the chord are crowded together as closely as possible, and open position spacing, where there are wider intervals between the notes of a chord. We looked at different ways to space a common chord, paying particular attention to those types of spacing that lead to the creation of effective and strong-sounding harmonies. Similarly, we studied the weaknesses of ineffective chordal spacing. Finally, we looked at chordal inversion, which concerns the particular note of the chord that is used in the bass.

Having looked at the two kinds of common triad, it is now time to look at the ways in which triads are brought together in the form of sequences—called *chord progressions*—that give to the music that uses them a sense of logic, progression, and forward motion. However, because chord progressions can be rather complex affairs, we will begin the next chapter by looking simply at the uses of the two most important chords of a given key—the chords of the tonic and the dominant.

6 Tonic and Dominant Harmony

I n the previous chapter, we looked at the voicing of common triads and how it is possible to voice a single triad in numerous ways. This is a very useful study because every chord used in a composition will at some time need consideration with regard to how it is voiced. But of course, compositions are not made from a single chord. Ordinarily, chords would be occurring in transit as they pass on to another chord within a chain of chords that logically follow one another. This chain is called a *chord progression*. Any composition or song that uses more than one chord—which includes most songs—will therefore involve the use of some kind of chord progression.

Chord progressions have a definite logic to them. And as a songwriter or composer, it is definitely advantageous to learn about this logic. But not only that—the use and treatment of chords historically has also led to certain customary practices, many of which still find favor with composers and songwriters. These customs are called *common practice*.

In earlier days, the logic behind chord progressions, together with these various customs concerning their use and treatment, was codified into what were called the *rules of harmony*, and any musician wishing to learn the arts of harmony would learn by simply adhering to these rules. Yet today we well know that it is pointless to prescribe rules with regard to what you can or cannot do in terms of musical harmony. This is because for generations musicians have been breaking these rules and coming out with perfectly acceptable music. Good examples of this are jazz and blues music. If no musician had ever broken the rules of harmony, jazz and blues simply would not exist. Bearing this in mind, it becomes apparent that it is not really productive to learn harmony by following rules—especially old-school rules—that try to restrict what you are allowed to do. For this very reason, this book will not lay down any rules. However, it will at times look at the principles upon which the rules of old were based, because in these principles there is often a certain concealed wisdom.

A good example of this is the idea of tonality. A lot of the old rules of harmony revolved around the importance of preserving a sense of tonality in a piece of music—one such rule being that every piece of music should end with the tonic chord. That this is a fairly pointless rule is proved by the fact that since then there have been many pieces of music that have successfully flouted this rule. But the idea of tonality that lies behind the rule is itself a very sound one.

Tonality is basically the idea that a chord progression makes more sense to the ear when it is heard to revolve around a central chord, which we call the *tonic chord*. This tonic chord is built on the first degree of either the major or the minor scale. To help you understand the importance of the tonic chord, think about the process of discussion. When we are discussing something, we are stringing together words into logical sentences. When we discuss a topic with other people, the discussion will often be heading toward a certain point—and that point will itself represent the topic around which the discussion is revolving. Having reached that point, the conversation will then come to a close for the simple reason that having reached that point, there is no purpose in any further discussion. A chord progression is very much like this. It is a sequence of chords that all revolve around the tonic and find their place in the chord progression through their relationship to the tonic. And ultimately, the chord progression will tend to culminate and resolve itself onto the tonic chord. So the tonic chord is in a sense like the point of a discussion.

Tonic and Dominant Harmony in the Major Scale

After the tonic chord, the next most important chord in a key is the dominant. This is the major chord built on the fifth degree of the scale. Therefore, in the key of C major, the dominant chord would have the notes G, B, and D. Figure 6.1 illustrates these two important chords of the key of C major with reference to a keyboard.

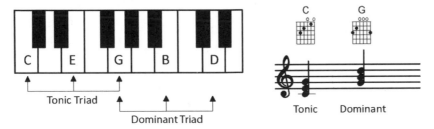

Figure 6.1   The tonic and dominant chords of the key of C major.

The tonic and dominant triads of a key have a very special relationship. This relationship has to do with their particular functions in maintaining a sense of tonality.

- The tonic chord represents the seat of tonality.

- The dominant chord represents the driver of tonality.

This driving quality of the dominant chord stems from the observation that compared to the tonic, the dominant chord has a great sense of tension about it. And historically speaking, this tension has been further loaded by composers who have added other dissonant chordal tones to the dominant, such as the seventh, ninth, eleventh, and thirteenth. And the chord that represents the optimal point of release for that tension is, of course, the tonic. In practical terms this means that the dominant chord always exerts a strong pull toward the tonic. This means that in chord progressions, the dominant tends to act in support of the position of the tonic triad as the tonal center. In this context the dominant chord is persuading the ear that the tonic is the tonal center of the music. Considered as a pair, therefore, the tonic and dominant chords represent two sides of the same principle, the principle itself being tonality. The tonic represents the seat of that principle; the dominant is its driver.

The importance of the tonic and dominant chords in tonal chord progressions therefore cannot be underestimated. As a pair they are as essential to one another as kick and snare are in the matter of drumming. So it is perhaps not surprising that there are a great number of songs that only use the tonic and dominant chords. Inevitably, these songs are very basic—for example, "Jambalaya," "Memphis," "I'm Going Back to Old Kentucky," "He's Got the Whole World in His Hands," "London Bridge," and so on. In fact, hundreds of such songs can be found. The reason these songs are pretty basic is that for their harmony they are relying on the simple nucleus of chord progressions—the tonic and dominant chords. Representing that simple nucleus, it is perhaps best to begin the study of chord progressions that involve only the tonic and dominant chords. Naturally, by doing so, our options are severely limited—which is perhaps a downside to this particular approach. But the upside is that we then become familiar with the core that provides the foundation for more complex chord progressions.

The Authentic Cadence

The driving role of the dominant chord finds its most appropriate use in cadences. A *cadence* is the characteristic way in which a musical phrase, section, or entire piece of music comes to a close. Although there are numerous different types of cadences used in music—the main ones of which will be explored in this book—the most important type of cadence is the one commonly used to bring a piece of music to a close. A concluding or closing cadence would normally be expected to be—but by no means is always—upon the tonic chord. And the history of traditional musical harmony shows us that composers and songwriters unanimously favor the dominant chord to precede the tonic. This is because for the ear, this progression from dominant to tonic chord—especially when both of the chords are in root position—has about it a sense of finality and inevitability that is quite unambiguous. For this reason, this type of cadence is called a *full close* or *authentic cadence*. Figure 6.2 shows an illustration of a perfect cadence in the key of C major.

To get a deeper appreciation of this cadence, each of the melodic movements between the four parts in the perfect cadence has been labeled using letters from (a) to (d). In (a) you can see a melodic movement from the seventh note of the scale—called the *leading note*—up to the tonic. This particular melodic movement is one of the strongest features of the dominant to tonic chord progression, having about it a strong sense of inevitability and finality as the leading note—only a semitone below the tonic—rises smoothly up to the tonic. In a perfect authentic cadence, the leading note to tonic

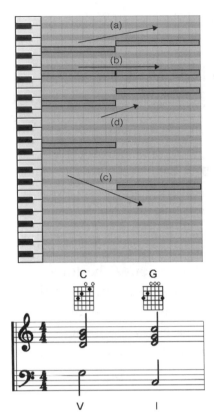

Figure 6.2   Progression from dominant to tonic chord.

movement would normally be in the uppermost part, where it can be heard most clearly and therefore have the maximum impact.

In (b) you can see the use of the note G as a pivot that connects the two chords together. This pivot is available because the fifth degree of the scale—the dominant degree—is common to both chords. As such, when voicing tonic and dominant harmony, the dominant degree represents a useful pivot note that connects tonic and dominant triads together. The existence of such pivot notes in harmony can be used to great practical advantage, as they offer points of continuity that interlink successive chords within a chord progression.

In (c) you can see a melodic movement from the root of the dominant triad (note G) to the root of the tonic triad (note C). Notice that this movement is that of a descending fifth, which is one of the most distinctive and powerful root movements possible in chord progressions. When occurring as part of a dominant to tonic chord progression, it really enhances that sense of the dominant chord falling to the tonic as the piece comes to a close.

Finally, in (d) you can see the fifth of the dominant triad moving smoothly in a stepwise manner up to the third of the tonic. This movement makes for smooth voice leading.

Where the leading note to tonic melodic movement is not in the upper part or where an inversion of the dominant triad is used, the cadence has a slightly weaker effect—that is,

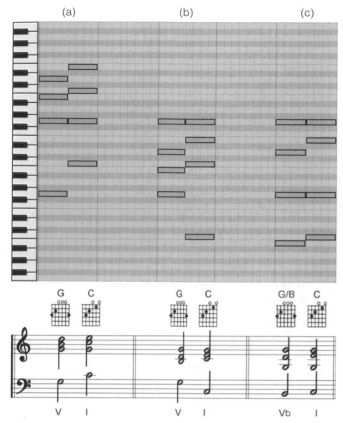

Figure 6.3 Variations of V-I progression.

it does not feel as conclusive (see Figure 6.3 (a) and (b)). For this reason it is termed an *imperfect authentic cadence*. This type of cadence is more likely to be used at a less conclusive point in the composition. Where the leading note occurs in the lowermost part, this means that the dominant triad is then being used in first inversion (c). When the dominant chord is used in first inversion, the cadence is not so incisive. This is because the leading note is then in the bass line, which means that the leading note to tonic movement is not so prominent.

Tonic and Dominant Harmony in the Minor Scale

The minor scale is an interesting case for the tonal system for the simple reason that in its natural form, it is a scale that itself does not have a major dominant triad. The significance of this can be understood by looking more closely at the minor key. Looking, for example, at the scale of A minor, we can see that the triad naturally occurring on the fifth degree is a chord of E minor (see Figure 6.4).

For this reason the character of a dominant to tonic chord progression in the minor key is much more mellow. Both tonic and dominant chords, after all, are minor. As well as this, the minor dominant chord does not progress to the tonic chord quite with the same incisive quality as it does in the major key. This is due to the lack of a leading note

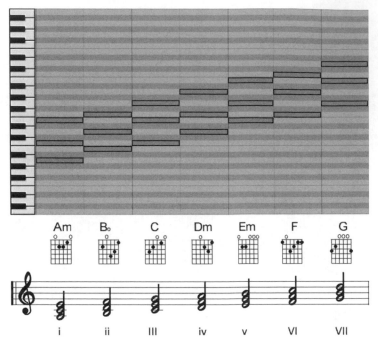

Figure 6.4 Triads in the minor key (A minor).

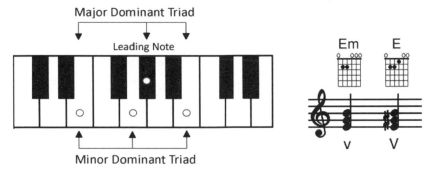

Figure 6.5 Minor and major dominant triads of A minor.

between the seventh and eighth (tonic) degree of the scale. This means that a perfect cadence in the minor key does not have the same driving quality as in the major key.

To remedy this weakness, composers of old used to sharpen the seventh note of the minor scale in order to provide both a major dominant triad and a leading note that lies a semitone below the tonic. You can see this illustrated in Figure 6.5. Observe how raising the third of the minor dominant triad not only converts the E minor chord into an E major chord, but it also gives a leading note up to the tonic.

The consequences of this alteration of the seventh degree of the minor scale are numerous. For a start, because a major dominant triad is being used, the dominant to tonic chord progression in the minor mode becomes much more incisive—solving the problem of the lack of a proper tonal driver in the minor key. Yet by sharpening the seventh degree of the scale to create a leading note, we are in effect stepping outside of the natural minor scale and creating an altogether new scale. In recognition of this fact, this new scale is called the *harmonic minor scale*. And it is strongly distinguished from the natural form of the minor scale by the rather exotic-sounding augmented second interval between the sixth and seventh degrees, as illustrated in Figure 6.6.

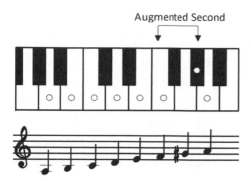

Figure 6.6   The harmonic minor scale.

This sharpening of the seventh degree of the natural minor scale also leads to the creation of some new, equally exotic-sounding chords in the minor scale. These are the augmented triad on degree three and another diminished triad on degree seven. We will consider how to use these in a later chapter. At present we can see that the harmonic minor scale only has four common triads, which in the key of A minor are Am, Dm, E, and F. All of the others are either augmented or diminished. Figure 6.7 illustrates triads available in the harmonic minor scale.

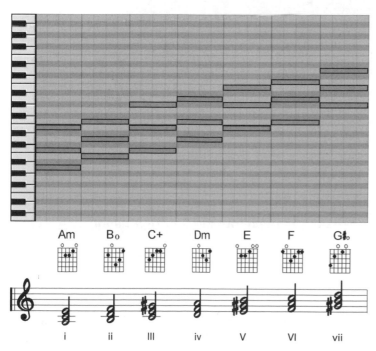

Figure 6.7   Triads in the harmonic minor scale—key of A (MIDI file 05, bars 37–43).

Harmony in the minor scale, therefore, is not such a straightforward affair as in the major scale, because there are not only multiple versions of the scale to contend with, but also the difficult option of different chords potentially being used on the same degree of the scale. For example, on the dominant degree, a major or a minor triad may be used depending upon the context and mood of the music. Suffice it to say it is best to approach the complexities of the minor scale in a gradual fashion.

For a perfect cadence in the minor scale, the major dominant triad would always be used in root position with the leading note in the uppermost part. See Figure 6.8 (a) for an example of this. Figure 6.8 (b) shows a progression from the dominant in root position to the first inversion tonic triad. Figure 6.8 (c) shows a progression from the dominant triad in first inversion to the tonic triad. And finally, Figure 6.8 (d) shows a second inversion tonic triad to dominant and tonic in root position progression. These provide a representative sample of tonic and dominant chord progressions in the minor key.

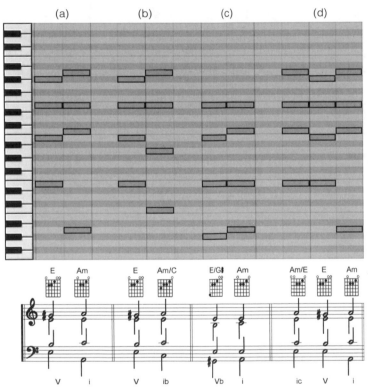

Figure 6.8   Dominant to tonic chord progressions in the minor key (key of A minor).

Chordal Inversions

When putting a harmony to a melody, you must not only decide which chord to use at a given moment, but also decide what is the best position of the chord. Each triad has three possible positions determined by the note of the triad that is in the bass line. Each position will significantly affect the profile of the chord and its quality to the ear.

Chords in root position, for example, where the root is in the bass, have a great quality of stability to them. Therefore, you would probably expect a chord progression to end on a root position tonic triad. Triads in first and second inversion are not as stable because the supporting root is absent in the bass line. For this reason, when these chords are used it feels like they are on their way to another chord. As such, they are more suited for use somewhere between the beginning and end points of the chord progression. Out of the three possible positions of a chord, the most unstable is the second inversion where the fifth is in the bass. As such, second inversion triads are perhaps the least used when compared to the other positions. And when they are used, they tend to be used in certain limited contexts. One such context is where the parts of the harmony are moving in contrary motion, the second inversion chord being used in between two more stable chords. Figure 6.9 shows an example of this in which the second inversion of the dominant triad occurs between a first inversion and a root position tonic triad.

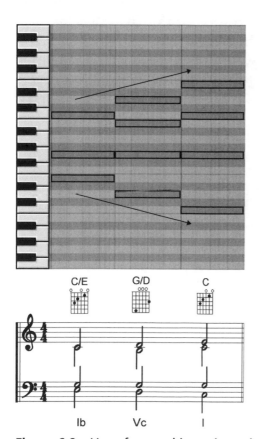

Figure 6.9 Use of second inversion triad.

Observe that because the second inversion triad is safely nestled between two more stable harmonies, the instability of the second inversion triad does not destabilize the harmony.

The Cadential Six-Four

One of the most well-tried uses of the second inversion triad—which uses its instability as a harmony to great advantage—is the cadential six-four, a cadential formula that originated in classical music. The figures six and four refer to the intervals above the bass in the second inversion triad, which are of course the fourth and the sixth. In the cadential six-four, the second inversion of the tonic triad is used as a pre-dominant chord—that is, a chord that precedes the dominant in an authentic cadence. Figure 6.10 shows two examples of the cadential six-four, which we can take a brief look at.

The important feature of the cadential six-four, seen in Figure 6.10 (a), is that the note that is common to both chords—in this case, note G—is held over in the bass line. This then enables the unstable tonic six-four chord to resolve nicely to the dominant, the sixth falling stepwise to the fifth, and the fourth falling stepwise to the third. A powerful effect that can be used to enhance this is to use a melodic suspension where the root of the tonic chord is held over into the range of the dominant chord. This causes a moment of dissonant tension, which is then released as the tonic resolves downward to the leading note. In Figure 6.10 (b), you can see an illustration of this in which the suspended note is marked with an asterisk. This note C, belonging to the previous chord of C major, is being held over while the other parts move to a chord of G. This lingering effect of a note from a previous chord refusing to give way to a chord change gives rise to a great moment of tension before the arrival of the dominant chord in full. In jazz

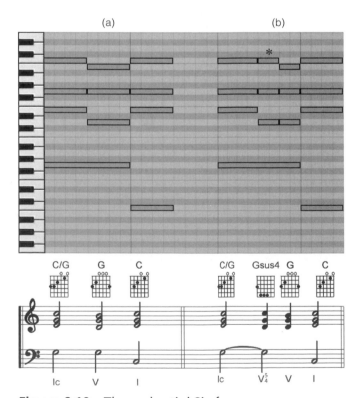

Figure 6.10   The cadential Six-four.

notation, the use of this suspension gives rise to a chord known as a *sus4 chord* (a chord of the suspended fourth) on account of the fourth being used as a substitute for the ordinary third of the common triad. See Figure 6.11.

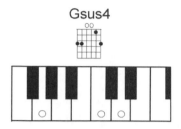

Figure 6.11   The sus4 chord.

Conclusion

This chapter began with the consideration of chord progressions and the notion that behind good chord progressions there is a certain logic. Coupled with this, we observed that there is also the notion of common practice, which concerns the ways in which chords and chord progressions have been commonly treated. We discussed the codification of all of this into the rules of harmony, and we observed that these days it is not really advantageous to be bound by rules that restrict what you can and cannot do. I noted, however, that the principles and values behind such rules are themselves often quite sound and that, therefore, there is a certain point in studying these principles.

We saw one such important value to be tonality, the establishment of which depends upon two important chordal functions: the tonic, which is the seat of tonality, and the dominant, which represents the driver of tonality. As these functions were considered to be so important, we studied in some detail the chords that represent those functions. This study thus looked at tonic and dominant harmony with reference to both the major and the minor scale. However, having covered this territory, it is now time to advance another step and bring another chord into the picture—the chord of the subdominant. This means that the topic of the next chapter will cover the use of three of the possible seven chords within a key.

7 The Three Primary Triads

In the previous chapter, we focused on what are probably the two most important triads in all of music—the tonic and the dominant triad. In this chapter we are going to bring another functional triad into the picture, the subdominant triad. Along with the tonic and dominant triad, the subdominant is a part of an important group of triads used in harmony, which are known as the *three primary triads*. Figure 7.1 offers an illustration of the three primary triads as they appear in the key of C major.

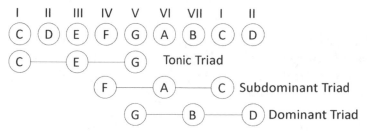

Figure 7.1   The three primary triads.

A Harmony for All Seven Notes of the Scale

The great feature about the three primary triads is that, as you can see from a glance at Figure 7.1, between them they define all seven notes of the scale. This means that—unlike tonic and dominant triads alone—with the three primary triads it is possible to harmonize complete melodies that use all of the notes available to us in a particular key. In effect, this means that the three primary triads offer all of the necessary resources with which to write a complete song. There are many such songs that do rely on the three primary triads for their harmony. Simply Google "three-chord songs," and you will find extensive lists of such songs. There again, like those songs that rely solely on tonic and dominant harmony, many of these songs are very basic. Yet they do include some very memorable popular tunes—tunes we often learned as children, such as "Amazing Grace," "Yellow Bird," "Rock of Ages," or the Christmas carol "Silent Night." Yet don't be fooled into thinking that three-chord songs are all just for children. Artists such as Bob Marley and Bob Dylan did wonders with the three-chord formula.

In this chapter we are going to get you to the point where you can harmonize complete melodies using this three-chord formula. And although by doing so you will be covering territory that has already been well covered by other composers and songwriters, being able to do so provides a solid foundation from which to start and be able to write more complex and sophisticated harmonies.

The Function of the Subdominant

To be able to use the three primary triads of a key, it is useful initially to have some idea of what they do—that is, their function within that key. We have already partly touched upon this topic in the previous chapter, where we considered the job of the tonic and the dominant triads. Here we saw that as a linked pair, the tonic and dominant triads set up the basic terms of a chord progression, these terms being evident in the simple I-V-I progressions we studied in the last chapter.

For the tonic chord, the dominant chord offers a strong pathway of progression. Therefore, we can move away from the tonic and arrive at the dominant (chord I-V). For the dominant chord, the tonic offers a means of bringing that progression to a satisfactory close (chord V-I), called a *cadence*. We can understand this more clearly when we compare an I-V-I progression to a journey, in which we go out from home (the tonic), engage in some activity (the dominant), and then return back home (the tonic). And if you are anything like me, when I am at home for any length of time, I often want to go out into the world and explore for a while. But when I do so, I reach a certain point where I begin to feel restless and want to return home. This is the relationship between the tonic and the dominant in a nutshell. In this way, the tonic chord represents a state of rest and the dominant chord a state of activity.

Bearing this in mind, let us now consider how the other primary chord—the subdominant—fits into the picture. The importance of the subdominant triad is that it enables this journey to be expanded into a more complete and satisfying cycle. It does this by offering an excellent substitute for the dominant chord. What I mean by substitute is a chord that can be used as an alternative to the dominant. And as a substitute for the dominant, one of the most fitting roles for the subdominant is as a pre-dominant chord. What I mean by pre-dominant is a chord that can come after the tonic but in advance of the inevitable arrival of the dominant. The most obvious chord progression that demonstrates this is I-IV-V-I, which represents a shorthand way of saying tonic triad to subdominant triad to dominant triad and then finally back to the tonic triad. In Figure 7.2 you can see an illustration of this cycle.

Sounding great when used in both major and minor keys, this option of being able to use a pre-dominant chord makes for a much more interesting, complete, and varied journey. If the tonic chord represents home, the pre-dominant is rather like the process of moving away from home and undertaking a journey. This means that the dominant then represents the high point of the journey prior to the process of returning home. Emotionally, this is a very satisfying cycle. It also has implications for the structural development of music in that complete sections of music can then be built up around either this particular cycle (I-IV-V-I) or one of its many possible variants. Two well-known examples of this are eight-bar and twelve-bar blues patterns, which in their simplest forms can be represented in the way shown in Figure 7.3.

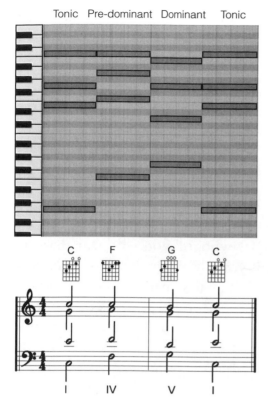

Figure 7.2   I-IV-V-I progression.

Eight Bar Blues Progression

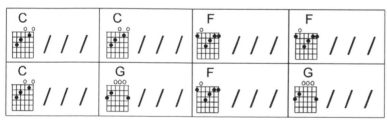

Twelve Bar Blues Progression

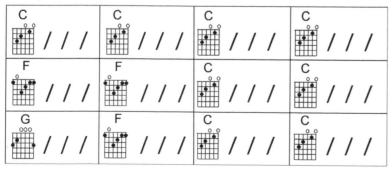

Figure 7.3   Eight-bar and twelve-bar blues chord progressions.

Looking at these progressions, you can see that both basically rely on the three important functions of the tonic, subdominant, and dominant. And although involving only three chords, these progressions are notable for their variety and the way in which the eight- or twelve-measure cycle can be varied in interesting ways. With just two chords—tonic and dominant—we cannot do this. All we can do is to rock back and forth between them.

Variations in the order of the three primary triads are possible because the subdominant does not have to serve as a pre-dominant, although it is an ideal chord for this purpose. A chord progression could equally go from I-V-IV-I. When a phrase or piece of music does end in this way—that is, with the subdominant as the penultimate chord—the cadence is called a *plagal cadence* (IV-I) as opposed to an *authentic cadence* (V-I). If you play a IV-I root position progression on your MIDI keyboard, you will hear that the plagal cadence (see Figure 7.4) has a majestic quality, and this quality has made it a favorite way of ending hymns and gospel tunes. You will sometimes hear a plagal cadence called an "Amen" cadence for this reason. However, despite this type of traditional formulaic use, the plagal cadence is just as popular in popular music, examples of which include the Rolling Stones' "Satisfaction," the Beatles' "Strawberry Fields Forever," or the Manic Street Preachers' "Motorcycle Emptiness."

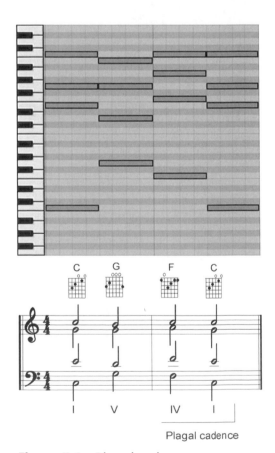

Figure 7.4   Plagal cadence.

An important part of the job of the subdominant is that, like the dominant, it helps to strengthen the position of the tonic triad. This becomes obvious when we realize that the root of the dominant is also the fifth of the tonic, and the fifth of the subdominant is the root of the tonic. If this sounds confusing, take a look at the placement of the arrows in Figure 7.5. The note C in the tonic triad is shared by the subdominant triad, and the note G of the tonic triad is shared by the dominant triad. From this we can see that the dominant and subdominant triads offer key support for the two most important notes of the tonic triad. This in turn gives to the tonic triad a sense of stability, which strengthens its position as the tonal center of the music.

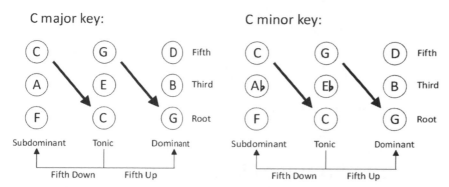

Figure 7.5   Relationship of roots of the three primary triads.

Note as well the respective positions of the chordal roots of these triads. While the root of the dominant triad lies a fifth above the tonic, the root of the subdominant lies a fifth below the tonic. This means that the subdominant therefore offers a nice counter-balance to the dominant. From this standpoint you can see why the basic I-IV-V-I chord progression is so satisfying, for it paints a picture of perfect tonal balance and equilibrium. From the tonic chord, we move to a chord whose root lies a fifth below and then to a chord whose root lies a fifth above, and then finally back to the tonic. This means that the fifth down root movement of the subdominant is counterbalanced by the fifth up root movement of the dominant. In this way, the tonic triad represents a point of tonal equilibrium between these two important triads—the dominant a fifth above and the subdominant a fifth below.

As representing the three primary triads of a key, the I-IV-V-I nuclear progression represents a great way of getting to know the ins and outs of a particular key. This can be achieved by playing these triads in a simple sequence such as you can see in Figure 7.6.

For the minor version, you simply swap the C major for a C minor triad and the F major for an F minor triad. The dominant triads remain major in both keys. When you have learned this sequence in both major and minor keys, it can then be transposed into other keys. When you can do this in all major and minor keys, you will be in a position of having at least a basic familiarity with every single key that is available to you.

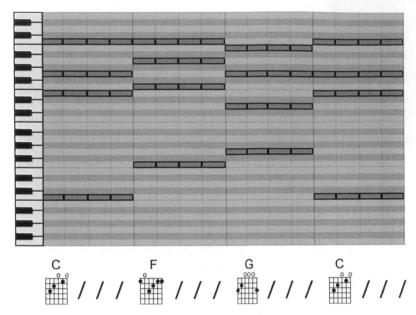

Figure 7.6   Keyboard sequence for the three primary triads.

Adding Three Parts above a Bass Line

Having considered what the three primary triads do, let us now put all of this into practice and develop some harmony using the three primary triads. Composers generally use two main approaches to writing harmonies. A harmony can be put to a given lead melody, or, alternatively, a harmony can be created above a given bass line. Ideally, we should be comfortable with both approaches, which means that both approaches need to be studied and given ample time and practice. In the exercises that belong with this particular chapter, there are some that require you to add a harmony over a given bass line. The chords required in each case will be indicated. This will involve adding three harmony parts above the bass line in order to give rise to a four-part harmony. All of the chord progressions will involve the three primary triads only.

Chord progressions involving the three primary triads present their own unique problems of voicing, particularly with regard to the voice leading as chord IV moves to chord V (or vice versa). These problems arise because the root of the dominant is a second above the root of the subdominant. For a start, this means that the two triads share no notes in common—which means that all of the parts have to move either in similar or contrary motion. The primary difficulty with this is avoiding consecutives. In the process of free composition, consecutives can be used to great effect and in many different ways. But this book is not about free composition. It is about the study of harmony, and an important part of the study of harmony—especially functional harmony, which has its origins in classical musical styles—are the principles of effective part writing. At this level consecutive octaves and fifths are definitely to be avoided.

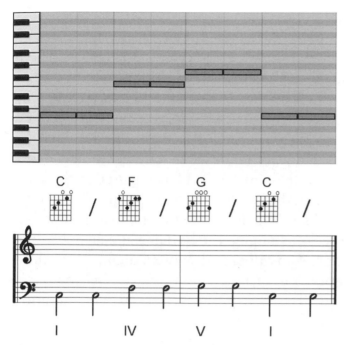

Figure 7.7   Three-chord bass line.

Now say, for example, that the task is to add three melodic parts above the bass line shown in Figure 7.7.

The progressions from I to IV and V to I present no real problems with regard to the voice leading. The problem, as we shall see, is the progression from chord IV to chord V. In Figure 7.8, you will see some of the possible ways of voicing a IV-V root position chord progression.

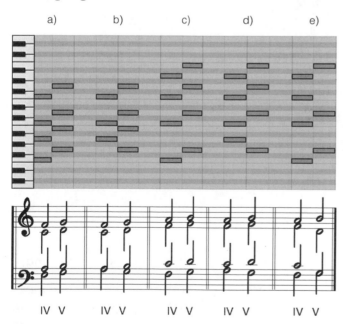

Figure 7.8   Different ways of voicing chord IV to V.

To voice a chord progression properly and to get good, smooth part writing, we need to get down really close and start to examine the voice leading of each possible progression. In terms of the examples in Figure 7.8, if the notes F and G are used in the lead as in example (a), then immediately this leads to consecutive octaves with the bass. Consecutive fifths are also apparent between the bass and one of the inner parts. The only way of harmonizing the notes F and G is to use the subdominant triad in first inversion as in (b), in which case the bass line needs to be changed. Both solutions are unsatisfactory. As a consequence, these two notes cannot be used in the lead given the restrictions of the bass line. In (c) we can see the notes A and B being used in the lead. Although this lead harmonizes the bass line in thirds, this also leads to problems in the part writing. Consecutive octaves and fifths result. Example (d) eliminates these but only at a price. The price is again the need for changing the bass line and also the doubling of the third of the F major triad. For reasons already discussed, doubling the third of a major triad is rarely a good solution for producing an effective harmony. In example (e), you can see a solution around all of these problems, although this solution is a bit awkward due to the jerky part writing in the lower parts.

From these examples we can appreciate that when adding a harmony above a bass line, particular care and attention needs to be taken with the progression from IV to V and vice versa. Realistically, there are only a number of limited solutions that respect the principles of good part writing. You can see some of these in Figure 7.9.

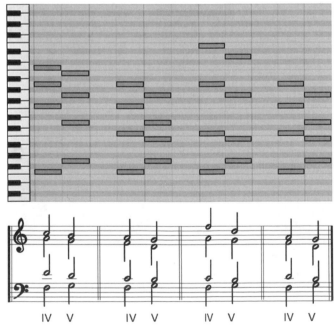

Figure 7.9 Progressions from chord IV to V, which respect the principles of good part writing.

Looking at these we can see that they all have something in common. The upper parts are all moving in similar motion downward relative to the bass, which is moving upward. In this way consecutives are avoided.

Harmonizing Melodies with the Three Primary Triads

Having considered the situation of creating a harmony above a given bass line, let us now approach the matter from the other perspective—that is, harmonizing a melody or lead in four parts. In doing so, only three chords will be used—the three primary triads of the key together with their respective inversions where appropriate. Although this kind of three-chord harmony is very basic, it does have the advantage of removing ambiguity when harmonizing a melody. This is because some of the notes of the scale have only one possible harmony. For example, looking at Figure 7.10, you can see the notes of the scale that are supported by the three primary triads.

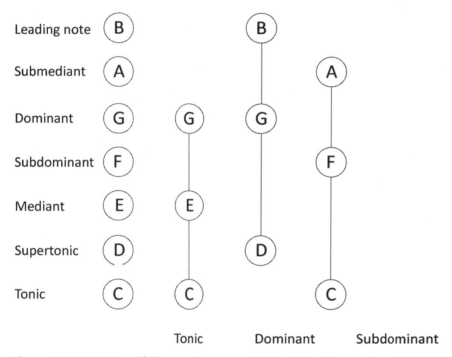

Figure 7.10   Notes of the scale supported by the three primary triads.

For note D of the scale, there is only one possible triad to use as a suitable harmony. This is the dominant triad where note D occurs as the fifth. Similarly, note E is supported only by the tonic triad, note F the subdominant triad, note A the subdominant, and note B the dominant. Finding a harmony for these notes is not problematic because there is only one option. There is only some degree of ambiguity in terms of the tonic degree C, which is supported by both the tonic triad and the subdominant triad, and the dominant degree G, which is supported by the tonic and dominant triad. In these cases, therefore, we are given a choice of which chord to use. The main factor that will influence that choice will be the context. The chord that is chosen must fit in logically with the rest of the chord progression.

Example Harmonization

Let us now harmonize a sample melody in four parts using only the three primary triads of the key. Figure 7.11 illustrates the melody.

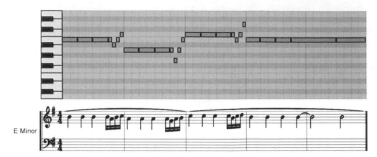

Figure 7.11   Melody in E minor to harmonize.

When trying to harmonize a melody, the first task is to study the melody as a whole, to look at its form and structure and the characteristic way in which it begins and ends. This is for the simple reason that the harmony that we add has to support and enhance that form and structure rather than work against it. One good way of looking at the structure of a melody is to reduce the melody down to its bare bones. This involves getting rid of everything that is not going to be essential to the harmony itself. This naturally includes note repetition and what are obviously melodic flourishes that are going to be occurring against the background of the harmony.

Looking at our melody to be harmonized from this perspective, we can see that it uses a lot of note repetition. It is also obvious that the relatively fast sixteenth-note melodic figure at the end of each bar is simply melodic decoration. So for harmony purposes, we can quickly eliminate these from the picture. This is because to harmonize every melody note would make the music sound absurd. We only need to harmonize the essential harmony notes. Doing so, we arrive at the reduction shown in Figure 7.12. Looking at this reduction, we can see that the melody has a basic question-and-answer format in that it consists of two phrases—the first phrase (the question) occurring in bars 1 and 2 and an answering phrase occurring in bars 3 to 5. These phrases are called the *antecedent* and the *consequent*.

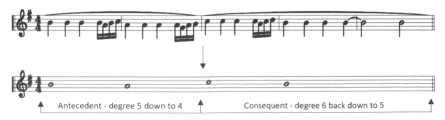

Figure 7.12   Melody from Figure 7.11 reduced to its bare essentials.

We can see from this illustration that the antecedent phrase is based around a descent from the fifth to the fourth degree of the scale, while the consequent phrase answers this with a similar descent from the sixth down to the fifth degree of the scale. Looking at the individual phrases themselves, we can see that they are based on sequential repetition. The term *sequential repetition* simply means the repeat of a melodic figure upon another degree of the scale. Therefore, in the first bar we have the melodic figure itself, which is centered on the fifth degree of the scale. In bar 2, the melodic figure is repeated but is centered on the fourth degree of the scale. In bar 3, the melodic figure is also repeated but this time is centered on the sixth degree of the scale. Finally, in bars 4 and 5, the melodic figure extends into a cadence centered around the fifth degree of the scale—the dominant scale degree. Taking all of these observations about the form and structure of the melody, we can arrive at the conclusions shown in Figure 7.13.

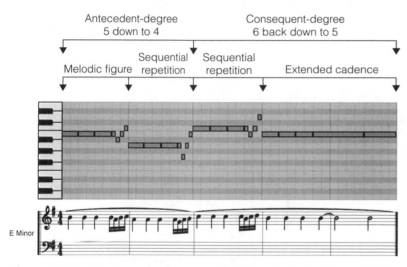

Figure 7.13 Form and structure of the melody in Figure 7.11.

Reading the Melody for the Best Chords to Use

The degree to which a melody is studied and broken down in this way is naturally a matter of choice. The methods of breaking it down are also fairly flexible. Figure 7.13 shows a technical approach to the breakdown, while a more intuitive approach to the study of the melody could work equally as well. The important point is that the melody needs to be properly scrutinized for its basic structure, because this puts you in a good position to read it with regard to the best chords to use when harmonizing it.

For example, looking at the melody given in Figure 7.11, it is extremely obvious that the last chord will be upon the tonic. And as the last chord is the final chord of the cadence, the chord preceding it will be the dominant. This in turn shows that for the notes that precede the dominant, we are looking for a good pre-dominant harmony. Looking at the melody in Figure 7.11, we can see that the fourth and fifth bars all repeat the same note—the fifth degree of the scale note B. Bearing this in mind, the most obvious answer to the use of a pre-dominant chord is the tonic chord in the second inversion, because like the dominant chord, it also uses the note B. The whole cadence thus implies the use of a cadential six-four.

Having sorted out the cadence, we can now look to the beginning of the melody. The first bar is centered around note B—the fifth degree of the scale. Within the range of the three primary triads of the key of E minor, only two of these chords could possibly be used. These are the tonic (Em) or the dominant (B). Because this is the first chord, the most sensible choice for this bar is the tonic chord. In bar 2 there is only one chord that could be used within the range of the three primary triads. This is chord iv—the subdominant chord (Am)—which is the only one of the three primary triads that offers a harmony for the fourth degree—note A. Similarly, in bar 3, which is centered around the sixth degree of the scale—note C—there is again only one implied option within the range of the three primary triads. That is the subdominant chord (Am).

Taking these observations we can now jot down the particular chords that would best be used in the harmonization. You can see these in Figure 7.14.

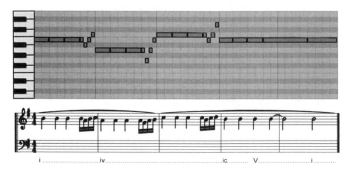

Figure 7.14   Chords to be used in the harmonizing of the melody in Figure 7.11.

Establishing a Harmonic Rhythm

Having a good idea about the chord to use, let us now think about the harmonic rhythm. Harmonic rhythm is the rhythm of the chord changes in a piece of music. Harmonic rhythm can vary—some pieces of music use a rapid type of harmonic rhythm, while in others the harmonic rhythm is slower. A very common type of harmonic rhythm is one or two chords per bar, although of course, like any other type of rhythm, if we allow it to become too rigid, the listener will soon lose interest in the music because the chord changes will begin to sound predictable and humdrum. So the best approach to harmonic rhythm is to set up a basic rhythm and then vary it at points in order to give it a sense of natural ebb and flow. Looking at the melody being harmonized, a harmonic rhythm is automatically implied by the phrasing of the melody. A basic one-chord-per-bar harmonic rhythm seems to be implied. In bars 2 and 3, because we only have the option of one chord—the subdominant—this means that we are going to need to create an impression of chordal change at this point. This, of course, is where chordal inversions become useful!

The harmonic rhythm toward the end of phrases often tends to vary, as it does in this example. This is in order to emphasize the tension that builds up toward the end of a section or piece of music. So during the final bars of a section, we can vary the rhythm to create an impression of culmination.

Sketching in the Bass Line and Adding the Inner Parts

Having a good idea of the best chords to be used, we can now sketch in a bass line part. The bass for the first bar would obviously be note E—the root of the tonic triad. The automatic choice of a bass for bars 2 and 3 would therefore be note A—the root of chord iv—the subdominant triad. Yet this chord occurs for two whole bars. To make the harmony more interesting, we can use the chord iv in first inversion in bar 2 and in root position in bar 3. This at least gives a sense of contrast and change within the range of the one chord that is used. And in this way, the harmonic rhythm is maintained. In the penultimate bar, a bass line on the fifth degree is automatically implied by the harmonies that we have chosen for it. To make this repetition of the note B in the bass more interesting, we can make the bass line fall an octave before it rises back up to the tonic chord root—note E for the final chord. See Figure 7.15.

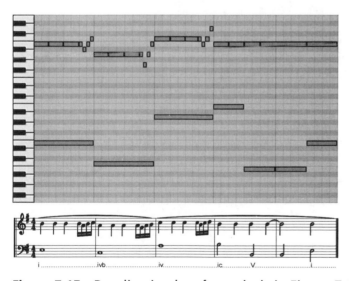

Figure 7.15   Bass line in place for melody in Figure 7.11.

Now that the bass line is in place, it is a simple matter of completing the implied harmonies by adding in the other two parts. In doing so, we make sure the chords are properly spaced and that the voices have their own natural melodic flow. In Figure 7.16, you can see the complete harmonization.

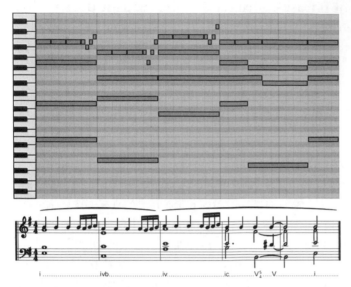

Figure 7.16   Adding the inner parts for the melody in Figure 7.11.

Notice that this harmonization is basically a collection of sustained notes. Although this would be suitable for, say, an organ or strings, what if you're writing this for, say, a piano? This brings us to a very important area that concerns the way in which the harmony is practically used in the music.

Adaptation of the Harmony for Various Forces

To harmonize a melody is one thing, while arranging that harmony in such a way that it sounds good on the instrument or instruments that will play the music is another. Having completed the harmony, therefore, we now need to consider the best way to arrange and adapt that harmony for the specific musical uses that it will be put to. This concerns the way in which the harmony is treated for the particular forces that are required. Let us now consider some of the different possibilities or ways in which this harmony might be used. Naturally, these ways will vary depending both on the instruments being played and on the particular style of music. The harmony written here could be used, for example:

- On a piano, perhaps as an accompaniment to a voice

- In a lead synthesizer arpeggiated riff for use in dance music

- As a series of string stabs for use in a hip-hop backing track

- To create an accompaniment pattern for another instrument

- As an arrangement of the melody for a gospel choir

The point is that whatever the style or type of music being written, there will come a certain point where the harmony will be used and adapted for the instrumental forces required and, perhaps more importantly, using the techniques appropriate for the particular style of music. There are many different ways of adapting a given harmony in this fashion, and each style tends to prefer particular methods above others. We will now consider some relatively common techniques of adaptation. One such application of this harmony could easily be made for piano. For this purpose, we find it very effective if the harmony simply follows the quarter-note rhythm of the melody line (see Figure 7.17).

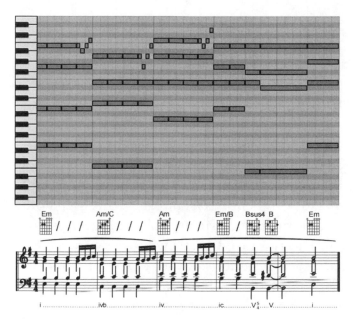

Figure 7.17   Arrangement of the harmonized melody from Figure 7.11 for piano.

If the lead melody were being played, say, on a flute, we could just as easily arrange the same harmony into a series of arpeggios that will accompany the flute—whether played on piano or harp. To adapt the harmony in this way, it is just a matter of taking your harmony, deciding on a particular arpeggio pattern, and sticking to it throughout the harmony. In this case each four-part chord is broken up, starting from the bottom upward (see Figure 7.18).

Naturally it is this consideration that turns the study of harmony into something that goes beyond a mere academic exercise. For this reason, in the exercises that follow, I will also sometimes present you with the particular musical situation in which the harmony is going to be practically used.

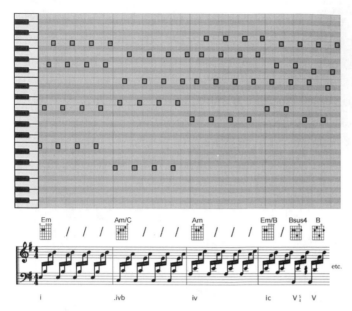

Figure 7.18   Harmony of the melody of Figure 7.11 arranged in arpeggios.

Conclusion

In this chapter we have seen that the three primary triads of a key are those that use the first, fourth, and fifth degrees of either the major or minor scale as their chordal root. We have also seen that the three primary triads offer chordal support for all seven notes of the scale and that therefore, through use of the three primary triads alone, it is possible to harmonize complete melodies. Those harmonized in this way are appropriately termed *three-chord songs*. Having looked at the functions of the tonic and dominant triads in the previous chapter, we looked at the particular function of the third primary chord—the subdominant. And in particular, we looked at the way in which the subdominant enables the creation of more extensive and structurally balanced chord progressions. We also saw how the subdominant chord features in the particular type of cadence known as a *plagal cadence*.

Having considered the three primary triads, we went on to study the ways in which they can be used to create a harmony. First, we looked at the creation of a harmony by adding three parts above a given bass line. Here we saw that particular care needs to be taken where the chords IV and V follow one another due to the difficulties in effective part writing that can be encountered.

From there we went on to consider the use of the three primary triads in harmonizing a melody line. Here we saw that this task was made easier by the fact that for some notes of the scale, only one possible chord could be used. A specimen melody was harmonized using the three chords. Here we learned that when harmonizing a melody, it is important first to look at the structure of the melody, for the simple reason that whatever harmony we do give the melody, it has to support and enhance that structure rather than working against it. The structure thus forms an important consideration when we go on to try to read the melody with regard to the best chords to use when harmonizing it.

Having harmonized that melody, we then looked at the different ways in which a basic harmonization could be treated and adapted to various purposes. This is an important part of the study simply for the reason that harmony is above all to be used practically in a piece of music. Any study of harmony should therefore include due consideration being given to the uses of the harmony—whether to add a harmony to a melody being sung by voices or to add an accompaniment figure to a melody or indeed a series of arpeggios. Finally, I pointed out that the exercises presented are merely an introduction and that these should be supplemented by the student seeking out well-known traditional three-chord songs and trying to harmonize those songs themselves.

Having covered this territory and built a firm foundation, it is now possible to widen the net and consider a more complete range of chords. The three primary triads are only three out of a possible seven triads in a key. In the next chapter, we will therefore consider the use of all seven of these triads in the process of creating a harmony.

8 | Secondary Triads

When we hear a chord progression, the three primary triads represent the main points of reference that our ear will continually pick up on. And although we, as listeners, might not be aware of this, it is through our hearing of the three primary triads in a chord progression that we gain an overall sense of the key of the music. This includes our awareness of a particular tonic or home chord and, of course, whether the key is major or minor.

Because of the important role that the three primary triads play for our key awareness and sense of tonality, the three primary triads will always be the most important chords that we will use in a chord progression. Yet they are by no means the only chords that we can use. A scale—major or minor—has seven degrees, and each degree may be taken as the root note of a particular chord. This means that a key is composed of a group of at least seven chords, any one of which might be freely used in a chord progression.

Secondary Triads

These other chords, exclusive of the three primary triads, are usually called *secondary triads*. Secondary triads tend to occur as points of transit on the way to or away from a particular primary triad. In doing so, they enable the creation of more complex chord progressions—that is, chord progressions that use a wider and subtler range of colors than the strong primary colors of the tonic, subdominant, and dominant triads.

In this chapter we will consider the various jobs of the secondary triads of a key and then explore the process of adding harmonies above a bass line that use the full complement of primary and secondary triads available to us. We will then go on to the harmonization of melodic leads using the complete spectrum of primary and secondary triads. In doing so, we will notice an important distinction between the major and the minor key. This distinction lies in the fact that harmony in the major key is often much simpler than harmony in the minor key. The reason for this is that the minor key includes various alterations of particular scale degrees, which can alter the profile of certain chords. This means that harmony in the minor scale is therefore a more complex issue.

Harmony in the Major Key

Because of the complexities of the minor scale, it is perhaps easiest to take a look at the secondary triads of the major key first. You can see four of these in Figure 8.1, in the key of C major.

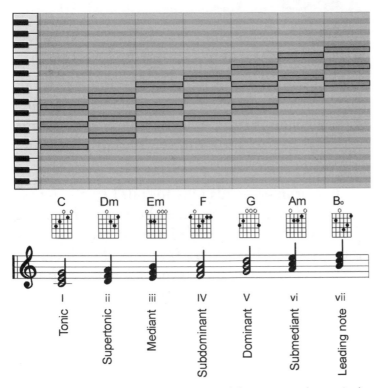

Figure 8.1 The three primary and four secondary triads.

In Figure 8.1, the notes used for the secondary triads are quarter notes, as opposed to the half notes used for the primary triads. This enables us to easily distinguish between them in the illustration. Looking more closely at Figure 8.1, we can glean some important information about the secondary triads of the major key. For example, we can see that while the three primary triads are all major, the four secondary triads are all minor except for one—the chord on degree vii of the scale—the leading note, which is a diminished triad.

This major key as a whole offers a nice, balanced range of three major and three minor common triads. Using both primary and secondary triads in our chord progressions therefore enables us to achieve a nice contrast between bright, major harmonies on one hand and darker and more somber minor harmonies on the other. This in turn gives us a wider and more emotionally expressive range of chords with which to write our music. In a moment we will consider each of the four secondary triads individually. But first we need to look at the range of secondary triads in the minor key.

The Complexities of the Minor Scale

In the minor key, our options for the use of triads are made much more complicated because of the alterations commonly applied to the natural minor scale. These are the sharp seventh degree of the harmonic minor scale (in order to give a leading note up to the tonic) and the sharp sixth degree of the melodic minor (originally introduced to get rid of that awkward augmented second melodic interval between the sixth and seventh degree of the harmonic minor scale).

In studies of classical functional harmony, the harmonic minor scale tends to be taken as the standard model for harmonization. Choosing one minor scale like this as a standard tends to simplify the study of harmony in the minor key. However, in much modern music, the different forms of the minor scale—natural, harmonic, and melodic—are often used and exploited for their own particular spectrum of harmonic colors. Therefore, studying harmony focusing primarily on the harmonic minor scale does not really do justice to modern practice.

To account for this, we need to recognize that the alterations made to the sixth and seventh degrees of the natural minor scale transform the profiles of the possible triads on each degree of the scale. This means that on some degrees of the scale, there is more than one chord possible. Figure 8.2 shows a list of the possible triads in C minor so you can see what is available in that key.

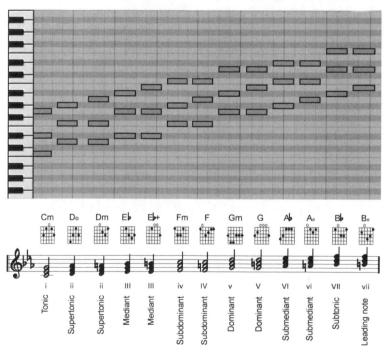

Figure 8.2 Primary and secondary triads in the minor key.

On the supertonic degree, there are two possible triads. There is the diminished triad present in the natural minor mode (D○) and also a minor common triad (Dm), which is created when the sixth degree of the minor scale is sharpened (as a part of the melodic minor mode). On the third or mediant degree, there are also two triads. There is the major common triad on degree three of the natural minor mode (E♭) and the augmented triad found in the harmonic minor mode (E♭+).

The subdominant degree also offers us two triads. There is the common minor triad on degree four of both the natural and harmonic minor mode (Fm) and the major common triad arising from the melodic minor form of the minor scale (F). The dominant degree of the minor scale also offers us two options. There is the minor dominant triad on the natural minor scale (Gm) and the major dominant triad on the harmonic and melodic minor scale (G). The two options for the submediant triad are the common major triad stemming from the natural minor mode (A♭) and the diminished triad (A○) stemming from the melodic minor mode. Finally, there is the major triad on degree seven of the natural minor mode (B♭) and the diminished triad on degree seven—the leading note—of the harmonic minor scale (B○).

Even this brief survey of triads available in the minor mode shows that the issue of choosing which chord to use for a chord progression or harmonization is made much more complex and difficult by the fact that there are so many choices available when compared to the major mode. In practice, some of these choices tend to be pushed right to the background, especially in popular music, which tends to favor the stable sound of common triads over the more unstable and unsettling sound of diminished and augmented triads. Not that the latter would never be used—they are used on occasion to deliberately create an unsettling effect. A good example is the first chord used in the introduction to Madonna's song "Like a Prayer." This chord is the diminished triad B-D-F, and considering that the key of the song is D minor, this would therefore be the submediant diminished chord (chord A○ as it appears in the key used in Figure 8.2). So it would be wrong to say that these triads are never used. They are used, but not as primary choices.

Because common triads do tend to be the first choices with songwriters and composers, we can eliminate some of the lesser-used triads given in Figure 8.2. This means that for more practical purposes, we can think of the minor key as being an array of the common triads shown in Figure 8.3—an array that at least helps to simplify the overall picture of harmony in the minor scale.

Having more triads than the major key, the minor key can offer some really interesting chord progressions. A good example is the Cm-E♭-F-A♭ chord progression used in "The House of the Rising Sun," made famous by the Animals. The progression from F major to A♭ major is particularly colorful and brings into play what is called a *cross-relation*. This is where you have, say, a flat in one part that is then followed by a natural in the other—in other words, note A of the F major triad forms a cross-relation with note A♭

of the following A♭ major triad. Suffice it to say, harmony in the minor scale can offer some interesting possibilities. But those possibilities are gained at the price of the greater complexity of that scale system. I'll say more on this when we discuss the concept of modal interchange in Chapter 19, "Modal Interchange."

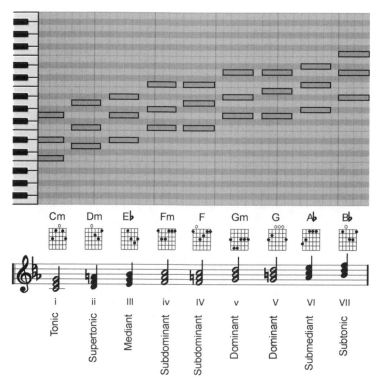

Figure 8.3   Common triads in the minor key.

Having considered the array of triads available in both the major and minor scales, let us now look at the individual functions of the secondary triads, beginning with the submediant triad—that is, the triad built on the sixth degree of either the major or the minor scale.

The Submediant Triad

The submediant triad is built upon the sixth degree of the scale, which means that its root lies between the leading note and the dominant. Figure 8.4 illustrates the position of this triad in both the major and the minor key.

When trying to understand the function of the chord on the sixth degree, the term *submediant* is very useful because it shows us that the root of the submediant lies midway between the roots of two important primary triads—the tonic and the subdominant. This in turn helps us to define the role of this particular triad in chord progressions. As a triad, the submediant is most often used as an alternative choice to the tonic when harmonizing the first and/or third degrees of the scale. This choice exists because the submediant and tonic triads share two notes in common, as you can see in Figure 8.5.

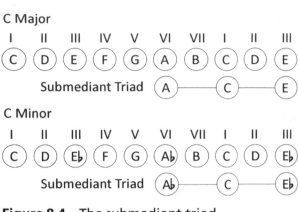

Figure 8.4   The submediant triad.

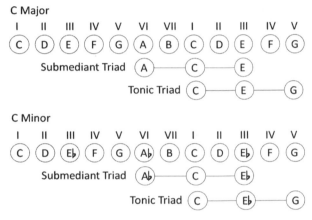

Figure 8.5   Relationship between the tonic and submediant triads.

In effect, this means that both first and third degrees of the scale can be harmonized with a major or a minor chord, depending upon the mood of the music required. This use of the submediant as an alternative to the tonic chord in certain situations is highlighted in the cadence known as the *deceptive cadence*. This is where the dominant chord, rather than progressing to the tonic as we would ordinarily expect in an authentic cadence, instead frustrates that expectation by progressing to another chord—typically the submediant. Figure 8.6 shows a deceptive cadence in which the subdominant chord leads into a cadential 6/4, the final chord of which would ordinarily be expected to be the tonic. Instead, the submediant chord is placed there as a substitute to form a deceptive closure, which thereby invites some form of continuation.

The effectiveness of a deceptive cadence is enhanced when used with this type of voice leading, where the outer parts move in contrary motion to converge upon the submediant triad.

Another use of the submediant chord is as an alternative to the subdominant with which it also shares two notes in common: the first and sixth degrees of the scale. This means that when putting a harmony to melodic notes using these scale degrees, the submediant

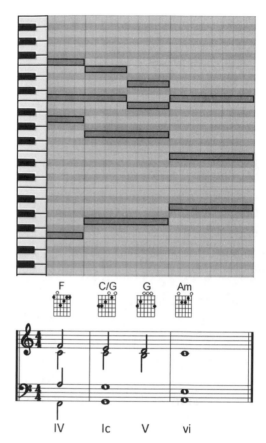

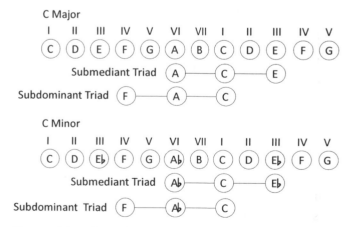

Figure 8.6   A deceptive cadence.

offers a nice alternative choice to the subdominant. The value of this choice lies in the fact that in the major key, the subdominant is a major triad and the submediant is a minor triad; while in the minor key, the opposite situation is encountered. This means that an option of major or minor chord is available when putting a harmony to these degrees of the scale. See Figure 8.7 for a diagrammatic representation of this information.

Figure 8.7   The relationship between the subdominant and submediant triads.

Another popular use for the submediant triad is as a chord of progression from either the tonic or the subdominant. In terms of the former, from the Beatles onward, entire passages of music have been created that simply rock between the tonic and the sub-mediant triads. A good example is Nirvana's song "About a Girl," the verse sections of which simply rock back and forth between the triads of G and Em. This gives rise to a hypnotic alternation of major and minor harmony that very few listeners can resist. In the minor key, this continual rocking back and forth between triads I and VI has become something of a cliché in dance music, having now been used in countless trance, hard trance, and hard dance tracks since the '90s.

This type of harmony is often called *static harmony* because it is reluctant to go beyond the tonic triad, and when it does it immediately returns to it. Another chord that is useful for this type of static harmony is chord IV—the subdominant. Just listen to the beginning of John Lennon's "Imagine," and you will get the idea.

When used along with the three primary triads, the submediant takes its place in a four-chord progression, which has proven itself to be one of the most popular chord combinations ever used by songwriters. In fact, a lot of the output of 1950s popular music relied entirely on this four-chord formula. The minor submediant chord contrasts nicely with the three major primary triads to bring a touch of mellowness and emotion into the chord progression. Examples of songs that use this progression, either in whole or in part, are Bob Marley's "No Woman No Cry," the Beatles' "Let It Be," LMC vs. U2's "Take Me to the Clouds Above," to name but a few. The most popular forms seem to be those illustrated in Figure 8.8.

I	V	vi	IV
I	vi	IV	V

Figure 8.8 Popular four-chord song formats.

The Mediant Triad

Another extremely useful secondary chord is the mediant triad built on the third degree of either the major or the minor scale. Figure 8.9 shows the position of the mediant triad in both the C major and the C minor scales.

Looking at the position of this triad in Figure 8.9, we can see that its root lies midway between the roots of two primary triads: the tonic and the dominant—hence its particular name, mediant. This name in turn helps us to understand its role in chord progressions. Sharing with the tonic chord two notes—the third and fifth degrees of the scale—the mediant triad offers an alternative choice to the tonic chord when putting a harmony to the third and/or fifth degrees of the scale. Figure 8.10 shows the notes the two triads share in common.

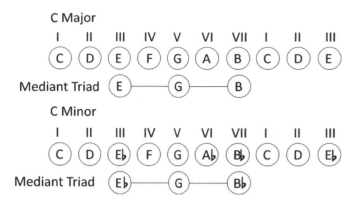

Figure 8.9   The position of the mediant triad.

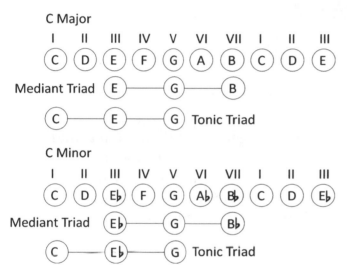

Figure 8.10   Relationship of the mediant chord to the tonic chord.

In Figure 8.11, we can see what happens when we insert the mediant as a substitute for the tonic chord. The progression begins with a classic I-IV-V progression, after which a return to the tonic chord might be expected. By inserting chord iii instead of the tonic, the chord progression is given further impetus to continue, carrying on through the chords IV, ii, and finally to a half close on the dominant chord. In this way, like the submediant, the mediant chord helps us to expand chord progressions beyond the limited range of the three primary triads.

For the dominant chord the mediant plays a similar role: offering a useful alternative to the dominant when putting a harmony to the fifth and/or seventh degree of the scale—both of which they share in common. This alternative option further enables the expansion of chord progressions beyond the limited circle of the three primary triads. This of course leads to the creation of chord progressions with much greater variety, color, mood, and atmosphere.

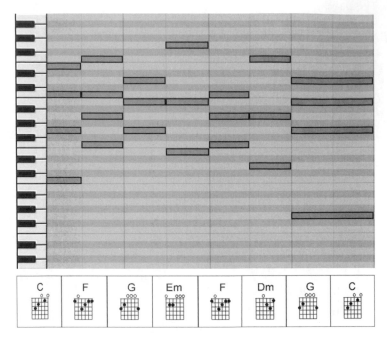

Figure 8.11   Progression in the major key involving the mediant chord.

Figure 8.12 illustrates the common notes shared by the mediant and dominant triads. Both natural and melodic minor modes are shown, as the mediant chord is different for each. In the natural minor, the mediant chord is a regular major common triad; while in the harmonic minor scale, the mediant is an augmented triad. Like the diminished triad, the augmented triad is essentially unstable. This instability is caused by the interval of

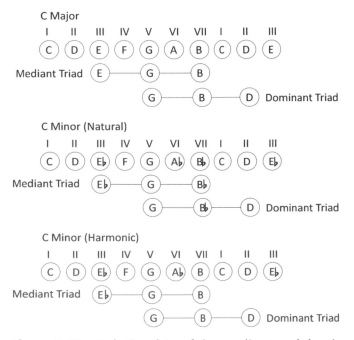

Figure 8.12   Relationship of the mediant and dominant triads.

an augmented fifth—a chromatic interval whose presence in a chord always tends to have an unsettling effect. Its use therefore tends to be limited to certain contexts. These are mostly related to the chord of the dominant thirteenth and will be further discussed in Chapter 18, "Thirteenth Chord."

Like the submediant, the mediant common chord offers a useful addition to the four-chord formula exploited by so many popular songs. The principal attraction to the mediant, instead of the submediant, as the fourth chord is the opportunity to use a rising bass line through the roots of the tonic, mediant, subdominant, and dominant triads. Rising bass lines have always been popular in music because they generate a feeling of escalating energy and excitement. You can see an example of this in the minor key in Figure 8.13.

As the bass rises up toward the dominant, there is a sense of culminating energy that peaks when the dominant chord is reached.

The Supertonic (and Subtonic) Triad

Another useful secondary triad is the supertonic triad. The name given to this triad—supertonic—refers to the fact that it is the chord whose root lies a scale step immediately

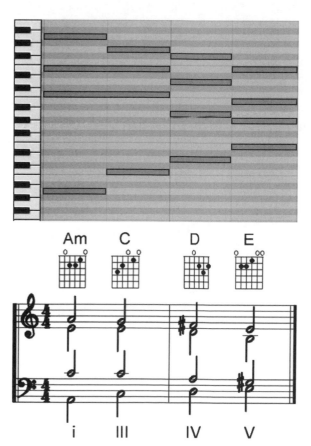

Figure 8.13 Rising bass line through the roots of chords i, III, IV, and V (key of A minor).

above the tonic. You can see this illustrated in Figure 8.14. Note that while in the major scale and the melodic minor scale, the supertonic is a minor common triad; in the natural and harmonic minor scale, the supertonic is a diminished triad. As a diminished triad it is essentially unstable, although when used it does add a nice dark quality to harmony in the minor key.

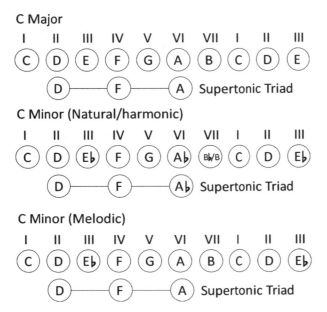

Figure 8.14 The position of the supertonic triad.

The supertonic triad offers a great alternative to the subdominant triad with which it shares two notes in common—these notes being the fourth and sixth degrees of the scale. You can see this by taking a look at Figure 8.15.

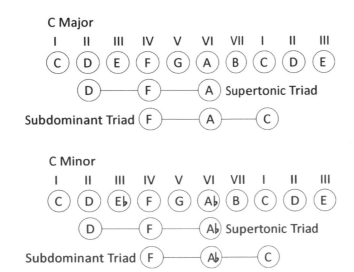

Figure 8.15 The relationship between the supertonic and subdominant triads.

As an alternative to the subdominant chord, the supertonic provides a valuable pre-dominant harmony. When used in this fashion, the cadential formula ii-V-I is born—a formula that is common to all types of popular music, particularly jazz, where ii-V-I represents one of the staple progressions of the harmonic language belonging to that style. When used in jazz, however, it is typically enriched through the use of chordal extensions such as the seventh, ninth, eleventh, and thirteenth. The great strength of the ii-V-I progression lies in the fact that the roots of these three triads are all a fifth apart. This gives the progression an inevitability that helps drive it toward the target chord, which is the tonic. See Figure 8.16.

The supertonic triad also shares two notes in common with the leading note triad. As such, the supertonic is often used prior to the leading note triad, the root and third being held over as the sixth rises up to the seventh degree. When used in this way, this re-presents a variation of the ii-V-I formula in which chord vii is representing—by proxy—the dominant chord.

The minor scale throws up another common triad not present in the major. This is the major triad whose root lies on the seventh degree of the natural minor scale. This means that its root lies a tone below the root of the tonic. Hence it has sometimes been called the *subtonic chord*—as opposed to the supertonic chord, whose root lies a tone above. See Figure 8.17.

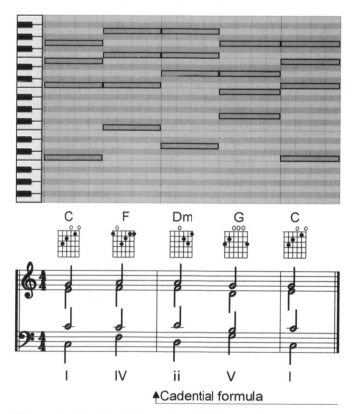

Figure 8.16 The ii-V-I cadential formula.

C Major

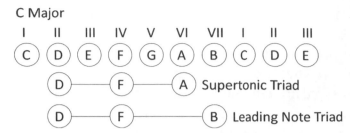

Figure 8.17   The subtonic triad of the minor key.

The great feature about the subtonic triad is that it offers chordal support for two notes of the supertonic triad—the notes D and F. But in doing so, it offers a more user-friendly major common triad, as opposed to the diminished triad found on the supertonic degree. One of the most popular uses of the subtonic chord is as a part of a falling bass line formula, beginning with the tonic of the minor key and falling down stepwise until the dominant is reached (8-7-6-5). See Figure 8.18.

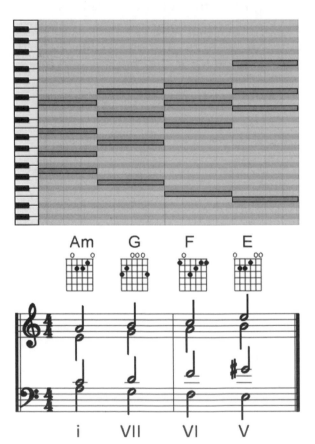

Figure 8.18   Subtonic as part of a falling bass line formula.

Sometimes called the *Flamenco progression,* or alternatively the *Andalusian cadence,* due to its distinctly Spanish feel, composers and songwriters have wasted no time in adapting this popular progression to their own purposes. From the '60s onward, many popular hits were written that exploit this progression (or any one of its possible variations obtained by changing the order of the chords). Listen to Ray Charles' "Hit the Road Jack" as one such example of the use of this very popular progression.

The Leading Note Triad

The leading note triad tends to stand alone amongst the group of secondary triads for the reason that it is not a common triad. It is a diminished triad, and the dissonant sound of the diminished fifth above the root of the chord gives it a strong sense of instability. Play the chord on your MIDI keyboard, and you will hear this for yourself. Figure 8.19 illustrates the leading note triad.

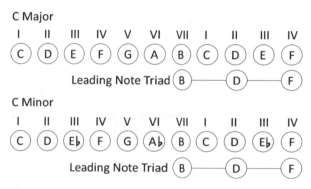

Figure 8.19   The leading note triad.

Because of the dissonance of the diminished fifth, which gives this particular chord its backbone, the leading note triad tends to sound best when used in first inversion—that is, with the third in the bass. When used in this position, both of the intervals above the bass line—the minor third and major sixth—are consonants. This gives the chord a slightly more stable profile. See Figure 8.20 for an illustration of this.

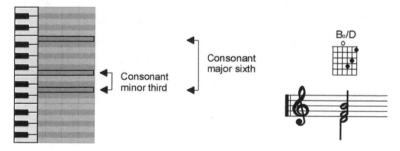

Figure 8.20   The leading note triad in first inversion.

In classical terms, the instability of the leading note triad was used to good effect in order to create a dominant substitute chord in which the tension of the dissonant fifth (or augmented fourth when inverted) was resolved to the third of the tonic triad. You can see this in Figure 8.21.

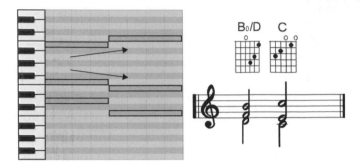

Figure 8.21   Resolution of the leading note triad.

As such, the main use of the leading note triad was as an alternative to the dominant. This means that everything that has already been said about the function of the chord of the dominant tends also to apply to the leading note triad.

When doubling a note in the diminished triad, the best note to double is the third. We would avoid doubling the root note because this is the leading note. And because the diminished triad often tends to stand in for the dominant triad, as the leading note progresses up to the tonic, we would therefore be forced to introduce consecutive octaves in those parts that carry the leading note.

Chord Progressions and Root Movement

Each of the secondary triads that we have so far looked at should be studied as individual chords, and you should make an effort to explore the ways in which one chord progresses into another. To do this, take, for example, the supertonic chord of the major key and study the way in which it progresses to the other triads of the key. In this way, you will gradually build up a picture of chordal interrelationships and which chords work best with other chords.

By doing this, you will soon discover that some progressions are much stronger than others. One of the major factors that determines this is the root movement between chords. Any common triad has a root, and when one common triad progresses to another, irrespective of what position or inversion the chord is in, the ear picks up on the relationship between the chordal roots. This relationship is called *root movement—* a factor that represents one of the most powerful guiding and driving influences behind chord progressions in general. This driving influence becomes more and more apparent as the harmonies that we use become more complex. So let us now consider root movement and the principles by which it works.

Looking, for example, at the major scale of seven notes, we can see that there are only so many kinds of root movement possible. There is root movement by seconds, by thirds, and by fourths—either rising or falling. All possible root movements represent one of these six possible kinds of root movement. Knowing this allows us to be more methodical in our exploration of chord progressions, because any chord can move in six possible ways. With reference to, say, the supertonic chord, you can see these six possible movements in Figure 8.22.

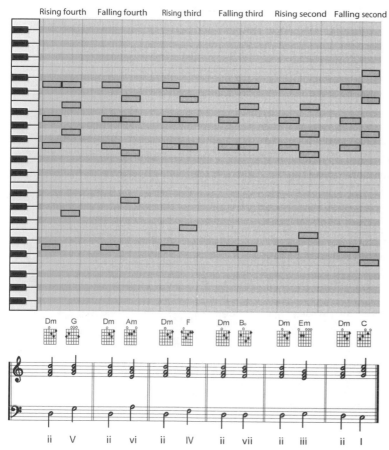

Figure 8.22 The six types of root movement with reference to the supertonic triad.

If you play the progressions in Figure 8.22 on your MIDI keyboard, you will soon discover that the strongest type of root movement is root movement by a fourth—either rising or falling. Looking at Figure 8.22, we can see that where there is root movement by fourths, this means that the two chords involved will always share one note in common. In the case of ii-V, this common note is D; while in the case of ii-vi, the common note is A. This common note creates a strong link between the two chords. Yet the two notes that the chords do not share in common ensure that the progression has a powerful sense of contrast. For a strong chord progression, therefore, root movement by fourths will always represent the first choice.

After root movement by fourths, there is root movement by a third. Where chordal roots move by thirds, the two chords will always share two notes in common. Looking back at Figure 8.22, we can see that in the case of ii-IV, the two common notes are

F and A; while in ii-vii, they are D and F. These two shared notes create a sense of continuity between the two chords. But because they share two notes in common, there is less of a sense of contrast between them—in other words, they have a great similarity.

Finally, there is root movement by seconds. Where root movement by seconds occurs, the two chords will share no notes in common. We can see this in Figure 8.22 in the case of both ii-iii and ii-I. Therefore, although there is a great sense of difference and contrast between the two chords, there are no common notes by which to link them. This means that there is less of a sense of continuity in the harmony than when root movement by fourths or thirds occurs.

All chord progressions represent a combination of these three kinds of root movement, which means that in effect any chord progression will be composed of one, two, or even a mix of all three basic root movement cycles. Figure 8.23 illustrates these cycles.

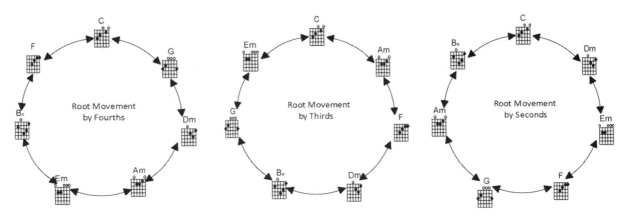

Figure 8.23 The three root movement cycles.

The first cycle on the left of Figure 8.23 shows chords connected by a common root movement of a fourth. Moving clockwise around the cycle represents a movement of a falling fourth, while moving counterclockwise represents a movement of a rising fourth. In this way, whichever direction we choose to go around the cycle, we can encounter all of the chords of a key as a part of that cycle. The same can be said for the other two cycles. The difference between them lies in the interval that represents the common root movement. In the case of the cycle on the right of Figure 8.23, the common root movement is a second, while the cycle in the center represents root movement by a third.

Whenever we create a chord progression for our music, we are in effect utilizing these cycles of connection between all of the chords of a key. Knowing these cycles, we can create chord progressions more systematically, and in this way we can always arrive at the best options for the next chord of our chord progression. Transposing these cycles into other keys and playing each of them through also represents a great way to get to know and explore other keys.

Conclusion

In this chapter I briefly introduced the various secondary triads that can be used within a given key. Here we observed that although such triads do perform a secondary function for the maintenance of tonality, they are all nonetheless very valuable in offering alternative pathways from and to the primary chords of a key. In offering these alternative pathways, secondary chords in turn lead to a great expansion in the coloristic possibilities of chord progressions. Major chordal influences can be contrasted with minor and vice versa.

Once you have become familiar with the secondary chords and are comfortable using them in chord progressions, you have reached an important point, for you now have access to all of the basic chords that can be used within a given key. This in turn makes available to you the basic resources from which all of the great composers and songwriters through history have created their music. From here on in, therefore, the study of harmony becomes a matter of building upon that very important foundation.

One such way of building upon this foundation is through the incorporation of dissonances into your harmonies. By dissonances, I mean notes that somehow clash with the harmony notes of the music. The conscious use of dissonances in this way is a method that has been used to enhance chord progressions for hundreds of years. The attraction to the use of these dissonances lies in the fact that they enable us to create chord progressions whose melodic parts are not only much more fluid and mobile, but also carry with them a great sense of expressive tension.

As you will soon discover as you go on to subsequent chapters of this book, there are many methods of incorporating dissonances into the chordal texture. One of the most important and basic of these is through melodic embellishment and decoration. As an introduction to the idea of the use of dissonance in harmony, this will provide the topic for the next chapter.

9 Repetition, Arpeggiation, and Melodic Decoration

So far, the exercises given for you to complete in this book have focused on note-for-note harmony. The result of this approach is a musical texture that is basically made up of a series of block chords. However, most of the music that we hear—unless it is a hymn being sung in church or a very basic harmonization—does not use plain and unadorned chords. In most music, there are a variety of rhythmic and melodic embellishments used to spice up what would otherwise be a series of very basic harmonies. In this chapter we are going to open up the study to include these various embellishments, and by doing so, we'll take the study of harmony much closer to actual real musical practice than simply textbook study.

Repetition

Repetition is one of the most powerful techniques that musicians have always used to bring more interest, variety, and energy to their music. Repetition occurs where a given harmony or harmony note is simply repeated. Through use of repetition in this fashion, a given harmony can be prolonged for the period of time in which the repetition takes place. When prolonged for an entire section or even a whole piece of music, the harmony is said to be *static*. Being static, the interest in the music then shifts toward elements such as the particular rhythm of the repetition. Static harmony is very popular in modern music, and styles such as house and Detroit techno have established a great precedent for the use of static harmony in modern electronic works.

As an example of repetition being used to bring interest to static harmony, in Figure 9.1 you will see an A minor chord that has been prolonged for a period of four bars. The interest, therefore, lies not so much in the harmony itself, but in the characteristic rhythm with which the harmony is repeated—this rhythm being a combination of successive groups of two and three sixteenth notes.

Any harmony note or notes might be prolonged indefinitely in this way—provided, of course, that the creator of the music can successfully maintain the listener's interest for that length of time. An obvious example of this is a bass line pattern that is repeated on the root note of a chord. This technique is common to all styles of electronic music, especially those aimed at the dance floor. In Figure 9.2, you can see an example of root bass repetition, where the rhythm of Figure 9.1 has been transferred to the bass line and the chord itself is sustained on other instruments.

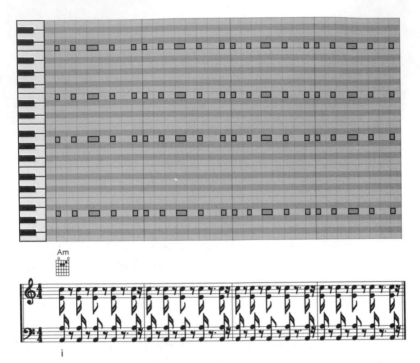

Figure 9.1 An A minor chord prolonged for eight bars using repetition.

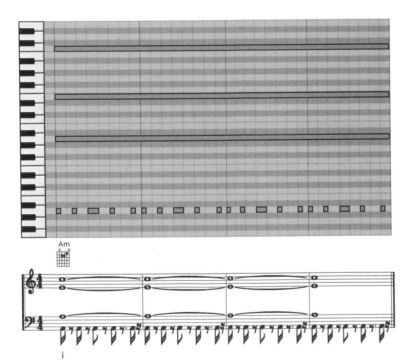

Figure 9.2 An A minor sustained chord over a root note bass line pattern.

Octave Repetition

A natural extension of the principle of repetition is octave repetition, which in its own way is also a very popular technique used to bring interest and variety to musical textures. The logic of calling octave changes a form of repetition lies in the observation that because a movement of pitch over an interval of an octave means that the note class remains the same—in other words, note C remains note C—then any decoration of a basic harmony that involves octaves is, I suppose, a form of repetition.

Repetition at the octave is a very important technique for creating additional interest to what is in effect a basic harmony. In Figure 9.3, you will see three applications of this technique, which have been labeled (a), (b), and (c).

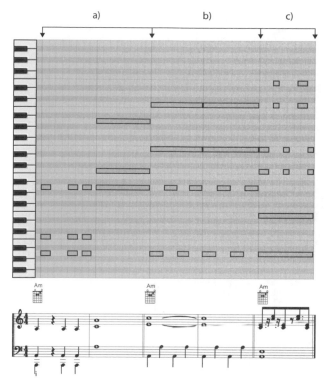

Figure 9.3   Three examples of repetition at the octave.

In example (a), a simple chord is repeated an octave higher. In addition to prolonging the harmony into the next bar, this has the effect of creating additional interest through the dramatic shift of the harmony up by an octave. In (b), we can see an example of a root bass that has been given additional interest by placing every alternate note up an octave. This type of bass line is commonly called a *walking bass*. Finally, in (c), a melody note is given additional interest by the way in which it rises and falls through the octave. All three of these are simple examples of creating additional interest to the music by using the technique of octave repetition. Naturally, once you know about the principle of octave repetition, you can investigate other methods using your own ingenuity.

Arpeggiation

For a number of centuries now, one of the most common and popular methods of bringing additional interest to a basic harmony has been arpeggiation. Arpeggiation is where the notes of a chord are played separately in succession. The pattern of arpeggiation concerns the particular order in which the notes of the chord are played, together with the characteristic use of note and/or octave repetition where appropriate. Figure 9.4 shows three well-known arpeggiation patterns. These have been labeled from (a) through to (d). Example (a) is where the chord has been arpeggiated from the bottom up, and example (b) is where the chord has been arpeggiated from the top down. In example (c) there is an alternation between rising and falling, while example (d) gives an Alberti bass pattern, named after the classical composer who popularized this particular pattern in his own music.

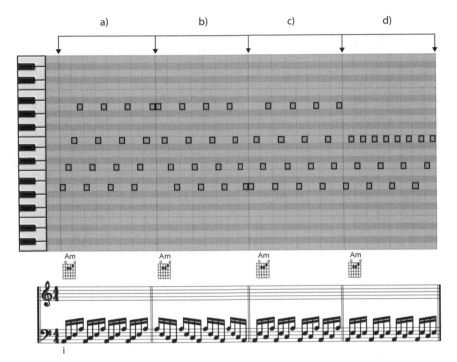

Figure 9.4 Four examples of arpeggiation.

Arpeggiation is a great way to create a sense of motion and forward movement within what would otherwise be a field of static harmonies. The potential applications of the technique are vast, and it can be used flexibly wherever there is a need to create a sense of motion. If it is being applied to an entire four-part harmony, first write your harmonies in sustained notes and then apply the particular arpeggio pattern you feel would suit your purposes. In this way, with reference to Figure 9.5, the plain harmonies as represented in (a) can become a series of rippling arpeggios, as you can see in (b).

Arpeggiation can also be used along with other techniques, such as repetition, to create interesting and fresh-sounding textures. A good example of the application of this is those house piano riffs of the '90s, which typically used a combination of repetition and arpeggiation to create an interesting repetitive pattern. You can see an example of such a riff in Figure 9.6.

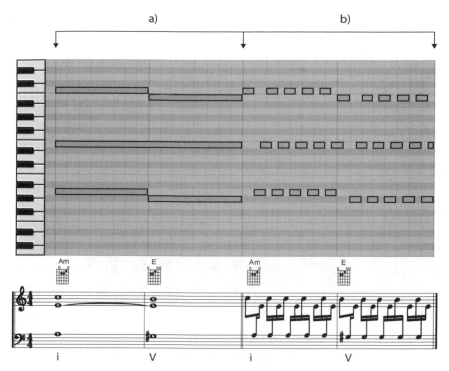

Figure 9.5 Arpeggiation of basic harmonies.

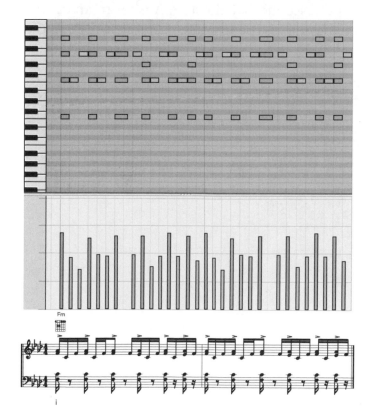

Figure 9.6 House piano riff.

Representing nothing more than the prolongation of a basic F minor harmony over the space of the two bars shown, ideally the arpeggiated notes should be set to a fairly low velocity (as the velocity lane of Figure 9.5 shows), in order for them to create simply a subtle effect of bristling motion.

Linear Decorations

A passage of music that uses a series of simple harmonies can also be given more interest through the use of melodic decoration. The focus of this decoration is the melodic movement of the individual parts of the harmony, and it is applied typically to the lead in order to give the lead part more melodic interest and variety. It is also often applied to the bass line, which will always benefit from a touch of melodic decoration to give the bass more interest and character. The inner parts tend to receive less attention because, often being given the role of filling in the harmony between the lead and the bass, they tend to be less mobile than the lead. But even the inner parts of harmony can benefit from a bit of melodic decoration to make them more varied and interesting.

By *melodic decoration,* I mean the use of notes that fall outside of the required harmony. Look, for example, at the lead melodic part of Figure 9.7. This lead uses two techniques to give the part additional melodic interest. First, the lead uses repetition—both straight repetition and repetition at the octave. Therefore, in both bars the note A is repeated, the difference between them being that in the second bar the note A is taken an octave higher. This leap of an octave between the bars gives the melodic part a sense of energy.

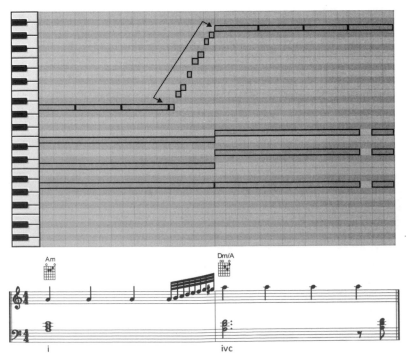

Figure 9.7   Lead that has been decorated through the use of repetition and a glissando.

The second technique the lead uses is a run or *glissando*. As the part rises up an octave from the low A of the first bar to the high A of the second bar, all of the notes of the scale that lie between them are briefly touched upon. This technique involving the use of numerous brief passing notes represents a common method of generating additional interest to a melodic part. And because these decorative notes are so fleeting, the ear readily perceives them as being simply embellishments of the melodic part.

Accented and Unaccented Embellishments

The notes used in the glissando of Figure 9.7 are hardly essential to the harmony. In fact, the notes B, D, F, G, and G♯ are not even a part of the chord of A minor that prevails over this bar of music. Not being a part of the harmony, they are therefore perceived by the ear as being simply a type of melodic decoration—a method of embellishing one of the parts in order to give that part more melodic interest. In the process of embellishing the melodic parts, notes that are not essential to the harmony will usually be used. These are called *unessential* notes. One of the most important qualities of these unessential notes is that, falling outside of the given harmony, they will form a dissonance with some elements of it. Forming a dissonance in this way, they will thereby introduce a much-valued element of tension to the harmony.

The position of the decorative note(s) relative to the beat—whether occurring on a strong or a weak beat—will have a strong bearing upon their impact. When used on a weak part of the beat, decorative notes are said to be *unaccented*. Unaccented embellishments are always less obtrusive, in that the dissonant element(s) that they introduce are less prominent. When used on a strong part of the beat, however, decorative notes are said to be *accented,* which means that the dissonances will be heard more prominently. This gives the dissonances a greater impact, but it also means that accented embellishments need to be handled with more care and attention. In the case of Figure 9.7, the unessential notes that are used to embellish the part are unaccented, in that they occur on a weak part of the beat. The dissonance that they introduce to the harmony is therefore less prominent.

Standard Types of Embellishment

Along with repetition and arpeggiation, melodic embellishment counts as one of the main techniques that composers have used to create complex-sounding music from very simple raw materials. These raw materials are, of course, the chords of harmony. By learning how to use repetition, arpeggiation, and melodic decoration, we too can learn how to create intricate and complex musical textures. The study of these techniques, however, is a rather complex one, because each composer/songwriter tends to embellish melodic parts in his or her own particular way. And if you produce your own musical tracks, you too will develop your own methods of decorating the raw chordal materials you use.

A good place to begin the study of melodic decoration is with those formulaic types of melodic embellishment that have established themselves over a long period of time as being fairly standard. This chapter will explain and illustrate the main types of these standard embellishments. All of those explained and illustrated have been in use for hundreds of years. And in one form or another, they are just as popular with composers and songwriters of today as they were hundreds of years ago.

Melodic Auxiliaries

One such standard type of decoration is the melodic auxiliary, an example of which is illustrated in Figure 9.8.

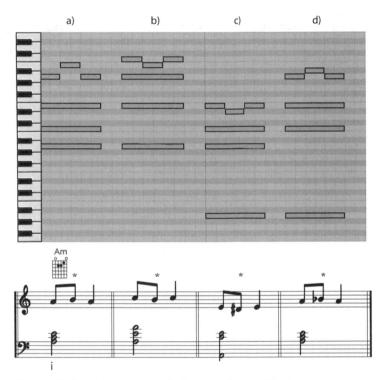

Figure 9.8   Diatonic and chromatic auxiliaries.

A melodic auxiliary is any note that lies either side of the harmony note—in other words, a single step above or below the harmony note in the scale. For this reason an auxiliary is also sometimes referred to as a *neighbor note*. What qualifies a decoration as being an auxiliary is the fact that it is used between two harmony notes that are the same. For this reason, this decoration can also be called a *returning tone figure* for the simple fact that it returns to the note from which it just left.

Look at Figure 9.8 (a) for an example of the use of an auxiliary. In this case the auxiliary is occurring on the weak part of the beat, so it is unaccented. The harmony is a simple A minor triad—the tonic chord of the key of A minor. Notice that the lead temporarily rises up to the note B, which is not a part of the triad. In fact, for the ear this note is discordant for the chord of A minor. Yet because the lead effects an immediate return to the harmony note, the decorative note B is not felt as being intrusive. In Figure 9.8 (b), you can see a similar returning tone figure, except it is occurring in the opposite direction. Rather than moving to and then returning from the note immediately above it in the scale, the lead instead moves to and returns from the note immediately below it.

There are two general types of melodic auxiliaries. There are *diatonic auxiliaries*, in which the note is a part of the major or minor scale of the key being used. Figure 9.8 (a) and (b) represent two examples of this. And then there are *chromatic auxiliaries*, in which the note is not a part of the scale being used—in other words, it is taken from outside of it from the other notes of the chromatic scale. Figure 9.8 (c) and (d) are representative examples of chromatic auxiliaries. In the case of (a), the lead temporarily falls and then returns from the note D♯, which itself is not a part of the A minor scale. In the case of (b), the lead temporarily rises and then returns from the note B♭, which is also not a part of the A minor scale.

Melodic auxiliaries can be used to good effect in any of the parts of the harmony, and when used appropriately, they can give the harmony a more mobile and fluid texture. They can be used to especially good effect when employed in more than one of the harmony parts. Figure 9.9 provides an example of this. This takes the form of a simple two-bar loop, the harmonies for which are a chord of Am in the first bar followed by a chord of Em in the second bar. In (a), two accented diatonic melodic auxiliaries are used—the notes G and B, neither of which belong to the Am chord—while in bar 2 another pair of accented auxiliaries are used involving the notes F and D—again, neither of which belongs to the prevailing Em chordal harmony.

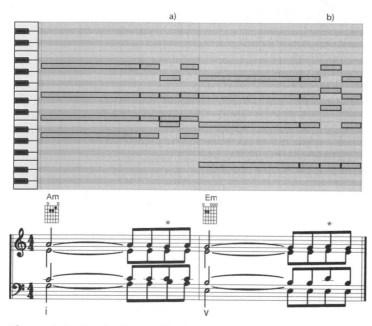

Figure 9.9 Melodic auxiliaries used in more than one melodic part.

Auxiliaries have always provided a great way of decorating the main harmony notes of a lead melody. Have a listen to the slow movement of the Spanish composer Joaquin Rodrigo's "Concerto de Aranjuez." There you will hear auxiliaries expertly used to considerably heighten the emotional intensity of the melody line. And as you listen, you will hear that the main melody is crafted from a careful combination of auxiliaries placed on various degrees of the scale. In fact, there is such an abundance of the use of auxiliaries in this work that right from the start you won't be able to help but notice them!

Variations of the Auxiliary

There are numerous variations of the melodic auxiliary, all of which can be used to good effect to bring more interest to harmony parts. One such variation is where an auxiliary skips a third in the opposite direction before returning to the harmony note. This is called a *changing note figure*. There are two ways in which a changing note figure can occur; these are illustrated in Figure 9.10. On the left, the harmony note rises up to the auxiliary and then falls back a third in the opposite direction before returning to the harmony note. On the right, the opposite situation can be seen.

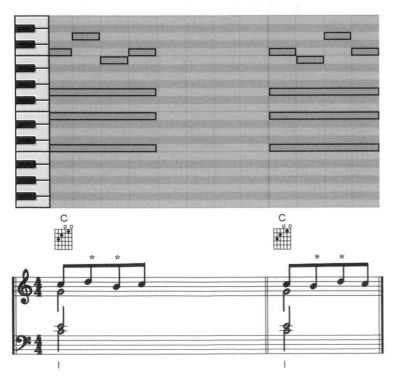

Figure 9.10   Two examples of a changing note figure.

For a famous example of the use of a changing note figure, think of John Williams's score to *Jaws*. Whenever the shark would move in to attack, there would be a repetitive changing note figure moving from E up to F, down to D, and back to E again!

Another variation is where the auxiliary skips down by a third to the harmony note of another chord. Sometimes called an *echapée,* this is a great way to introduce an element of tension into the harmony. You can see two examples of this technique in Figure 9.11. The first, (a), is an accented auxiliary that falls down by a third to the B of the E major dominant triad, while in (b) we can see the use of an unaccented auxiliary, which rises a third up to the root of the subdominant major triad.

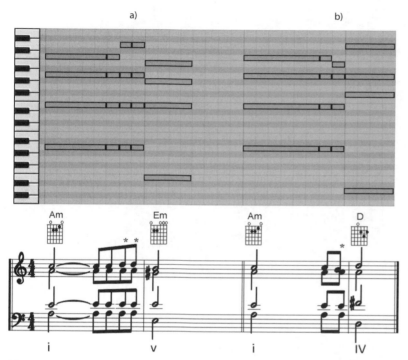

Figure 9.11   Variation of auxiliary treatment.

An auxiliary can also be effective when a harmony note skips up or down to it. In Figure 9.12 you will see an example of numerous auxiliaries being treated in this way. Each auxiliary is marked with a star. Some of these auxiliaries, you will notice, are chromatic auxiliaries—that is, notes not belonging to the diatonic scale of the key in question, which is A minor.

Passing Notes

When instead of returning to a harmony note, an auxiliary moves to another harmony note in the same direction, the decorative note is said to be a *passing note.* Passing notes are typically used to fill out the interval of a third, and on occasion a larger interval, such as a fourth. Figure 9.13 shows three examples of passing notes. In (a), you can see rising passing notes filling out the third between notes E and G in the lead and C and E in the bass. In (b), you can see an example of a falling passing note, while in (c) you can see an example of two consecutive passing notes filling out the interval of a fourth.

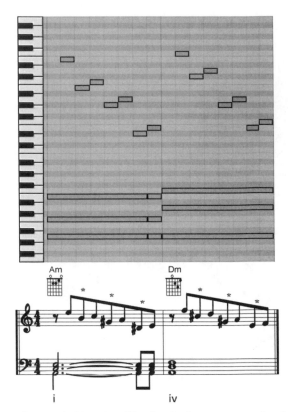

Figure 9.12   Auxiliaries being approached by leap.

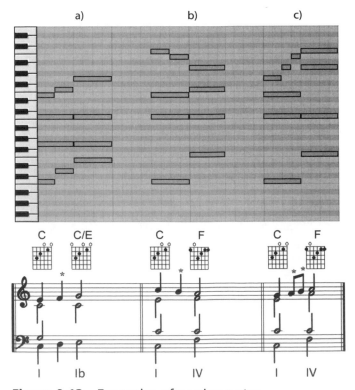

Figure 9.13   Examples of passing notes.

Passing notes are perhaps one of the most common types of melodic decoration that composers use. Because they serve a purpose of filling in gaps that occur between harmony notes, their use gives the harmony a smooth, mobile, and flowing texture. And the dissonant notes they introduce help to impart a sense of subtle tension to the music.

As is the case with any type of melodic decoration, passing notes can be used effectively on both accented and unaccented parts of the beat. When used on an accented part of the beat, the dissonance introduced by the passing note is more prominent. In Figure 9.14, you can see two accented passing notes being used, each marked by an asterisk. In the first half of bar 2, the note B in the lead is an accented passing note occurring between the drop of a third from C down to A. In the fourth quarter of the bar, you will see another example of an accented passing note being used in the lower part on the bass staff, which again involves note B, but this time going in the opposite direction. The accented passing notes are marked with an asterisk.

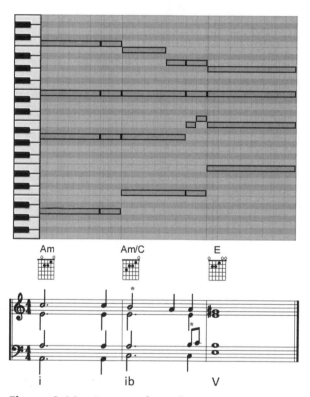

Figure 9.14   Accented passing notes.

Passing notes that belong to the major or minor scale of the key being used are called *diatonic passing notes*. Passing notes can also be chromatic. A chromatic passing note borrows from those notes of the chromatic scale not belonging to the diatonic scale of the key. The most typical use of a chromatic passing note is to fill in the interval of a major second between the voice parts. This creates a moment of tension as the chromatic note then resolves either upward or downward to the harmony note, as the case may be. Where the chromatic note occurs as a rising passing note, it is typically notated as a sharp. Where it is being used as a falling passing note, it is notated as being a flat. This is because these symbols naturally reflect the directional tendencies of the passing note.

Figure 9.15 shows two examples of chromatic passing notes. In (a), you can see an example of a rising chromatic passing note that fills out the whole tone between the notes G—the fifth of the C major triad—and the note A, which is the third of the F major triad. In (b), you can see an example of a falling chromatic passing note introduced between the notes G of the G major triad and the F of the F major triad in first inversion, which follows.

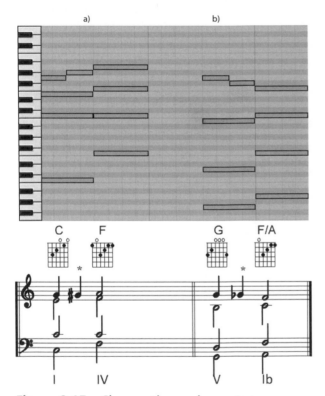

Figure 9.15   Chromatic passing notes.

Use of chromatic passing notes effectively opens up the whole chromatic scale for the purposes of melodic decoration, and it is a common effect to hear numerous successive notes of the chromatic scale being used to fill out the gaps between harmony notes. This type of decoration is typical of styles such as ragtime, bebop, and other such jazz-inspired styles where chromatic runs are the norm. It is also popular in film musical scores, especially when used for humorous purposes. I am sure you have all heard the effect of a falling chromatic run on the glockenspiel being used when somebody falls down the stairs!

The Appoggiatura

A related type of decoration to the passing note is the appoggiatura. The difference between a passing note and an appoggiatura lies in the fact that the appoggiatura approaches the dissonant note through a leap. Otherwise, as a decoration it behaves just like a regular passing note—that is, it moves stepwise up or down to the harmony note. Figure 9.16 shows two examples of appoggiaturas. The first example, (a), is an appoggiatura approached by leap from above. The appoggiatura note—F♯—is dissonant with the E major triad, and the fact that it is accented creates a strong feeling of tension, which then resolves as the appoggiatura moves stepwise up to the harmony note of G♯. The second example, (b), is an appoggiatura note approached from below. The appoggiatura is note C, which again is a dissonant to the G major harmony. As in the previous example, the appoggiatura resolves stepwise to the harmony note, which has the effect of releasing the tension.

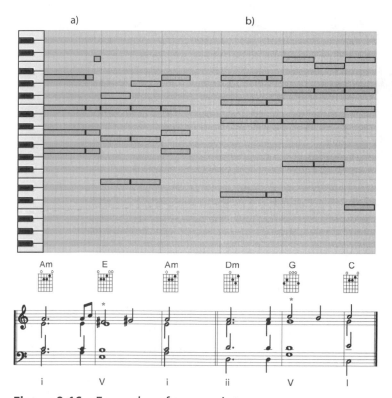

Figure 9.16 Examples of appoggiaturas.

The Suspension

The suspension is one of the time-honored methods of bringing variety and interest to a harmony. The principle of the suspension is that a note belonging to the previous chord is held over into the next chord, with which it forms a dissonance. This creates a powerful moment of tension, which is then released when the suspension falls stepwise to the harmony note. As treated conventionally, a suspension has three phases, which are called *preparation, suspension,* and *resolution.* Figure 9.17 (a) illustrates these. In the first phase, the note to be suspended—in this case, note C—is prepared by being presented as a harmony note of the previous chord (i). Then when the chord changes, as at (ii), the note is said to be suspended, creating as it does a dissonance with an element of the new chord. In this case, as you can see in (ii), the note C has a dissonant relationship with the note D. Finally, there is the resolution, which represents the release of the tension caused by the suspension, as shown in (iii), where the suspension is pushed downward to settle on a note that is consonant with the new harmony.

It is also possible to use suspensions that rise rather than fall. These are referred to as *retardations.* Figure 9.17 (b) shows an example, where the note D is prepared, retarded in the sense of being held over, and then resolved stepwise in an upward direction.

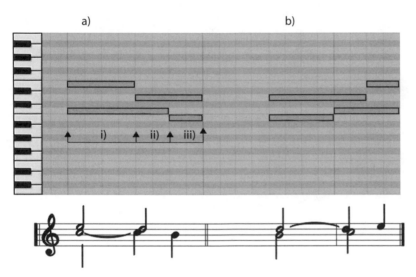

Figure 9.17   The suspension and the retardation.

Suspensions are typically applied to the intervals of the fourth, seventh, and ninth, as you can see in Figure 9.18. In (a), you can see a suspension of a fourth, also called a 4–3; in (b) a suspension of the seventh, also called a 7–6; and in (c) a suspension of the ninth, called a 9–8. Retardations tend to work best when applied to the seventh and the ninth.

A favorite technique of classical composers was to introduce a chain of suspensions, which would often culminate upon the dominant chord of a new key. In Figure 9.19, you see an example of a suspension chain that starts out in the key of C and finishes up with the dominant chord of the relative minor key—this being the key of A minor.

The Anticipation

The opposite of a suspension is an anticipation. An anticipation occurs when a harmony note of the next chord is played early to create a dissonance, which is then resolved when the next chord arrives. See Figure 9.20.

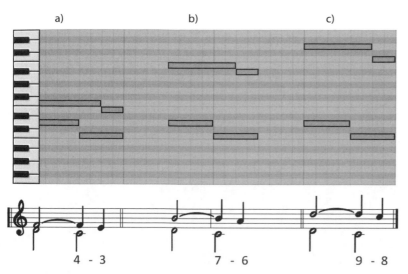

Figure 9.18   Three kinds of suspension.

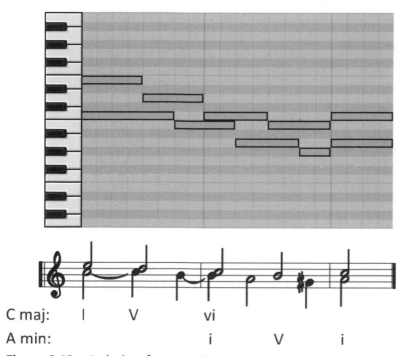

Figure 9.19   A chain of suspensions.

Anticipations are another method of introducing that required element of tension into the harmony. In Figure 9.21, you can see a chain of anticipations being used to decorate what would otherwise be a succession of plain block chords. The anticipations give the harmony more of a gritty, biting quality.

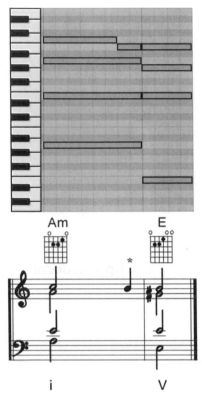

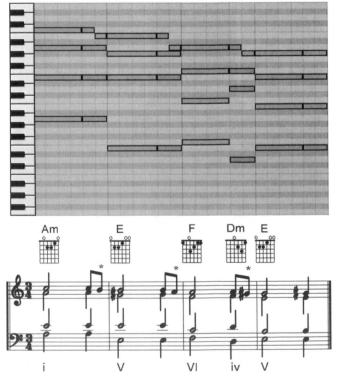

Figure 9.20   A melodic anticipation.

Figure 9.21   A chain of anticipations.

Conclusion

This chapter covered the main techniques of melodic decoration that composers have tended to use when writing music within the parameters of traditional tonal harmony. In certain situations, plain, unadorned chords may be required for a particular piece of music. And of course, there is nothing wrong with using chords in this way if through this use we can achieve our musical purposes. Plain and simple harmonies can often carry a great power, especially in the hands of a skillful composer. Have a listen to the composition for solo piano called "Für Alina" by the Estonian composer Arvo Pärt. This music has a certain power to it that in large part stems from the fact that the composer has stripped down the basic materials of harmony as far as it is possible to go; that is, he uses just two parts—two parts of simple, plain, and unadorned note-against-note harmony.

In many musical situations, however, composers feel the need to spice up and decorate the harmony, to introduce some elements of gritty tension to it, or to impart more life and mobility to the melodic parts. This is where melodic decorations come into their own as methods by which this can be achieved. At the beginning of this chapter, I pointed out that composers tend to develop their own individual methods of melodic decoration. Although this is generally true, it is a wise move to learn those techniques that have already proven themselves to be universally useful. Having done this, you are then in a prime position to develop those techniques further and introduce the element of your own individual approach and thinking on the matter.

10 The Chord of the Dominant Seventh

The chords that most computer musicians, songwriters, music producers and composers use today have a long history of use behind them, one that stretches back many centuries. This sense of continuity between different ages is probably due to audience preferences. Audiences still love the sound of good old triadic harmony, and as long as they do, there will be musicians producing music that uses the chords of C, G, and F major. This leads us to the curious thought that in effect, today's songwriters are writing their songs with the same basic chords that Claudio Monteverdi used to fashion his madrigals in the seventeenth century!

What has changed, though, is the attitude toward what is regarded as being a proper chord. For a long period in the history of Western music, only the triad was recognized as a true chord. This meant that any note that was not a part of a triad was regarded as being foreign to the harmony. Any foreign notes that were used were therefore treated as a form of melodic decoration—along the lines of those standard types of embellishment studied in the previous chapter. However, as embellishments became standardized, they gave rise to numerous common formulas, which gradually crystallized into chords in their own right.

A good example of this would be a falling passing note being introduced between the root of the dominant chord and the third of the tonic chord in a perfect cadence. You might have used this yourself as you completed the exercises in the previous chapter. Figure 10.1 shows this cadence, with a passing note. The key is C major.

In Figure 10.1, you will see that this passing note—F—has been marked with an asterisk. It occurs between the G of the dominant triad and the E of the tonic triad, which means that melodically, it nicely fills the gap between those two notes. The interest in this passing note lies in its implications for the harmony.

The most important implication lies in the fact that as the passing note is introduced, two dissonances are formed. These are illustrated on the keyboard presented on the right side of Figure 10.1. If you look at the figure, you will see that there is the dissonance of a minor seventh formed with the root of chord V, which is G, and then there is the dissonance of an augmented fourth with the third of chord V, which is note B. These dissonances generate a certain tension, and this tension gives to the notes involved a powerful tendency or impetus to move in a particular way. The seventh has

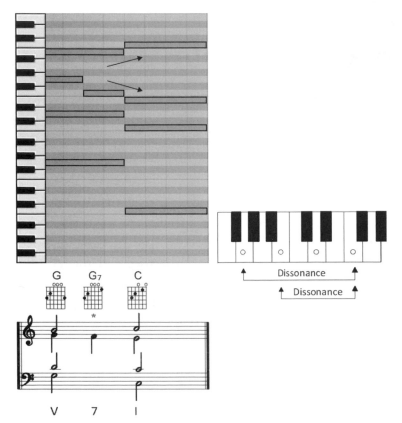

Figure 10.1   Dissonant passing note used in V-I cadence.

acquired an urge to resolve downward, while the third has an urge to rise upward. When they move in this way to the harmony notes of the tonic triad, the tension generated by the dissonance is then released. The direction of the resolution of this tension is indicated in Figure 10.1 by the arrows seen on the Piano Roll view.

This process of tension-release is so effective that as a result of the use of this passing note, the dominant chord has acquired a greater pulling power toward the tonic triad. Because of this increase in its pulling power, the chord formed at this moment—the dominant triad together with the dissonant seventh of the passing note—eventually came to be regarded by musicians as being preferable to the original dominant triad. And so, gradually, a new chord was born in practice and later recognized in theory. This four-note chord, which today we call the *dominant seventh,* is illustrated in Figure 10.2.

As you scrutinize this chord, notice that a dominant seventh chord is represented by the same symbols used to represent a triad, except for the addition of a small 7 after it.

Once it was recognized as a chord in its own right, there was no stopping the force of the dominant seventh. Every composition made abundant use of it, and it entered into music as a standard part of the harmonic language. Some composers overused it, and their music became little more than a two-chord trick—tonic and dominant seventh chord. Other composers, such as Beethoven and Mozart, worked wonders with the

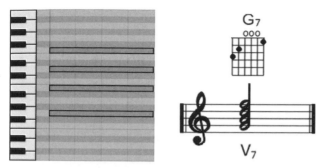

Figure 10.2   The dominant seventh chord.

dominant seventh chord. And in one form or another, composers have been using it in their music ever since. The importance of the dominant seventh chord in musical harmony therefore cannot be overstated. For more than 300 years, this chord has been consistently exploited for the tremendous pulling power that it exerts toward the tonic triad. And as a result of our use of that power, what we call *tonality*—and the whole key system that depends on it—has been enhanced beyond measure. In this way, the dominant seventh chord represents the driver of the entire tonal system.

Here it is notable that even in much of today's popular music, the dominant seventh chord is used in the same way that it always has been. That is, as an enhancement of the dominant triad, especially where the dominant progresses to the tonic at a perfect cadence. Its use in this way is fairly standard, and it occurs in all styles of popular music that use traditional harmony. This means that you will probably find a V7-I cadence in most songs you care to look at.

Treatment of the Dominant Seventh Chord

Surrounding the use of the dominant seventh chord are certain tried and trusted conventions that stem from the particular way in which the chord has been heard. Although I would not suggest sticking to those conventions in your songwriting, I do suggest learning what they are so that you can get the best out of your further study of musical harmony.

The best clues as to the traditional treatment of the dominant seventh chord in harmony lie in its origins as a passing note. When used as a traditional enhancement of a V-I cadence, the seventh of the dominant would ordinarily fall down to the third of the tonic chord, while the third of the dominant triad—the leading note—as we would expect, would tend to rise upward. This would apply in both major and minor scales. See Figure 10.3 for an illustration of this type of resolution.

In the case of Figure 10.3 (a), you can see a progression from the dominant seventh chord to the tonic chord of the major key. The interval that gives the dominant seventh chord its tensile power is the augmented fourth between the seventh and the third of the

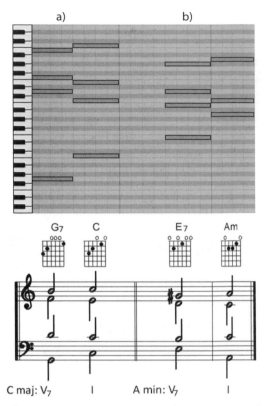

Figure 10.3 Conventional treatment of the dominant seventh chord in major and minor keys.

chord—notes F and B. Forming an augmented fourth (or diminished fifth when inverted), this dissonance resolves well to the third and root of the tonic triad. In Figure 10.3 (b), you can see the dominant seventh chord of the minor key resolving in the same way. So the normal pattern of treatment for the dominant seventh chord is that the seventh falls by a half step, while the third—the leading note of the key—rises by a half step up to the tonic. And this is the type of resolution that you would look for in your four-part writing when treating the dominant seventh chord.

To be able to effect this resolution, it is necessary sometimes to omit a note from the dominant seventh chord. The seventh cannot be omitted (see Figure 10.4 (b)), because the chord would then revert back to being a simple dominant triad. To omit the third would be to leave out the leading note whose rise upward so well defines the tonic (c). I suppose it is possible to omit the root of the dominant seventh chord, because it means the dissonant augmented fourth is still kept as a part of the chord. Yet when the root is omitted, the chord becomes a leading note triad (d). So when omitting a note from the dominant seventh chord, you would normally omit the fifth (e).

Should a note need to be doubled, we would avoid doubling the seventh and third of the dominant seventh because these are the tendency tones that give the chord its pull toward the tonic triad. If one of these were doubled, we would then need to introduce consecutive octaves.

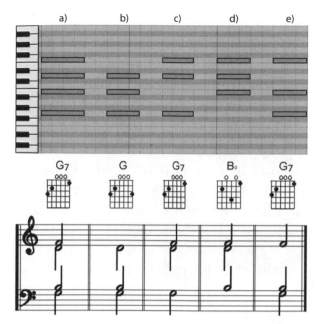

Figure 10.4   Omitting notes from the dominant seventh chord.

Inversions of the Dominant Seventh Chord

The dominant seventh chord is the first four-note chord that we have looked at so far. While a triad only has two possible inversions, a seventh chord has three possible inversions. There is a root position with the root in the bass (see Figure 10.5 (a)), a first inversion with the third in the bass (see Figure 10.5 (b)), a second inversion with the fifth

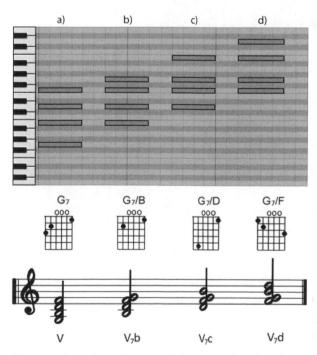

Figure 10.5   The four positions of the dominant seventh chord.

in the bass (see Figure 10.5 (c)), and finally a third inversion with the seventh in the bass (see Figure 10.5 (d)). Figure 10.5 also includes the symbols by which these are represented, both in jazz notation and conventional Roman numeral notation.

Of the four positions of the dominant seventh chord, the strongest is undoubtedly the root position. In a perfect cadence, we would expect the dominant seventh chord to be used in this position (see Figure 10.6 (a)). In the first inversion, the third—or leading note—of the key is in the bass. As the leading note rises upward, the seventh falls nicely down to the third of the tonic triad. This position has an ideal open spacing when the seventh is in the lead (see Figure 10.6 (b)). In the second inversion, the fifth is in the bass. This position is approached well from the first inversion of the tonic triad (see Figure 10.6 (c)). Finally, in the third inversion, the seventh is in the bass. As the seventh tends to fall stepwise, this means that this position automatically implies resolution to a tonic chord in the first inversion. As the seventh falls, the upper parts move nicely in the opposite direction (see Figure 10.6 (a)).

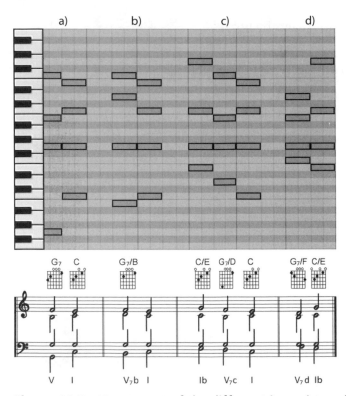

Figure 10.6 Treatment of the different inversions of the dominant seventh chord.

Irregular Progressions of the Dominant Seventh Chord

When the dominant seventh chord is used, the listener would ordinarily expect the tonic chord to follow—which means to say that the tonic chord represents the regular pathway of progression of the dominant seventh chord. But there are numerous factors that can affect the decision to follow this regular pathway of progression. One such factor is that the composer might be leading the listener on a deceptive route, in which case the dominant seventh chord will then progress to a chord other than the tonic. This, as we discussed in Chapter 8, is known as a *deceptive cadence*. And because the dominant seventh chord has a stronger pull toward the tonic than the ordinary dominant triad, this means that a deceptive cadence that involves the dominant seventh has a stronger impact upon the listener.

For a deceptive cadence, the submediant is undoubtedly the best option. Sharing two notes in common with the tonic triad, they are very similar. The dominant seventh chord contracts nicely into it, as you can see by taking a look at Figure 10.7 (a). The subdominant offers another option in terms of alternative pathways than the tonic triad, although the root of the subdominant is at the same time the seventh of the dominant seventh chord. This means that when the dominant seventh progresses to the subdominant, the resolution of the seventh downward is curtailed. For the ear, this has the effect of simply delaying or suspending the feeling of dominant tension. This means that the subdominant would represent a good option at, say, a plagal cadence, where the seventh of the dominant will eventually fall stepwise by means of the plagal cadence (see Figure 10.7 (b)).

Another option involving the subdominant is to return to the dominant seventh chord immediately afterward, setting up the possibility for an alternating vamp between the two chords. This has the effect of maintaining a continual feeling of dominant tension (see Figure 10.7 (c)). A dominant seventh to mediant progression has a certain weakness

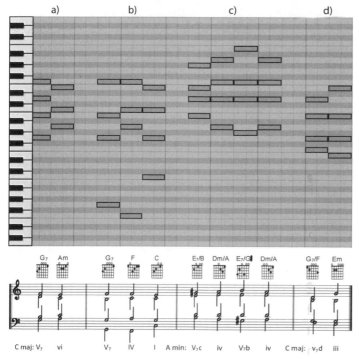

Figure 10.7 Alternative dominant seventh chord pathways.

about it due to the fact that the fifth of the mediant is the leading note. It might represent a viable option, though, when the dominant seventh chord is used in the third inversion. In this position it opens out nicely to the mediant triad of both the major and the harmonic minor scale. But like the dominant seventh to subdominant progression, it simply delays or suspends the feeling of dominant tension. As such, its use creates an expectancy of an immediate return to the dominant seventh chord (see Figure 10.7 [d]).

Another popular type of irregular progression of the dominant seventh chord is to another dominant seventh chord—a favorite technique used by composers to prolong a feeling of dominant tension. We'll talk more about this in Chapter 20, "Secondary Dominant Chords."

Conclusion

This chapter showed that the dominant seventh chord is in effect a triad that has been embellished with its own dissonance—the seventh. Probably originating from the use of a melodic decoration, that dissonance soon moved from a melodic to a harmonic dimension to result in the creation of a new chord—the dominant seventh. We discussed the way in which the dominant seventh chord enhances the perfect cadence. We then went on to look at the treatment of the dominant seventh chord and how important it is to at least bear in mind and be aware of traditional methods of treatment of the chord of the dominant seventh. This treatment focused upon the perceived functions of the tendency tones of the dominant seventh chord—the seventh, which has a tendency to fall stepwise to the tone of the scale below, and the third (the leading note), which displays a tendency to rise up to the tonic. Having considered these tendencies, we went on to look at the different inversions of the dominant seventh chord. Finally, we looked at irregular progression of the dominant seventh chord—that is, chords that the dominant seventh chord can progress to aside from the expected tonic chord. Having studied the dominant seventh chord, we can now go on to study the other seventh chords that it is possible to use within the range of a given key.

11 Secondary Seventh Chords

In the previous chapter, we considered the important role of the dominant seventh chord as the driver of tonality. Because the dominant seventh chord plays such an important role in this respect, it is called a *primary seventh*. In addition to the dominant seventh, there are numerous other seventh chords that can be used within a given scale—major or minor. These are obtained by adding a seventh to each triad of the scale. Therefore, applying this principle to the seven triads of the C major scale, we get the spectrum of chords shown in Figure 11.1.

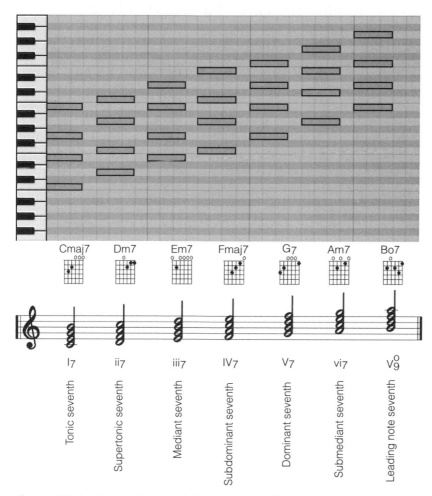

Figure 11.1 Seventh chords in the major key.

You can see from Figure 11.1 that each seventh chord is named according to the note that provides its root. Therefore, the seventh chord on degree one of the scale is called the *tonic seventh,* while the seventh chord on degree two of the scale is called the *supertonic seventh,* and so on. In chordal notation, these seventh chords are represented by a Roman numeral that signifies the degree of the scale that represents the root of the chord. The tonic seventh is therefore represented as I7, the supertonic seventh as ii7, and so on.

Exclusive of the dominant seventh chord—G7—all other seventh chords of a key are termed *secondary seventh chords.* This is for the simple reason that secondary sevenths play a lesser role as far as the maintenance of the tonality of the music is concerned. This means that secondary sevenths are not specifically used to strengthen or reinforce the sense of tonality or key in the music. Rather, they are used as enhancements and embellishments of the triad that represents their foundation. That being said, there are some secondary seventh chords that, because of their particular makeup, have about them a sense of dominant tension. Due to this tension, such chords are often used to represent the dominant seventh—by proxy—in certain contexts. The nature of those contexts will become clear as we delve into the subject of seventh chord harmony over the next few chapters.

Secondary seventh chords have a similar history and origin to the dominant seventh chord. This means that they are basically triads to which an embellishing dissonance has become attached. And this is what gives secondary seventh chords their characteristic sound. They are all dissonant chords—some mildly so, with others being more acutely dissonant. As dissonant chords, this does not mean that secondary sevenths sound unpleasant. On the contrary, they have a great richness and relative complexity of sound that causes musicians and audiences alike to love their particular sound. And above all, they provide a brilliant contrast to the completely consonant and stable sound of common triads. As such, seventh chords provide an excellent way to bring a feeling of expressive tension into our music.

The Seventh as Dissonant Note

When a seventh is added to a triad, each triad is converted into a tetrad of four notes. Each of the four notes of this tetrad has a name. They are called the root, third, fifth, and seventh. In Figure 11.2, you can see this illustrated with respect to the tonic seventh chord of the C major key.

The addition of a seventh to the tonic triad, as illustrated in Figure 11.2, completely transforms the sound of this particular chord. Therefore, if you care to play the chord Cmaj7 on your MIDI keyboard, you will immediately hear the difference between Cmaj7 and the C major triad on its own. With the seventh included, the otherwise completely consonant triad has been destabilized by the presence of the dissonant seventh. All seventh chords carry about them this sense of dissonance. Not that to

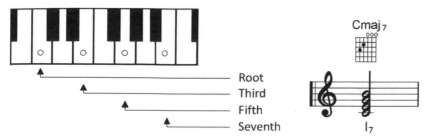

Figure 11.2   Tonic seventh chord.

modern ears this makes seventh chords sound unpleasant—on the contrary, when compared to triads, seventh chords have a more complex, richer, and even warmer sound. And for many of us, seventh chord harmony sounds distinctly modern when compared to simple triadic harmony.

The reason for this is that in today's music, composers and songwriters tend to use sevenths quite freely. And it is not uncommon for many (if not most) of the chords being used in a modern composition to be sevenths or even more complex sonorities, such as ninths, elevenths, and thirteenths. Because of this, harmony that uses an abundance of sevenths tends to have a very modern and contemporary feel to it. And once you begin to explore seventh chord harmony, you will also no doubt want to take advantage of this modern-sounding resource of expressive warmth and feeling that seventh chords have to offer.

Approaching Seventh Chords

There are a number of different ways to approach a seventh chord. And by that I mean the pathway of progression to a seventh chord. One way of approaching the seventh chord, which represents the most traditional method, is to prepare the dissonant seventh by sounding its note in the chord that precedes it. This imparts to the dissonance a mildness of impact that makes it more acceptable to the ear in passages dominated by mostly triadic harmony. You can see an example of this in Figure 11.3(a), where the seventh note B is already present in the E minor second inversion triad that precedes it. This approach leads to a nice point of tension in the harmony.

Another way of approaching a seventh is through use of a passing note between two consonant chordal tones. In Figure 11.3(b), you will see the seventh note B occurring in the bass as a passing note between the roots of the tonic and submediant triads. The dissonant seventh—occurring in the bass—imparts to the bass a melodic impetus to fall and thereby resolve the dissonant seventh. This represents a favorite technique with modern songwriters, a good representative example of which can be found in the song "Fix You" by Coldplay.

An equally valid, although more modern method of approaching the seventh chord is through another seventh chord in which the dissonance is not even prepared. This technique is typically used in jazz harmony. Therefore, in Figure 11.3(c), you will see a

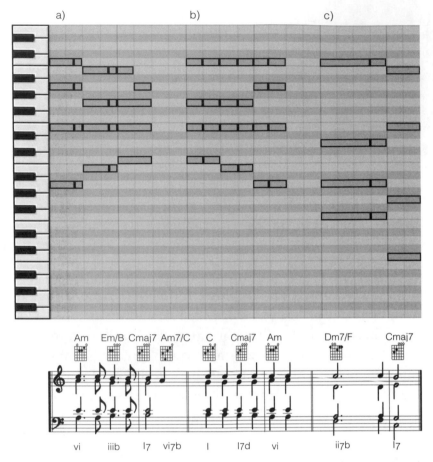

Figure 11.3   Some traditional and modern ways of approaching a seventh chord.

supertonic seventh chord in first inversion progressing to a major seventh chord in root position. In traditional harmony this type of progression tends to be avoided because it can sound rather harsh, especially where the sevenths are moving consecutively between the parts. However, in more modern terms, where the seventh has increasingly come to be regarded as being an essential part of a chord, this is quite normal practice.

Treatment of Seventh Chords

Because of the presence of the dissonant seventh, seventh chords always sound like they want to move, to go somewhere. As such, seventh chord harmony is very dynamic, being full of dissonant notes that, in a conventional sense, act as a driving force that gives the voices that carry them an impetus to move, to progress, to resolve the tension. The study of seventh chord harmony, therefore, is basically about learning how to handle tension and dissonance in our music. So perhaps it comes as no surprise to learn that there are different ways of going about this.

One approach to the dissonance of seventh chords is to resolve the dissonance to a point of consonance within the chord that follows. The voice that carries the seventh would normally be the voice that carries out that resolution. This resolution causes a release of the tension inherent to the seventh chord. Therefore, a common pathway of progression for the tonic seventh chord Cmaj7 is toward the subdominant triad, the chord of F major. Here the dissonant seventh—note B—resolves stepwise to the third of the subdominant triad—note A (see Figure 11.4(a)). Yet in effecting that resolution, it is equally possible to progress to another seventh chord—in this case, the subdominant seventh itself (see Figure 11.4(b)). In this way, although each dissonant seventh resolves downward by step, the feeling of gritty tension in the harmony is maintained through movement from one seventh chord to another.

A good example of this type of treatment of seventh chords is the introduction to Alicia Keys's song "If I Ain't Got You." Here, successive seventh chords are played as an arpeggio, in which the note of resolution of each seventh is at the same time part of another seventh chord. In this way a descending chain of connected seventh chords is created (Cmaj7, Bm7, Am7, Gmaj7, and so on). Yet another approach is to regard the seventh as being an essential part of the chord, such as in jazz. Here the seventh need not be prepared or resolved.

If these different types of approach sound confusing, it is because we are dealing with two sets of values: traditional values, which grew up around the use of the common

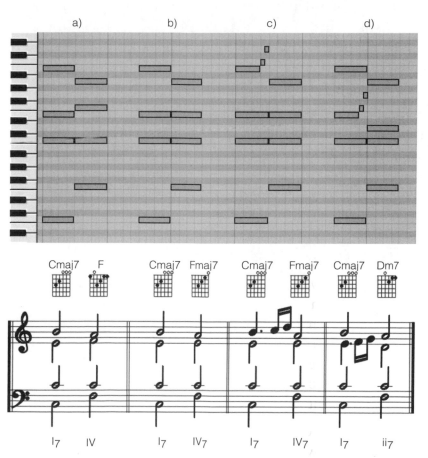

Figure 11.4   Pathways of progression for the tonic seventh chord of the major key.

triad as the unit of harmony, and more modern values, which often see the seventh as being intrinsic to the chord itself. So the type of approach to use with seventh chords all depends upon the musical context. In an environment dominated by triadic harmony—that is, common chords—seventh chords sound best when treated in the traditional manner—the seventh being resolved, for example. However, in an environment where the use of more dissonant chords is the norm, such as we find in jazz, the seventh can be treated more freely.

Inversions of Seventh Chords

Because a seventh chord has four notes, this means that a seventh chord can be used in four different positions. Each position is determined by the note of the seventh chord that is being used in the bass. You can see all four positions, together with typical voice leading applications, in Figure 11.5. In root position, which is represented as Cmaj7 or I7 for the tonic seventh chord of the major key, the root is in the bass, which means that the dissonant seventh will be somewhere in the upper parts. Here it is quite usual to have the seventh in the lead, because this imparts to the lead a sense of dynamic movement (see Figure 11.5(a)). In the first inversion, represented as Cmaj7/E or I7b, the third of the seventh chord is in the bass. This is a very stable position, as the seventh often appears inverted as a whole or half-tone depending upon the type of seventh chord

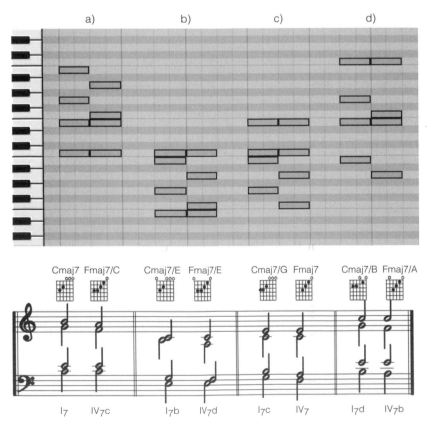

Figure 11.5 The four positions of a seventh chord.

(see Figure 11.5(b)). In second inversion, represented as Cmaj7/G or I7c, the fifth is in the bass. In this position the fifth and seventh tend to fall stepwise in thirds (see Figure 11.5(c)). Finally, in third inversion, represented as Cmaj7/B or I7d, the dissonant seventh itself is in the bass, encouraging the bass line to resolve the seventh through downward stepwise motion (see Figure 11.5(d)). To become familiar with these positions, it is a good idea to play them through separately and study their characteristic sonority.

Figured Bass Notation of Seventh Chords

Although in Figure 11.5 I am using alphabetic notation for the inversions of seventh chords, you will sometimes see these inversions represented by numbers. These numbers originate from the Baroque practice of the figured bass, whereby each chord was represented as a series of figures printed below each note of the bass line. These figures were then used by the performers of the music to realize a harmony above the bass line.

Later, for the purposes of harmony studies, these figures were used as shorthand to represent the various positions of chords. Therefore, for example, when a seventh chord is being used in root position, there is a seventh, a fifth, and a third being heard above the bass note. A root position seventh chord could therefore be represented by a Roman numeral that signifies the root, together with the numbers 7, 5, and 3, which indicate the intervals over the bass when the chord is used in this position.

Similarly, when a seventh chord appears in the first inversion, there is a different configuration of intervals over the bass, because now the seventh chord appears as a sixth, fifth, and third over the bass note. In the second inversion, the seventh appears as a sixth, fourth, and third over the bass. And finally, in the third inversion, the seventh appears as a sixth, fourth, and second over the bass.

Using this type of notation, all four positions of a seventh chord may be represented as shown in Figure 11.6. The top line indicates the position of the chord, from root position through to third inversion. The second line shows the intervals that occur above the bass in each position of the seventh chord. The third line shows the way in which these figures were then conveniently abbreviated. And finally, the fourth line shows the more recent method of representing chordal positions by letters of the alphabet.

Inversion:	Root	First	Second	Third
Intervals:	$I\begin{smallmatrix}7\\5\\3\end{smallmatrix}$	$I\begin{smallmatrix}6\\5\\3\end{smallmatrix}$	$I\begin{smallmatrix}6\\4\\3\end{smallmatrix}$	$I\begin{smallmatrix}6\\4\\2\end{smallmatrix}$
Abbreviation:	I_7	$I\begin{smallmatrix}6\\5\end{smallmatrix}$	$I\begin{smallmatrix}4\\3\end{smallmatrix}$	$I\begin{smallmatrix}4\\2\end{smallmatrix}$
Letters:	I_7	I_7b	I_7c	I_7d

Figure 11.6   Figured way of representing seventh chords.

Later in this book, when we look at chromatically altered chords, we will realize the value of this figured system, because through it we can indicate which notes of a chord have been altered and how.

Types of Seventh Chords

There are numerous different types of seventh chords. The exact type is determined by the type of triad to which the seventh has been added—major, minor, augmented, or diminished—and the type of seventh itself—major or minor. It is a very useful exercise to sit at the keyboard and play these different types of seventh chords in order to become familiar with their particular sound and color. The types that we encounter within the major and minor keys are shown in Figure 11.7.

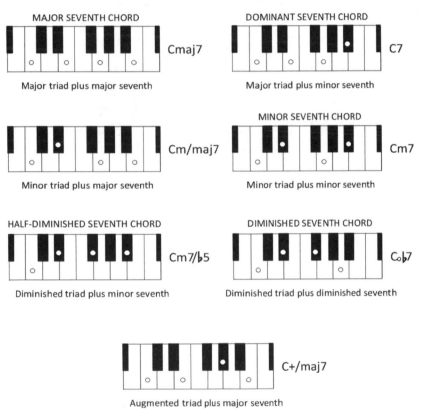

MAJOR SEVENTH CHORD   Cmaj7
Major triad plus major seventh

DOMINANT SEVENTH CHORD   C7
Major triad plus minor seventh

Cm/maj7
Minor triad plus major seventh

MINOR SEVENTH CHORD   Cm7
Minor triad plus minor seventh

HALF-DIMINISHED SEVENTH CHORD   Cm7/♭5
Diminished triad plus minor seventh

DIMINISHED SEVENTH CHORD   C♭7
Diminished triad plus diminished seventh

C+/maj7
Augmented triad plus major seventh

Figure 11.7 Main types of seventh chords.

Above each chord, you can see the name by which the chord is commonly known.

Conclusion

This chapter has served as an introduction to seventh chord harmony. It has shown that the seventh represents the first extension of the triad—an extension that loads a given triad with a dissonant factor: the seventh itself. We discussed the difference between primary and secondary seventh chords, and I pointed out that there is only one true primary seventh chord, the chord of the dominant seventh. We then looked at the derivation of sevenths—that is, how to create a seventh chord from the foundation of a triad. This came down to adding a fourth note to a triad in the form of the seventh above the root. Looking at the tonic seventh chord of the major scale as a representative example, we observed how rich and complex the sound of a seventh chord is. From there, we went on to consider the various pathways of approach to a seventh chord, of which we considered three main ones. Once we considered the pathways of approach, we could then logically look at how seventh chords tended to progress toward other chords. There we observed that it is possible to progress either to a triad, by resolving the seventh stepwise, or equally to another seventh chord, which still enabled that stepwise resolution. Alternatively, we also saw that the seventh could be treated as an essential part of the chord and therefore not necessarily prepared or resolved—as is typical of modern jazz. We examined the four positions of each seventh chord, along with the way in which those positions are used, represented, figured, and symbolized in various forms of chordal notation. Having done this preparatory study, we can now consider seventh chord harmony in the major and minor scales. We will begin this in the next chapter, with seventh chord harmony in the major scale.

12 Seventh Chord Harmony in the Major Key

When studying seventh chord harmony, it is a lot more convenient to begin with the major key. This is because the minor key uses numerous forms of minor scale—natural, harmonic, and melodic—which makes the study of seventh chord harmony in the minor key more complex. However, because there is only one form of major scale and therefore only one seventh chord associated with each degree of the scale, the major scale offers us a nice, simple, and clear inroad to the study of seventh chord harmony in general.

One of the first places to begin the study of seventh chord harmony is to become familiar with each of the seventh chords associated with each degree of the scale. This familiarity is gained by studying the particular type of seventh chord that occurs on each degree of the scale, together with the various regular pathways of progression that suit that particular chord. So let us begin this study by considering the tonic seventh chord of the major key. The key we will focus upon here is C major.

The Tonic Seventh Chord

The seventh chord occurring on degree one of the scale is composed of a major triad to which has been added a major seventh. Figure 12.1 illustrates this chord.

This particular chord is of the type that musicians call a major seventh chord. In jazz notation this is abbreviated to maj7. Please bear in mind that the abbreviation maj refers to the type of seventh, not to the triad to which that seventh has been added. Therefore, the notation Cmaj7 consists of two components. The C signifies a C major triad, and the maj7 refers to the extension—that is, the seventh added to that triad.

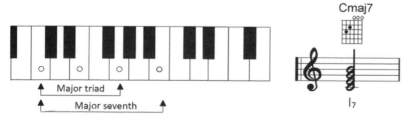

Figure 12.1 The tonic seventh chord of the major key.

147

A major seventh is a sharp dissonance, as you will hear if you play the two notes of a major seventh—from C up to B—on your keyboard. When combined with a major triad, as in the chord Cmaj7, the result is a bright but sharp sonority that contrasts beautifully with the various minor seventh chords in the key (such as the supertonic and mediant sevenths). The typical pathways of progression for this chord are based on the felt need for this sharp dissonance to resolve downward by a half step. Therefore, the seventh in chord Cmaj7 would typically find resolution upon the scale step immediately below it.

The strongest available progression is to a chord whose root lies a fourth above; in other words, the subdominant—chord IV—either the triad or seventh chord (see Figure 12.2 (a)).

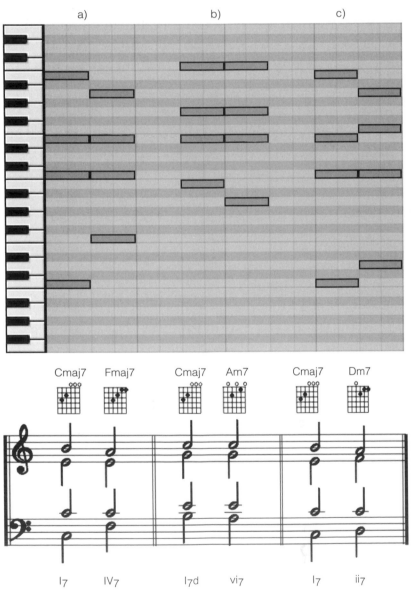

Figure 12.2 Typical pathways of progression for the tonic seventh of the major key.

After that are the chords of the submediant—chord vi (see Figure 12.2 (b))—and the supertonic—chord ii (see Figure 12.2 (c)).

It is recommended that these progressions are played in different keys to gain a sense of tonic seventh chord progression.

The Supertonic Seventh Chord

On degree two of the scale, we have the supertonic seventh, which is illustrated in Figure 12.3.

The supertonic seventh has a different composition to the tonic seventh. Composed of a minor triad to which has been added a minor seventh, this chord is appropriately called a minor seventh chord.

A minor seventh is a mild dissonance, in contrast to the major seventh of the tonic seventh chord, which is a sharp, biting dissonance. This gives to the minor seventh chord a soft, dark, mellow quality that offers a great means of contrast to the brighter colors of the major seventh chord.

The most common and popular use for the supertonic seventh chord is as a pre-dominant chord. The seventh resolves beautifully to the leading note, while the third is at the same time the seventh of the dominant. And the root movement between the two chords—a rising fourth—makes this progression very strong and distinctive. We have already discussed the value and popularity of the ii-V-I progression, particularly with reference to the perfect cadence. Sevenths can be used to beautifully enhance both the power and the drive of the distinctive ii-V progression, as you can see in Figure 12.4 (a). Another viable pathway of progression for chord ii7 is to the seventh on the leading note—see Figure 12.4 (b). This progression is not as strong as the ii7-V7 progression on account of the fact that the two chords share three notes in common. Consequently, as one chord moves to another, only one note needs to change. Finally, in Figure 12.4 (c), we can see the supertonic seventh in two different positions participating in a dominant-colored loop.

The progressions in Figure 12.4 need to be played in as many major keys as possible and also supplemented by your own studies and experiments with pathways of progression from the supertonic seventh chord.

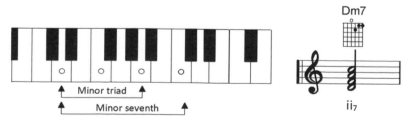

Figure 12.3   The supertonic seventh chord.

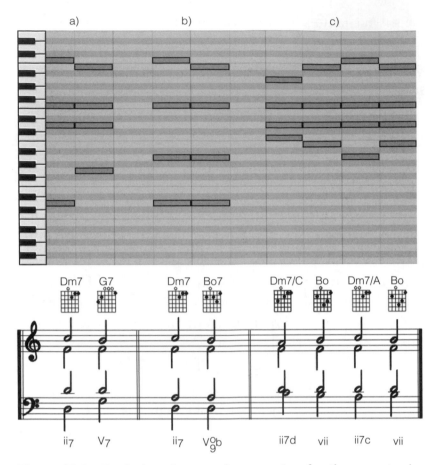

Figure 12.4   Typical pathways of progression for the supertonic seventh.

The Mediant Seventh Chord

The seventh chord on degree three is called the *mediant* seventh chord, and like the supertonic seventh, it is also a minor seventh chord (see Figure 12.5). Consisting of a minor seventh placed over a minor triad, minor seventh chords are distinguished by their soft, mellow, and emotionally expressive sound, which makes them a firm favorite with songwriters.

The regular pathway of progression for this seventh chord is to chord vi, either the triad or the seventh. In the case of Figure 12.6 (a), the seventh is taken. Chord I proves a viable alternative pathway (see Figure 12.6 (b)), and when the mediant seventh

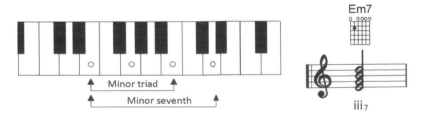

Figure 12.5   The mediant seventh chord.

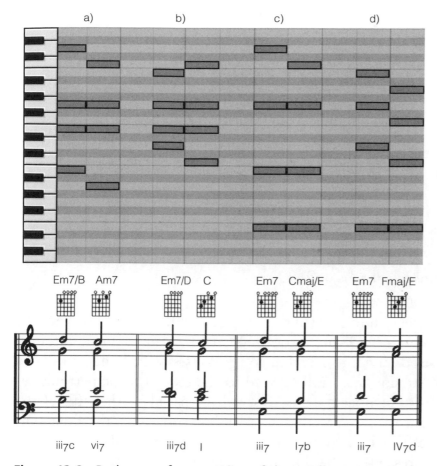

Figure 12.6   Pathways of progression of the mediant seventh chord.

progresses to the tonic seventh, the fifth of the mediant seventh becomes the seventh of the tonic chord (see Figure 12.6 (c)). Chord IV is also viable in certain part-writing contexts. In Figure 12.6 (d), the mediant seventh progresses to the subdominant seventh in the third inversion through retention of the bass note E, which is at the same time the root of the mediant seventh and the seventh of the subdominant.

The Subdominant Seventh Chord

The subdominant seventh on degree four of the scale is a major seventh chord. Like the tonic seventh, the subdominant seventh is also composed of a major chord to which a major seventh has been added. Because both the tonic seventh and the subdominant seventh are the only major seventh chords in the major scale, they belong together as a group (see Figure 12.7).

Sharing the same bright, distinctive sound, these chords are often found in close association with one another in chord progressions, such as in Neil Young's "Nowadays Clancy Can't Even Sing," Bob Dylan's "You're Gonna Make Me Lonesome When You Go," and so on.

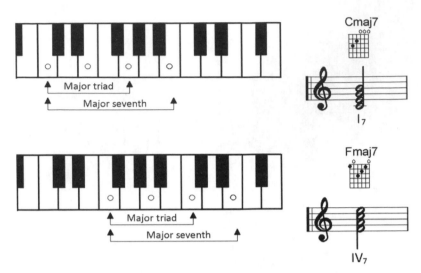

Figure 12.7 Major seventh chords in the major scale.

The regular pathway of progression for the subdominant seventh of the major key is to the seventh on the leading note—involving a root movement of an augmented fourth (see Figure 12.8 (a)). The subdominant seventh also progresses well to the supertonic seventh, the seventh of the subdominant falling well to the root of the supertonic seventh chord. The seventh of the supertonic is also well prepared by the fifth of the subdominant (see Figure 12.8 (b)). In certain voice-leading situations, the dominant seventh chord makes for an effective pathway of progression. The example given avoids consecutive sevenths by progressing to the dominant seventh chord in the third inversion (see Figure 12.8 (c)).

The Dominant Seventh Chord

We discussed the seventh chord on degree five of the scale—the dominant—in the previous chapter. So there is no need to consider the regular pathways of progression of this chord. However, it is worth bearing in mind that the dominant seventh has a rather unique sound on account of the fact that it consists of a major triad to which a minor seventh has been added. This gives rise to the diminished fifth interval between the third and the seventh (see Figure 12.9). It is undoubtedly this interval that gives the dominant seventh chord that restless urge to find a resolution in the tonic chord.

The Submediant Seventh

The seventh chord on degree six of the scale—the submediant seventh—is a soft minor seventh chord whose composition is exactly the same as the supertonic and mediant sevenths—that is, a minor triad to which a minor seventh has been added. As such, the submediant seventh belongs in a group of minor seventh chords along with the supertonic and mediant seventh chords (see Figure 12.10).

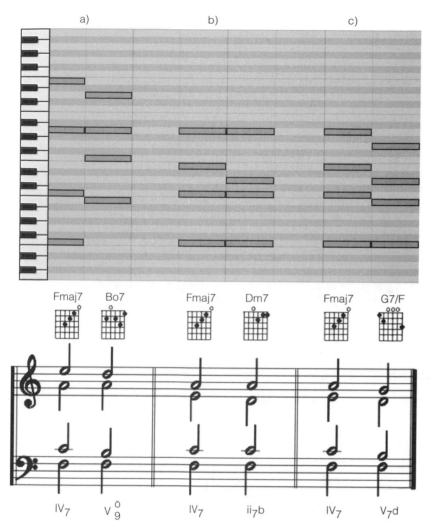

Figure 12.8 Pathways of progression of the subdominant seventh chord of the major key.

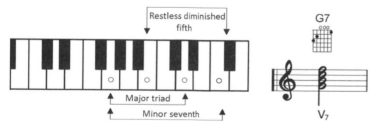

Figure 12.9 Composition of the dominant seventh chord.

The submediant seventh progresses particularly well to chords of the supertonic—involving a root movement of a rising fourth (see Figure 12.11 (a) and (b)). Another effective pathway of progression is to the subdominant, either triad (c) or seventh (d). In (e), the submediant seventh progresses to the leading note seventh. The two upper parts move in parallel fifths, although because one of the fifths is diminished, this does not count as consecutive fifths.

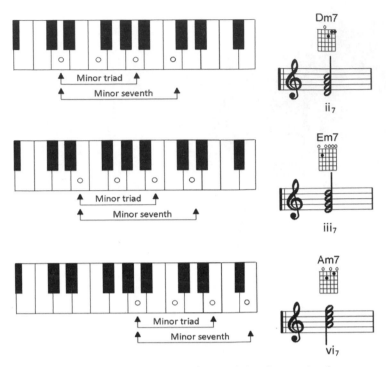

Figure 12.10 Minor seventh chords in the major key.

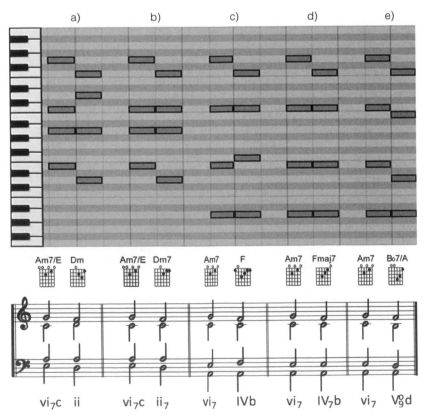

Figure 12.11 Regular pathways of progression of the submediant seventh of the major key.

The Seventh on the Leading Note

The final seventh chord in the major scale is the seventh chord on the leading note of the scale. This chord has a very distinctive sound due to its particular composition of a diminished triad to which has been added a minor seventh. Sometimes also called the *half-diminished seventh chord*, this particular chord has about it a definite dominant feel. In fact, all chords built up from the foundation of the diminished triad tend to have a dominant feel about them. This is due to the presence of the dissonant diminished fifth, which imparts to those chords in which it is present a restless sense of instability. This restless instability, when coupled with the dominant root, undoubtedly provides the essential motor that drives dominant harmony in general. For this reason, the seventh chord on degree seven of the scale is often understood as being a chord of the dominant ninth whose root is absent.[1] This means that ultimately, the root of this chord is really the dominant degree itself. You can understand this more clearly by perusing Figure 12.12.

Figure 12.12 shows the location of the missing root on the dominant degree. Being considered to have a missing root, this is why the seventh on the leading note can be represented in chord numeral notation as a chord of V—signifying its dominant function—the small o above the 9 signifying the missing root.

As a chord that has about it a distinct dominant color, the seventh on the leading note provides a good alternative pre-dominant chord to the supertonic or subdominant, the seventh falling nicely down to the root of the dominant itself (see Figure 12.13 (a)). Other viable pathways of progression are to the mediant seventh (see Figure 12.13 (b)) or even the tonic chord itself (see Figure 12.13 (c) and (d)).

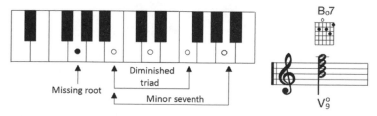

Figure 12.12   Half-diminished seventh chord as incomplete dominant ninth.

The Sequential Cycle

By looking at the best regular pathways of progression for seventh chords—as we have been doing—it now becomes possible to make a number of basic observations. The first observation is that in nearly all cases, the strongest pathway of progression for a given seventh chord is to a chord whose root lies a fourth above. Knowing this, we can arrange all of the seventh chords of the major key into a cycle of chords whose roots are

---

[1] Walter Piston, *Harmony*, Fifth Edition (W.W. Norton & Co. 1987). "The Incomplete Major Ninth."

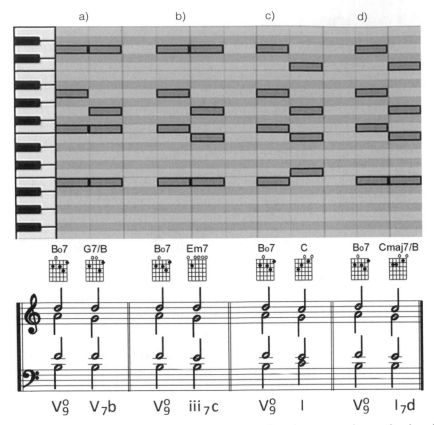

Figure 12.13   Pathways of progression for the seventh on the leading note.

all respectively rising upward by a fourth. This gives rise to the series of chords in C major that you can see in Figure 12.14.

The great thing about this cycle is that each chord within it not only prepares the seventh of the next chord in the cycle, but also resolves the seventh of the previous chord in the cycle. This gives rise to a never-ending chain of connected seventh chords that sounds very effective. Chains of chords like this are normally used in a sequence, a sequence being the repetition of the same melodic material upon a different pitch. The application of this will become obvious if you look at Figure 12.14, in which a sequence involving all of these seventh chords is created.

Beginning with the tonic seventh, the entire cycle is gone through until we land back again with the tonic seventh. The sequence is very clear visually as we look at the pattern of falling notes that repeats itself every two bars. Naturally, this is a very basic sequence, one that can be elaborated in an infinite variety of ways and using many types of melodic decoration.

When creating chord progressions for use in compositions, we don't necessarily have to begin with the tonic chord. It is possible to begin the cycle anywhere and use any segment of the cycle that is required. The famous ii7-V7-I cadence is a perfect example of this, using three of the chords that belong to this cycle. The only problem with using this

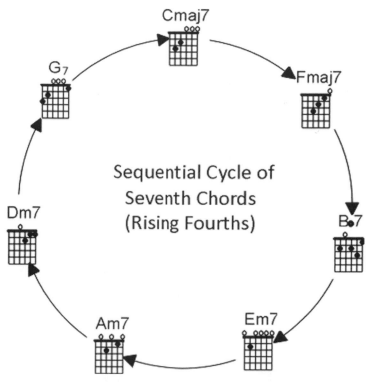

Figure 12.14 Seventh chords arranged in a cycle of root movement by a rising fourth.

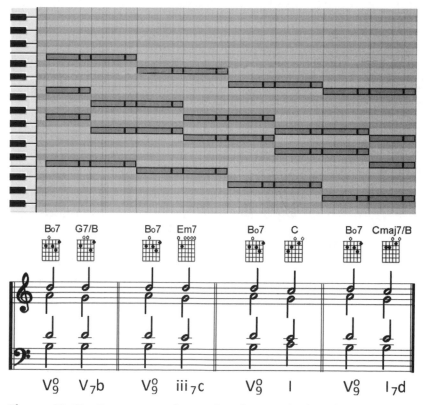

Figure 12.15 Sequence using cycle of seventh chords.

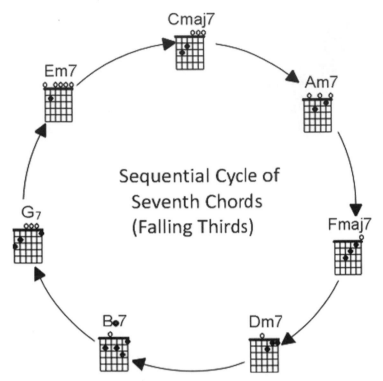

Figure 12.16   The falling thirds cycle.

cycle in compositions is that it is so effective that it has already been used a million times before. Play it through, and you will hear shades of countless songs from many eras, all written in such a way as to exploit this natural-sounding sequence of seventh chords. One way to overcome this problem is to approach the cycle with some original thinking and create a variant of it. One popular variant that has been developed in jazz improvisation is to substitute each of the minor seventh chords with a dominant seventh. Try playing it through this way and see how it sounds.

In looking at the regular pathways of progression of seventh chords, it became apparent that in addition to a rising fourth root movement, a falling third root movement was also effective. Therefore, another popular variant of the sequential cycle of seventh chords is the falling thirds cycle. In this cycle, all of the seventh chords of the major key are linked by a chain of connected roots that fall by a third each time.

In common with the rising fourths cycle, each chord that belongs to this cycle both resolves the seventh of the previous chord and prepares the seventh of the next chord. In this way, all seven chords become linked in a never-ending cycle. And like the previous cycle of rising fourths, the cycle can begin anywhere, and any segment of it can be used either as a chord progression or at least as a part of one. Figure 12.17 adapts the sequence previously used in the rising fourths cycle in order to follow the falling thirds cycle.

Both of these cycles are great ways to explore and get to know different keys. This is done by transposing them into the key required and playing them in that key. They are

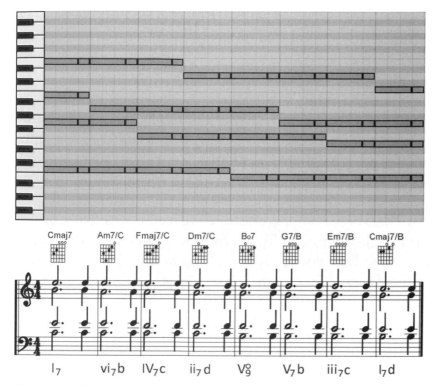

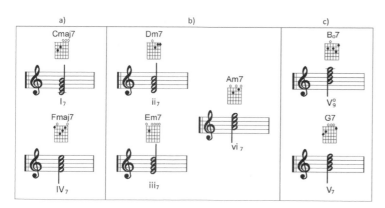

Figure 12.17   Sequence written using the falling thirds cycle.

also a fine way to generate musical ideas. This is done at the keyboard by playing the chords with the left hand and improvising a lead melody with the right.

Three Types of Seventh Chords

As a result of our survey of the seventh chords in the major key, we can see that they divide into three groups. There are the major seventh chords (see Figure 12.18 (a)), the minor seventh chords (Figure 12.18 (b)), and finally the two chords that perform dominant function for the key (Figure 12.18 (c)).

Figure 12.18   Three groups of seventh chords in the major key.

Each type of seventh chord has its own particular color, feel, and mood, and it is the contrast between these different types that makes seventh chord harmony so interesting.

Conclusion

This chapter examined seventh chord harmony in the major key. It looked at each of the seventh chords in that key, examined their composition, and traced the regular pathways of progression of each seventh chord. It needs to be stressed that these are simply regular pathways and that once these are known about and have been studied and understood, it then becomes necessary to explore the pathways of progression for each chord individually for yourself. Having explored the various regular pathways of progression of each chord, we saw that these could in effect be reduced to two basic cycles of progression—a cycle of seventh chords linked by a root movement of a rising fourth and a cycle of seventh chords linked by a root movement of a falling third. These observations will be extremely useful as we now approach seventh chord harmony in the minor key.

13 Seventh Chord Harmony in the Minor Key

When compared to the major key, seventh chord harmony in the minor key appears to be less straightforward. This is because the minor key does not really have a consistent scale system. There are numerous variations of the minor scale, each of which leads to significant changes in the profiles of particular seventh chords belonging to the minor key. Therefore, combining all three forms of the minor scale of the key of A, we obtain the range of notes shown in Figure 13.1—any one of which may at any given time require its own particular harmony.

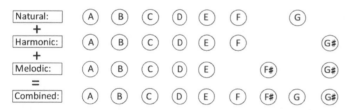

Figure 13.1 Combined range of notes used by the three forms of the minor scale.

Looking at this combined scale resulting from the fusion of all three forms of minor scale, we are left with a scale of nine notes. As well as this, from note E upward, we have a full chromatic scale of notes to contend with. The implications of this for seventh chord harmony in the minor key is that there are many more options available in the minor key than in the major. This can be easily demonstrated if we now take the combined scale illustrated in Figure 13.1 and work out all of the possible seventh chords that are available to us within the range of that scale. Figure 13.2 shows this result.

Compared to the major key, which offers only seven seventh chords, we can now see that the minor key offers double this amount. When studying seventh chord harmony in the minor key, it is therefore necessary to be aware of all of these options and when and where to use them. To this end, it proves very useful to look closely at each option, to examine where it fits into the picture of minor key harmony, and to look at the particular regular pathways of progression that belong with each of these chords. In this chapter we will start with this process, although any references made need to be followed up with your own experimentation with these chords at the keyboard.

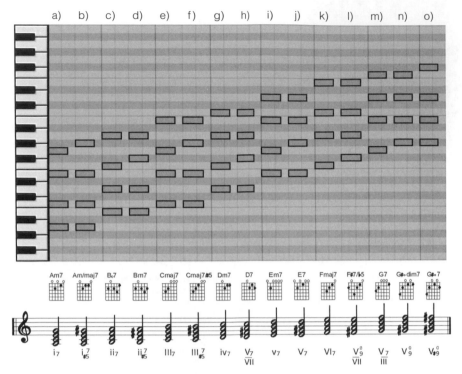

Figure 13.2 Seventh chords in the minor key.

The Tonic Seventh

The tonic seventh of the natural minor scale (see Figure 13.2(a)) is a straight minor seventh chord. The traditionally felt tendencies of the seventh of a chord to resolve stepwise suggest that this chord probably originated as a result of using a falling passing note between the first and sixth degrees of the scale (see Figure 13.3(a)). Regular pathways of progression for this chord are therefore toward those chords that offer chordal support for the sixth degree of the scale. Figure 13.3 shows some examples of this.

b. The major subdominant triad of the melodic minor mode

c. The regular subdominant minor triad

d. The subdominant seventh

e. The submediant triad

f. The submediant seventh chord

In the harmonic minor scale, due to the sharpening of the seventh degree, the profile of the tonic seventh chord is changed. Here we encounter a major seventh being heard over a minor triad (see Figure 13.2(b)). This is a seventh chord that we don't find in the major key, so when this particular chord is used, it immediately puts us into the territory of the minor key. However, due to the minor triad, which gives the chord its foundation, and the presence of a sharp, dissonant major seventh, this chord has a very distinctive

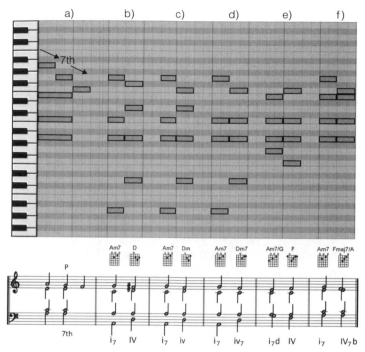

Figure 13.3   Regular pathways of progression of the tonic seventh of the minor mode.

color—a color that is probably not to everybody's taste. I personally find this tonic seventh chord very atmospheric, although it is a chord that is probably more at home in jazz styles of music. (See Figure 13.4.) The reason for this is that in jazz, often every chord that is used is a seventh, ninth, or even more complex chord. So the musical texture itself is so loaded with dissonance as to make a chord like this just one of many, often equally dissonant chords.

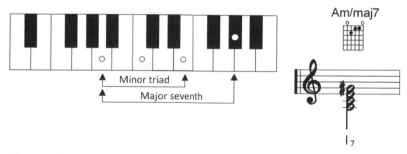

Figure 13.4   An exotic, jazzy-sounding tonic seventh chord of the minor key.

Whether to use the seventh from the natural or harmonic scale therefore comes down to the mood you are after. The seventh of the natural minor scale has a dark, mellow color, while the seventh from the harmonic minor scale has a much more exotic and distinctive color.

The Supertonic Seventh

There are two supertonic sevenths available in the minor scale. The regular supertonic seventh from the natural minor scale (see Figure 13.2(c)) is a half-diminished seventh chord. As such, we need to bear in mind that this chord also performs a dominant function for the relative major key—in this case, C major. When using chords shared by both the minor and the relative major key (another can be found on degree seven of the natural minor scale), the dominant implications of the chord for the relative major key need to be counterbalanced by an obvious resolution in the home key (usually by progressing to chord V7). In this way, there can never be a doubt in the listener's mind about the key of the music.

The other supertonic seventh, illustrated in Figure 13.2(d) originates from the melodic minor scale where the sixth—note F—is sharpened to give note F♯. This particular supertonic seventh is a welcome addition to the seventh chords in the minor scale because it offers the option of using a supertonic seventh, which, unlike the half-diminished seventh chord just considered, is not loaded with restless dominant tendencies.

Figure 13.5 depicts some regular pathways of progression for the supertonic seventh of the minor mode.

a. The dominant triad

b. The dominant seventh

c. The diminished seventh

d. The mediant seventh chord

The Mediant Seventh

The mediant seventh of the natural minor scale is a crisp major seventh chord (see Figure 13.2(e)). Because this chord uses the natural seventh of the minor scale, this means that it ignores the leading note. This means that the mediant seventh chord is also shared with the relative major key, where it counts as the tonic seventh. Where chords belonging to both the minor scale and its relative major are being used, the identity of the key is often decided by nothing more than context and the chords used that surround it. Therefore, when using, say, a sequential cycle of seventh chords that involves this particular seventh chord, the tonality would sway in favor of the minor key only through reference to the dominant seventh chord of that key. We can demonstrate this by looking back to the sequential cycle of seventh chords originally presented in Figure 12.14. In Figure 13.6, you can see the first few chords of this sequential cycle. What now sways this cycle in favor of A minor as opposed to the C major key in which it was originally presented is the dominant seventh chord of A minor arriving in the final bar. This makes the tonal context of the chord progression clear to the ear.

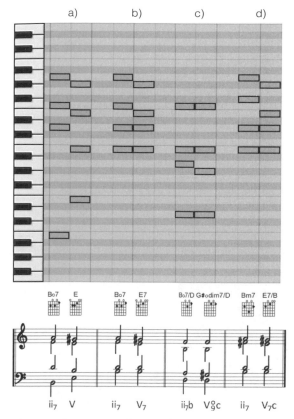

Figure 13.5 Regular pathways of progression for the supertonic seventh of the minor mode.

In the case of the mediant seventh chord that does include the leading note—C E G ♯ and B—as shown above, there cannot be any ambiguity of key, as the leading note is present. But like the tonic seventh (Am/maj7), which also has the leading note, this chord has an unusual profile being made up of an augmented triad to which a major seventh has been added.

This makes for a very exotic-sounding seventh chord, which is again very much home in jazz styles.

The Subdominant Seventh

On the subdominant of the minor scale, there are two options. First, there is the minor seventh chord belonging to the natural and harmonic forms of minor scale, illustrated in Figure 13.2 (g). The other seventh chord that is available comes from the melodic minor scale—Figure 13.2 (h). This is actually a dominant seventh chord belonging to another key. As such, it counts as a secondary dominant seventh, the uses of which we will consider in a later chapter.

The subdominant seventh, like the supertonic seventh, is very useful in pre-dominant contexts. This is because the note of resolution of the seventh is the fifth of the dominant triad, while its root is the dominant seventh itself. The subdominant seventh also

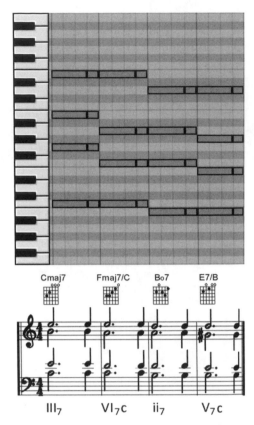

Cmaj7   Fmaj7/C   B♭7   E7/B

III₇   VI₇c   ii₇   V₇c

Figure 13.6   Sequential cycle of seventh chords in the minor key.

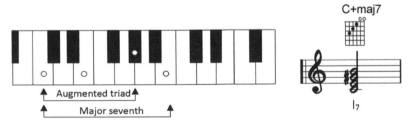

C+maj7

Figure 13.7   Mediant seventh chord of the harmonic minor scale.

progresses well to the supertonic whose root is the note of resolution of the sub-dominant seventh. The regular pathways of progression for the subdominant seventh chord (as depicted in Figure 13.8) are therefore:

a. Supertonic triad

b. Diminished seventh (dominant ninth with omitted root)

c. Supertonic seventh chord

d. Dominant triad

e. Dominant seventh

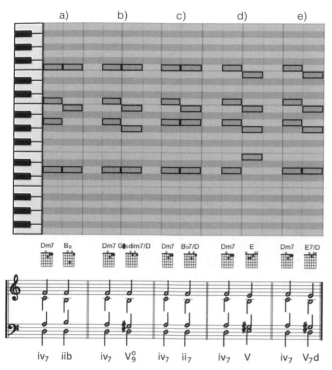

Figure 13.8   Regular pathways of progression for the subdominant seventh chord of the minor key.

The Submediant Seventh

On the submediant degree of the minor scale, there is the major seventh chord illustrated in Figure 13.2(k). The submediant seventh makes an excellent chord of approach to a ii-V-I cadence (see Figure 13.9(a)), the seventh of the submediant resolving down to the third of the supertonic seventh. The submediant seventh also progresses well to the subdominant seventh whose root is the note of resolution of the submediant seventh (see Figure 13.9(b)). An equally effective pathway is to the seventh chord on the leading note (see Figure 13.9(c)).

The chord on the sharpened submediant—that is, the sharp sixth of the melodic minor scale (see Figure 13.2(l)) is another secondary dominant chord. That is to say it is a chord that effectively belongs to another key. We could also argue that because the sharp sixth of the minor scale is often only introduced for melodic convenience—in other words, to get rid of the augmented second between the sixth and seventh degrees of the scale—that this sharp sixth is not really an effective minor key root note. It is simply an altered note introduced in order to improve the melodic profile of the voice parts in the minor key.

The Seventh Chord on the Leading Note

The chord on the natural seventh of the A minor scale is a dominant seventh chord: G B D F. You might recognize this chord as the dominant seventh of the key of

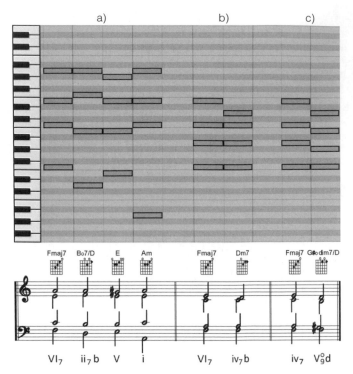

Figure 13.9 Regular pathways of progression of the submediant seventh chord.

C major—the relative major key to A minor. Bearing in mind the leanings of dominant seventh chords, using this particular chord would encourage an immediate shift of tonality toward the relative major key of C. This means that ordinarily, this chord would be used in the context of either modulating to the relative major key or at least making some kind of temporary reference to it. I'll make more mention of this in the next chapter, when we consider the process of modulating to closely related keys.

When the seventh note of the natural minor scale is sharpened, we manage to avoid the dominant seventh chord on the natural seventh degree. And instead, we encounter a powerful leading note sonority called the *diminished seventh chord,* which is illustrated in Figure 13.10.

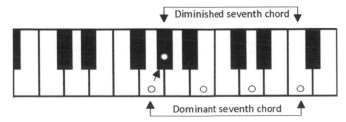

Figure 13.10 The diminished seventh chord obtained when the leading note of the A natural minor scale is sharpened.

The diminished seventh chord has always aroused great interest from those who study musical harmony because of its remarkable properties. All of the other seventh chords that we have looked at so far have been either major or minor seventh chords. The seventh on the leading note is totally unique in that it is only seventh chord that has a diminished seventh. In explanation of this, it is necessary to point out that a diminished seventh is basically a minor seventh interval that has been further shrunk by a semitone. Figure 13.11 illustrates this essential difference between a minor seventh interval and a diminished seventh.

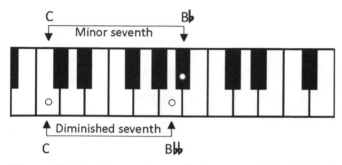

Figure 13.11   Comparison of minor and diminished seventh intervals.

The presence of this diminished seventh gives this chord a unique sound and color all of its own. And although in today's music this particular color is not to everybody's taste, the diminished seventh chord is nonetheless a valuable addition to the range of chords of dominant colors. I say *dominant color* for the simple reason that the diminished seventh is a chord built around the interval of the tritone. In fact, there are numerous tritones in the diminished seventh chord, as you can see in Figure 13.12. There you will see the diminished seventh chord as it appears as the leading note seventh of the key of A minor.

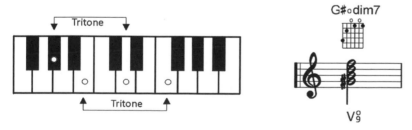

Figure 13.12   Tritones in the diminished seventh chord.

Like all other chords built around the tritone, the diminished seventh is literally charged with dominant tension. And containing two tritones, we could say that it is turbo-charged. To demonstrate this, we just need to observe the tendencies of the notes within the chord. The leading note upon which the diminished seventh chord is built rises smoothly up to the tonic, while the diminished seventh itself resolves nicely down to the fifth of the tonic chord. And the diminished fifth resolves equally well, down to the third of the tonic triad (see Figure 13.13(a)).

Alternatively, containing, as it does, three notes in common with the dominant seventh of the key, the diminished seventh resolves nicely down to the root of the dominant seventh chord. This makes it an effective pre-dominant chord for the minor key (see Figure 13.13(b)). And as an agent of dominant function, the diminished seventh chord can also take a deceptive route, such as to chord VI, for example (see Figure 13.13(c)).

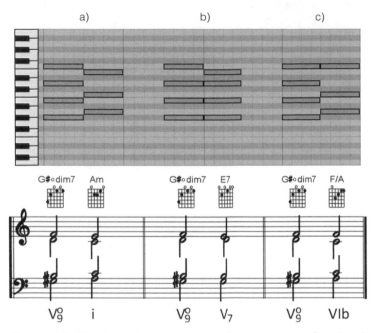

Figure 13.13   Regular pathways of progression for the diminished seventh chord.

Notice that the diminished seventh chord is not represented here as chord vii7. This is because, like the half-diminished seventh chord on degree vii of the major scale, the diminished seventh chord can be considered to be a dominant ninth chord with the root omitted.

Conclusion

From the standpoint of a traditional approach that has its roots in Western classical music, the seventh is generally viewed as a decorative addition to an ordinary triad. This is to say that seventh chords are viewed as points of tension occurring between otherwise stable triadic harmonies. The triads themselves therefore represent the points of resolution and discharge of the tension produced by seventh chords. There is a great body of modern music that still uses this type of approach to seventh chord harmony. This includes many folk and traditional songs, religious and gospel music, popular songs and ballads, and so on.

There again, this is but one approach. In jazz and a lot of other popular music, the seventh chord is treated as a self-sufficient harmony in its own right. In effect, this means that jazz musicians use seventh chords rather in the same way that classical musicians used triads. For jazz, therefore, chordal harmony begins with the seventh chord, and every chord that is used will have its own particular extension. Within this context the need for resolution of dissonance in a traditional sense is virtually redundant, because every chord used will be loaded with its own particular dissonant qualities. That said, the direction of the chord progressions may often be determined by regular pathways of progression for the simple reason that these sound best to our ear. The sequential cycle of rising fourth roots is a prime example—a cycle that has long been one of the firm favorites for jazz improvisation.

The type of approach to use, therefore, depends upon the particular context and the style of music being written. That there are different approaches to the use of the same material dispels the idea that rules need to be laid down for the treatment or use of chords in general. This means that as you get to know the resources of harmony, you should really use your own ear and decide what sounds right for you—irrespective of how anybody else might have used particular chords.

14 Modulation

All of the chapters of this book have so far have focused upon the study of harmony as it pertains to one particular key—either major or minor. Now it is time to look to the possibilities harmony offers for the change of key—a process called *modulation*. To modulate means to move from one key to another. This involves a change in what the listener perceives to be the tonic chord. This means that the qualities of the tonic chord must thus be transferred to a new chord. When this new chord has been established as the tonic, the music is said to have changed key.

Composers and songwriters have been using modulation in their music for hundreds of years now. The main reason for this is that modulation represents one of the best ways of refreshing a listener's interest in a piece of music. An analogy to try to explain this is that of terrain. A key is rather like a place that we occupy—a place that has its own particular layout and terrain. Too much of the same place, and we begin to get bored. We need a change of scenery. A change of key is like going off to a new place and entering into new territory. Within that territory, we might not do anything that is significantly different, yet our interest is renewed by the fact of the change. There are new sights, sounds, atmospheres, and places to explore. From this standpoint, each key is like a different territory, and movement between keys is moving from one territory to another. Ideally, this move should lead to a refreshment of the listener's interest in the material—although if this is done cynically, the move can disastrously backfire!

The uses of modulation all depend upon the type and style of music that we consider. There is a lot of music in the world that just does not modulate. It remains in the same key throughout. This can be for numerous reasons. Hindu classical music does not modulate because the primary value of this music is not in its tonality. The primary value of this music lies in modality—the exploration of the individual characteristics of a given musical mode or raga. Another reason may lie in the way in which the music is put together. A lot of loop-based dance music does not modulate because it relies upon repetition and processes of buildup and breakdown using the same basic material, so contrast is obtained in the music through these processes of building up and breaking down. This means that in many cases, modulation would be a fairly pointless process.

Modulation tends to become an issue when there is a need to build larger and more extended musical structures. The epitome of this is classical music, with its well-defined formal areas and contrasts. Being built up from contrasting thematic sections of music, these contrasts are enhanced through the use of modulation, especially modulation from the major key to the minor key or vice versa. And the very size and scale of some of these structures—that is, the sonata, symphony, or concerto—made modulation a vital tool for the achievement of variety, interest, and structural unity.

A more modern example where modulation is commonly used as a structural tool is popular song formats. These usually necessitate the creation of clear contrasts between sections such as verse, chorus, bridge, or middle-eight. As the music moves between one section and another, changes of key are used as a means of highlighting and enhancing those contrasts. A song that begins in the minor therefore might modulate to the relative major for the chorus. This upward shift from the minor to the relative major key not only enhances the mood of the chorus, but it also imbues the music with a new energy and vigor. Hopefully, at least… As far as popular music is concerned, modulation has always been one of its greatest blessings and curses. Done well, modulation can sound brilliant, but done badly—as we have all heard countless times on the radio—it can ruin the entire song. Much of this comes down to the reason why modulation is being used. Is a key change being used because it lifts the song, or is it being used as a simple songwriting gimmick to the refresh the listener's interest in already tired material?

Your interest in modulation will therefore depend upon the type and style of music you write. Is modulation a normal practice in that style, or is it unheard of? If it is a normal practice, what types of modulation are typical? And how frequent are they? And even if modulation is not commonly used in your style of music, how about trying it out? And what happens when you get an offer to do a musical project that requires you to use modulation, such as a computer game soundtrack where modulation can be used to considerably heighten the drama and tension of the gameplay? Suffice it to say, modulation is an integral part of our music, and the more we can learn about it, the better.

Relationships between Keys

When music modulates, there is felt to be a movement from one key to another. This means that there are two keys involved. There is the already established key, and there is the key that represents the intended destination. If the key of destination is a fairly remote one, then other keys might be briefly passed through along the way. But these modulations tend to be brief and transitory.

The process of modulation has two main features. There is the journey that is taken from one key to another, and there is the way in which we get there. The journey itself concerns the distance traveled between keys. This is to do with the fact that there are some keys that represent a relatively short journey, while others require a more extended or even abrupt journey. In a traditional sense, the distance traveled is measured by how closely related the two keys are. This closeness of relationship is generally determined by how many notes the two keys have in common. The more notes two keys have in common, the closer the felt relationship between them. Therefore, if our established key is, say, C major, the two most closely related keys would be G and F major. This is because G and F major both have six notes in common with the key of C major.

Closely Related Keys

To discover all of the most closely related keys to a given home key, we can consult the master map of key territories, which we looked at in Chapter 3. This map is the circle of fifths, which charts all of the possible keys within a circular arrangement that links all possible keynotes by fifths.

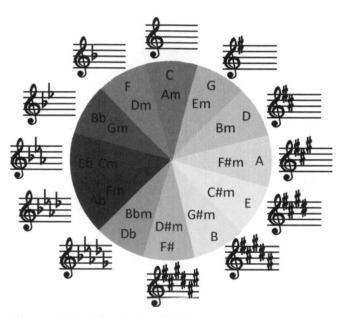

Figure 14.1   The circle of fifths.

Looking at the key of C major at the top of the circular diagram, we can immediately see that the two most closely related major keys are those whose keynotes are a fifth up (G major) and a fifth down (F major). This is because the key of G major requires only one sharp, which means that the other six notes are identical to the C major scale. Similarly, the key of F major requires only one flat. So again, F major has six notes that are identical to the C major scale.

The Relative Major/Minor Connection

The circle of fifths also shows us that there is another important key that is closely related to the key of C major. This is the relative minor key of A. The closeness of the relationship between these two keys can be gauged from the fact that they both use the same set of notes, the difference between them lying in the note that is perceived as the tonic. This key relationship is different than the relationship with F and G major by the fact that it also involves a change of mode. To change key from C major to the relative minor is also to change mode—from major to minor.

Because the key of C major has a close relationship to the relative minor key of A, C major also shares a close relationship with those keys whose tonic notes lie a fifth above and below the key of the relative minor. This is because a fifth above the tonic of the relative minor, we have the tonic of the key of E minor, which, like G major, uses only one sharp. And a fifth below the tonic of A minor, we have the tonic of the key of D minor, which, like F major, only uses one flat. Summarizing these observations then gives us a picture of those keys that can be considered to be most closely related to the key of C. Figure 14.2 portrays these keys.

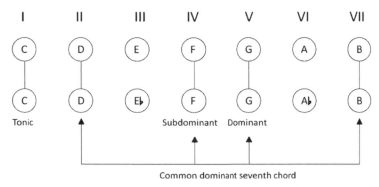

Figure 14.2   Closely related keys to C.

Here it is no coincidence to see that these keys all relate to those degrees of the major scale upon which common triads occur. Because of this, we can see that modulation, rather than weakening the sense of tonality, serves to strengthen it. It does this by representing the relationships upon which tonality depends as independent key centers in their own right. These key centers are then treated as satellites of the main key.

The Parallel Major/Minor Connection

Another criterion that can be used to demonstrate a link between keys is the strong connection between those keys that share the same tonic note. Therefore, for example, the key of C major uses exactly the same tonic as the key of C minor. On these grounds, there is a common link between the two keys. This link is strengthened by the fact that both keys possess the primary roots of C, F, and G as well as having the same dominant seventh chord (see Figure 14.3).

This link between keys that share the same tonic is called the *parallel major/minor link*. Therefore, the key of C minor is the parallel minor key to C major, and the key of C major is the parallel major to the key of C minor. However, because a modulation is said to be a change of key, this being qualified as a change of tonal center, then to move between C major and minor is perhaps not a true modulation. Nonetheless, it can be a great way to achieve contrast in our music.

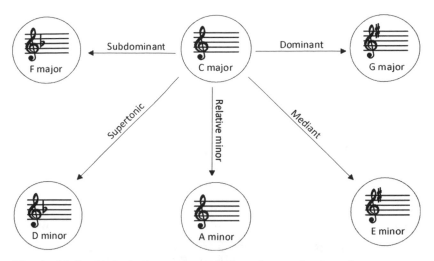

Figure 14.3   Links between parallel major and minor keys.

Distantly Related Keys

A distantly related key is regarded as one that shares few notes in common with the home key. Looking back to Figure 14.1, you can immediately see that the key of F♯ major shares only one note in common with the key of C major. The two keys are therefore viewed as being very distantly related. So it is perhaps appropriate that they appear at diametrically opposite points on the circle of fifths. In the same way, all keys that are diametrically opposite to one another on the circle of fifths represent a maximum possible distance between keys. Figure 14.4 depicts these diametrically opposite key relationships.

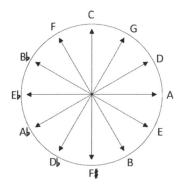

Figure 14.4   Diametrically opposite key relations.

Therefore, A major with its three sharps is diametrically opposite to E♭ major with its three flats, and so on. Although the two keys are therefore distantly related, this does not prevent a modulation between them. It is just that a modulation of this sort is more radical and tricky, and achieving such a modulation often requires ingenuity on behalf of the composer/songwriter. The guitar solo of Queen's "Bohemian Rhapsody" is a fine example of such a modulation.

Different Types of Modulation

Having considered the degree of closeness between keys—in other words, the distance one needs to travel—next it is time to consider how to get there. Numerous ways of changing key have been developed over time. Some methods are suitable for closely related keys—such as diatonic and chromatic modulation—while there are others that are only suitable for distantly related keys, such as abrupt and enharmonic modulation. In this section we will consider the four most common types of modulation.

Abrupt Modulation

Abrupt modulation is a sudden change of key that comes without warning or preparation. As such, abrupt modulation represents the simplest type of modulation that is possible. In popular music, abrupt modulation is typified by a sudden key shift up one, sometimes two, or even more semitones, often coming toward the end of a track, in which the previous section is then just repeated in the new key. The effect is one of increasing energy and excitement at best and rising hysteria at worst.

Countless popular songs have used this type of modulation. In fact, it is an effect that has literally been done to death. Sometimes derogatorily referred to as the *truck-driver's gearshift,* it has now come to be associated with the very worst of songwriting—a common trick to be pulled out of a songwriter's hat when he cannot think of a decent way to end a song. That being said, in skilled hands or approached from a new or different perspective, it is possible that abrupt modulation may yet yield some more surprises.

Diatonic Modulation

Diatonic modulation is where the change of key is effected through use of chords that belong to both keys. A classic example of this is the Beatles' song "Penny Lane," in which the verse is in B major, and the chorus is in A major. To modulate from B major to A major, the chord of E is used, which is chord IV in B major and chord V—the dominant—of A major. This common chord is thus used as a pivot chord in order to create a bridge to cross over to the new key. Because this type of modulation necessitates that the two keys share some chords in common, it is only really suitable for modulation to the more closely related keys. Suffice it to say, the fewer chords that two keys share in common, the lesser the opportunities for effecting a successful diatonic modulation between them.

The possibility of using pivot chords therefore arises from the fact that any one chord can perform a role for more than one key. Therefore, the chord of C major is chord I of the key of C major, chord IV of the key of G major, chord V of the key of F major, chord VI for the key of E minor, and so on. The chord of C major thus provides a useful pivot chord for modulation into all of the keys just mentioned. Its effectiveness in this context lies in persuading the ear to accept its function in the new key. This is accomplished by placing the pivot chord in a context in which it can be reinterpreted as a chord of the new key. Through use of such pivot chords, you can achieve a smooth transition be-tween different keys. This transition is then made complete by a dominant to tonic cadence in the new key. Figure 14.5 provides an example of pivot chord modulation.

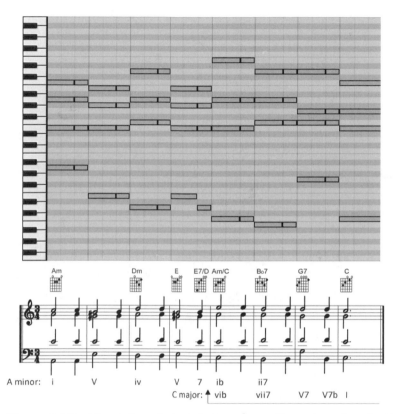

Figure 14.5 Pivot chord modulation from the minor key to the relative major key.

The pivot chords in this case are the A minor triad of bar 5, which is chord I in the home key and chord vi in the target key, and the B half-diminished seventh chord in bar 6, which is chord ii7 in the home key and chord vii7 in the target key.

So basically, pivot chords are common territory that is shared by both keys. If you want to use a diatonic modulation, therefore, the first stage is to take note of those chords shared by the two keys. Being aware of these, you can then direct the modulating chord progression toward those pivot chords. Culminating with a V-I progression onto the new tonic chord, the diatonic modulation will then have been effected successfully.

Chromatic Modulation

Chromatic modulation can be used for modulation to keys that are or are not closely related, as the case may be. Chromatic modulation is effected through introducing chromatic alterations of diatonic scale degrees. By chromatic, I mean notes that do not belong to the diatonic scale of the key in question. Let us consider some examples of these chromatic notes. In Figure 14.6, you can see the notes of both a rising and a falling scale of C major together with all of those notes that are considered to be chromatic for the key of C major. The chromatic notes are the notes without tails. And within the Piano Roll view, these chromatic notes have been marked with arrows.

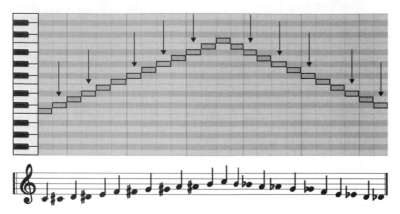

Figure 14.6   Chromatic notes for the key of C major.

By including these chromatic notes, along with the regular diatonic notes of the scale of C major, we obtain a complete chromatic scale. Notice, however, that the scale is notated differently depending upon whether it is rising or falling. This type of chromatic scale is called the *melodic form* of chromatic scale, and for a very good reason. Notice that any chromatic note preceded by a sharp is a rising chromatic note obtained by sharpening the previous note. Rising chromatic notes are notated in this way because they are assumed to be chromatic passing notes that are leading smoothly up to the note that follows. In contrast to this, any chromatic note preceded by a flat is a falling chromatic note obtained by flattening the previous note. And it is notated as a flat because it, too, is assumed to be a chromatic passing note that is falling down to the degree that follows. So the chromatic notes are written in such a way as to reflect their use as passing notes either to the scale degree above them or to the scale degree below them. In this way, a rising chromatic auxiliary would be written as a flat, and a falling chromatic auxiliary would be written as a sharp.

Chromatic modulation is most commonly effected by using these chromatic notes as part of a tritone that acts as a dominant agent of the new key. You can see two very simple examples of this in Figure 14.7. In Figure 14.7(a), the root of a C major triad in the first inversion has been sharpened in order to create a chromatic passing note up to note D. This passing note is highlighted with an arrow. If you look at the implications of this for the harmony, the C major triad has been converted into chord vii of the supertonic key of D minor. This means that the chromatic passing note is being heard in a context where it sounds like the leading note of a new key. And the note D, to which it smoothly rises upward, is thus heard as being the new tonic. In this way, the D minor chord that follows has been successfully tonicized by being preceded by a chord of dominant function for that new key. Chord vii, of course, containing within itself a tritone, is a strong agent of dominant function.

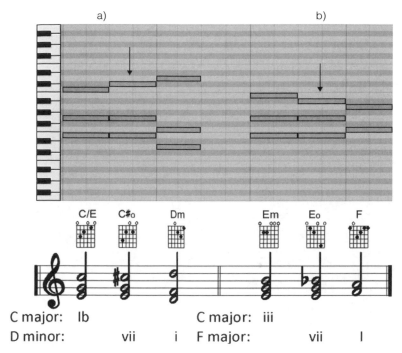

Figure 14.7 Use of tritone as an agent of chromatic modulation.

In Figure 14.7(b), you can see a similar thing happening through the use of a falling chromatic passing note, which is therefore written as a flat. Here, the fifth of the mediant triad has been flattened. This converts the mediant chord into the leading note triad of the key of F major. This triad, containing within itself a tritone and therefore acting as an agent of dominant function, serves to tonicize the following F major triad.

The important feature of chromatic modulation, therefore, is that the chromatic notes are presented in a context where they are acting as agents of dominant function—in other words, as a part of a tritone. And when these chords are accompanied by the dominant root, the effect of tonicizing the succeeding chord is even more powerful. To illustrate this point, in Figure 14.8 you can see the leading note triads used in Figure 14.7 converted into dominant seventh chords. This makes the process of tonicizing the following chord more convincing.

To be a true chromatic modulation, the chord progression must not cadence to the new tonic, but also depart from it as a new tonic chord. Otherwise, the modulation is said to be transitory—a brief visit to another key as a means of broadening the horizon of a chord progression. I'll say more on this in Chapter 20, "Secondary Dominant Chords."

Enharmonic Modulation

Enharmonic modulation is used to modulate to remote keys. This type of modulation is termed *enharmonic* because it largely depends upon the process of the enharmonic respelling of chords such as the dominant seventh, diminished seventh, and augmented triad. These chords are therefore being used as an enharmonic pivot chord between the

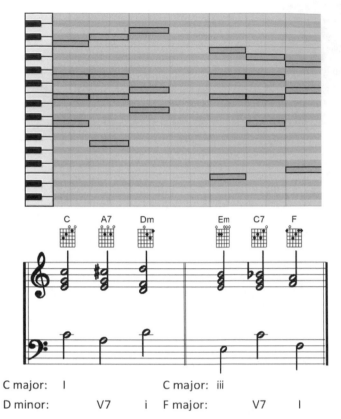

C major: I   C major: iii

D minor: V7   i   F major: V7   I

Figure 14.8   Chromatic modulation using dominant seventh chords of the new key.

two keys. If this sounds rather esoteric, it is because enharmonic modulation is rather esoteric, belonging as it does with the province of advanced classical and jazz musical composition. However, once you understand the simple principle behind enharmonic modulation, it ceases to be such a mystery, and you can even bring it into use in your own compositions.

Let us first consider the principle behind enharmonic modulation, which is the process of enharmonic respelling. This is based on the idea that the same note—B, for example—can also be written as note Cb. Although in terms of their pitch, notes B and Cb are the same note, in terms of their place in the scheme of key relations, they are very distant from one another. Therefore, while we can find note B in the key of C, in the circle of fifths we only encounter the note Cb when we reach the key of Gb major. And from the standpoint of the scheme of key relations represented by the circle of fifths, the key of Gb major is about as far from the key of C as it is possible to get.

Now that you understand the principle of enharmonic respelling, let us see how and why it applies to certain chords. It applies to the dominant seventh and the diminished seventh chord because they contain the interval of the tritone. The tritone is probably the most tonally unstable musical interval that there is. This instability, as we have seen numerous times already, is used to good effect when it is employed as an agent of dominant tension. Through enharmonically respelling the tritone, we can actually redirect its tension and harness it to a dominant chord from a different key. Let us now see how.

In the key of C major, there is only one tritone, and this uses the notes F and B. As a part of the dominant seventh chord of that key, the tritone tends to resolve in a certain way, the B—leading note—rising up to the tonic note C, and the F resolving stepwise down to the third of the tonic triad, which is E (or E♭ in the case of the minor key). However, we could also respell the same tritone as F and C♭. Spelled in this way, we find the same interval being used in the dominant seventh chord of a totally different key—the key of G♭ major. By enharmonically respelling the interval in this way, therefore, the tritone acquires different implications for resolution. While the tritone F and B resolves outwardly to the sixth E and C—in other words, the tonic chord of C major (see Figure 14.9(a))—the tritone C♭ and F resolves inwardly to the notes B♭ and G♭—that is, the tonic chord of G♭ major (see Figure 14.9(b)).

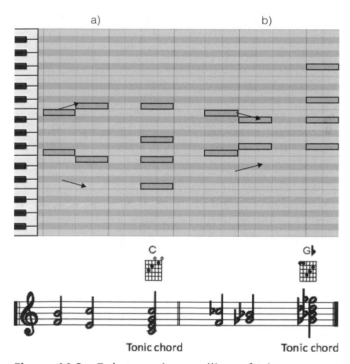

Figure 14.9   Enharmonic respelling of tritone.

The same tritone therefore effectively offers us a connection with both the keys of C major and G♭ major. In this way, through the process of enharmonic respelling, the tritone gives us a subtle doorway that connects keynotes that are diametrically opposite on the circle of fifths. (Revisit Figure 14.4 for an illustration of this.)

Wherever we find a chord that has a tritone in it, that tritone can be respelled in order to enter into the territory of a new key. In this sense, the chord that carries the tritone is being used as a pivot that links the two keys. An important chord for the process of enharmonic modulation, therefore, is the diminished seventh chord. This is because the diminished seventh chord consists of numerous equal interlocking tritones. Figure 14.10 illustrates the tritones that can be found in the diminished seventh chord.

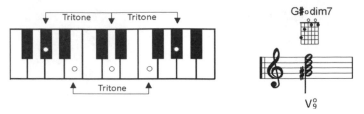

Figure 14.10   Interlocking tritones in the diminished seventh chord.

Because each tritone can be enharmonically respelled, the diminished seventh chord offers the possibility for a literal feast of enharmonic respelling! So let us now see how we can apply this enharmonic respelling to the process of enharmonic modulation. First of all, let's take the diminished seventh chord of the key of A minor, which is spelled G♯, B, D, and F. In the previous chapter, we saw that this chord performs a dominant function for the key and that its regular pathway of progression is to the tonic chord of that key—in this case, A minor. And in progressing to the tonic chord, as an agent of dominant function, the diminished seventh chord has a tonicizing effect upon the A minor triad to which it resolves (see Figure 14.11(a)). However, using exactly the same notes that we would play on the keyboard, we can respell this diminished seventh chord as being A♭, C♭, D, and F (see Figure 14.11(b)). Spelled in this way, the diminished seventh chord is the leading note seventh of the key of E♭ minor. And again, taking the same notes, we could spell the chord as being A♭, B, D, and F— which gives us the leading note seventh of the key of C minor (see Figure 14.11(c)). And finally, again taking the same notes, we could spell the diminished seventh chord as being E♯, G♯, B, and D. This gives us the leading note seventh of the key of F♯ minor (see Figure 14.11(d)).

In this way we can see that the same chord offers us a doorway between four different keys. By using that chord as a pivot, we can therefore move freely between any of these keys. This is the magic of enharmonic modulation.

Another chord that is susceptible to enharmonic respelling is the augmented triad on degree three of the harmonic form of the minor scale. If our starting key is A minor, the augmented triad would be spelled as C, E, and G♯ (see Figure 14.12(a)). However, we could also spell the same augmented triad as B♯, E, and G♯. This would make the augmented triad chord III of the C♯ minor scale (see Figure 14.12(c)). We could also spell the same triad as C, E, and A♭—which would make it chord III of the F minor scale (see Figure 14.12(b)). In this way, the same chord links three rather remote keys on the circle of fifths.

Using this idea of enharmonic respelling, we can then create chord progressions that move quickly through the territories of different keys. In Figure 14.13, you can see an

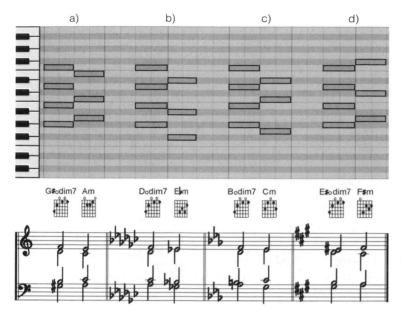

Figure 14.11 Enharmonic respelling of diminished seventh chord.

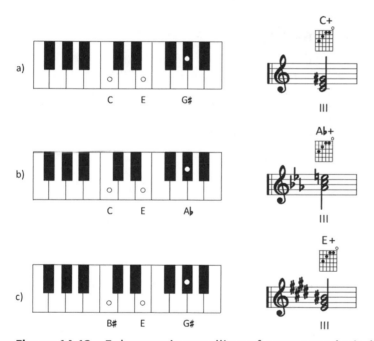

Figure 14.12 Enharmonic respelling of augmented triad.

example in which chords that use the augmented triad are enharmonically respelled to modulate between the three keys illustrated in Figure 14.12. The chord progression both begins and ends in A minor but modulates through the keys of F minor and C♯ minor on the way:

Naturally, the effect of such chord progressions is never settling. This is for the simple reason that the tonality itself is unsettled, rapidly moving through different keys

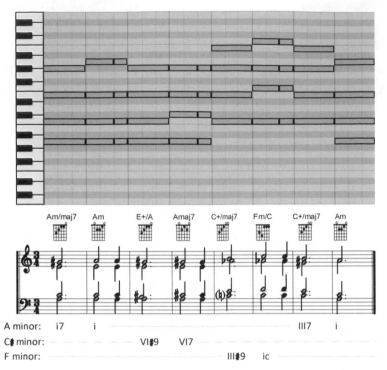

Figure 14.13   Rapid enharmonic modulation through remote keys.

without ever remaining in the one key for very long. Inevitably, this leads to complexities in both the notation and the symbols used to represent the chords. This is why many modern composers who produce written scores often do not bother with key signatures—the changes of key are so rapid as to make it tiresome to indicate every key change with a change of key signature.

Learning How to Modulate

The best way to learn how to use modulation effectively is to compose chord progressions that modulate using the techniques shown. For diatonic modulation, you first need to work out which chords are common to both keys. This will enable you to develop a pivot zone occupied exclusively by those chords. This zone would then culminate in a dominant to tonic progression into the new key.

For chromatic modulation, it is worthwhile to spend some time exploring different ways of imparting dominant tension to those particular chromatic notes used to enter into the new key. Each chromatic note can be effectively harmonized with numerous chords of dominant function. Examples are the leading note triads and sevenths, the dominant seventh, and the diminished seventh chord. Try them all out and see how they sound.

For enharmonic modulation, it is valuable to examine each chord that uses a tritone, or even other such intervals, and look at the different ways in which these intervals can be enharmonically respelled. Having discovered these, then look at the implications of those respelled intervals for resolution onto chords belonging to the target key.

Conclusion

This chapter focused on the practice of modulation from the perspective of the study of musical harmony. First, we looked at the relationships between different keys and how modulation itself has two aspects. There is how far one travels between keys, and there is the process of getting there. In terms of the distance traveled, we saw that there were closely related keys and keys that are more distantly related to one another. We looked at different types of modulation in terms of their suitability for use from this standpoint. This included four main types of modulation: abrupt modulation, diatonic modulation achieved through the use of pivot chords, chromatic modulation achieved through the use of chromatic chords, and finally, enharmonic modulation achieved through the use of a pivot chord that is respelled enharmonically. Having considered and introduced modulation, it is now time to advance our knowledge of basic chords even further and consider the uses of those chordal extensions other than the seventh. This includes chords of the sixth, ninth, eleventh, and thirteenth.

15 Suspended and Added Note Chords

In Chapters 5 through 8, we focused our studies on the use of triads in harmony. Following on from this, after an initial study of different ways of embellishing and decorating a basic triadic harmony (Chapter 9), we went on to study one of the most important extensions of the triad—the seventh (Chapters 10 through 12). Probably originating through the use of melodic embellishments, we saw how that decorative seventh gradually transferred to the vertical dimension of the harmony itself. From this standpoint, a seventh chord could be viewed as being nothing more than a triad embellished with a dissonance.

As an embellished triad, the seventh chord counts as only one possibility among numerous other possibilities we have yet to consider. These include those other important extensions that musicians use in their music, such as chords of the ninth, eleventh, and thirteenth. It also includes various chords that musicians often use as substitutes for common triads, such as suspended chords and added note chords. By studying these extensions and chord substitutes and learning how to incorporate them into our own music, we are able to take a great leap forward in our ability to write and produce music. This means we now have access to much more of the great wealth of musical harmony as it is currently understood.

The focus of this chapter will be on those chords that musicians sometimes use as simple substitutes for or alternatives to ordinary common triads. There are numerous types of chord that belong to this category, the main ones being *suspended chords* and *added note chords*.

Suspended Chords

Suspended chords originate when one of the melodic parts is being used as a suspension. When we looked at suspensions in Chapter 9, you might recall that at the moment of the suspension, there is a point of tension that is then released as the suspension resolves down to the appropriate harmony note. A suspended chord is one that incorporates the dissonance of the suspension as a part of the chord itself. Figure 15.1 illustrates the most common types of suspended chords.

a. The sus2 chord in which the sus2 is used as a substitute for the third of the triad

b. A variation of the sus2 chord—the sus9 chord, in which the second is placed an octave higher

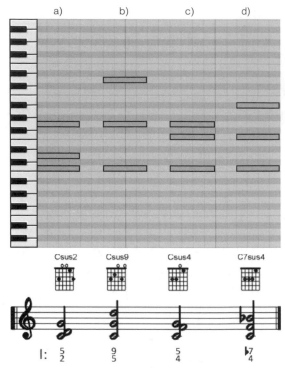

Figure 15.1 Suspended chords.

c. The sus4 chord, in which the sus4 is used as a substitute for the third of the triad

d. The 7sus4 chord, in which the sus4 is used as a substitute for the third of a seventh chord—usually a chord of the dominant seventh

Creating and Playing a Suspended Chord

When studying harmony, there is no substitute for listening. Follow the steps in Figure 15.2 to create a suspended chord and then play it on the keyboard and listen to its qualities.

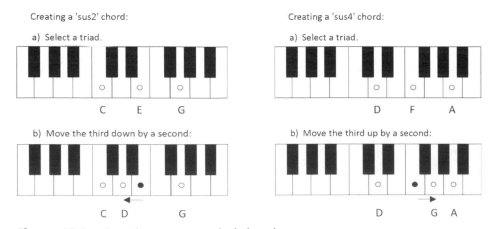

Figure 15.2 Creating a suspended chord.

Origins of Suspended Chords

To illustrate the origins of these common types of suspended chords, Figure 15.3 offers four examples.

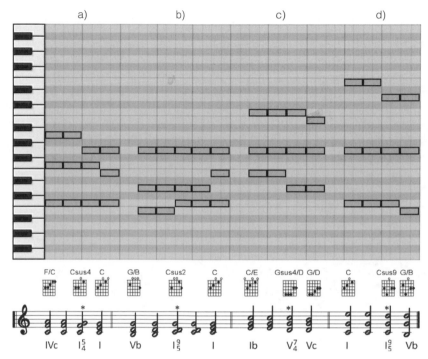

Figure 15.3   Examples of suspended chords.

In Figure 15.3(a), you can see the origin of one of the most common types of suspended chords—the sus4 chord, which in this case incorporates note F as the suspended fourth held over from the F major triad that precedes it. As a part of the suspended chord itself, the note F is replacing the ordinary third of the C major triad—note E.

Figure 15.3(b) is an example of a sus2 chord, in which note D is the suspended second of the note C below it. As a chord in its own right, the sus2 uses the second as a substitute for the ordinary third of the chord. In Figure 15.3(c), you can see a sus4 chord being used in a different position, in which the suspended note appears as a seventh over the bass note D. Finally, in Figure 15.3(d), you can see an example of a sus9 chord, in which the suspended note D forms a ninth with the bass note C. As such, the sus2 and sus9 chords are directly related—in the sus9 chord, the second is an octave higher, while in the sus2 chord, the ninth is an octave lower.

Uses of Suspended Chords

When thought of as resulting from a suspension, suspended chords regularly resolve in the ways shown in Figure 15.3. However, composers and songwriters soon discovered that suspended chords can also be used effectively as substitutes for what would otherwise be plain triads. Therefore, rather than using, say, a chord of C major, one could use say a Csus2 chord instead. When using suspended chords in this way, the dissonant notes do not need to be prepared or resolved, for they are regarded as being an essential part of the chord itself.

You can see an example of this in Figure 15.4, in which a Csus2 chord is being used as a substitute for an ordinary C major triad. The Csus2 chord is marked with an asterisk over the staff where it occurs. The resulting harmony is a nice, gritty replacement for the ordinary common triad. There is another suspended chord in the final bar. This chord is treated in a more regular, conventional way—in other words, the dissonance is both prepared and resolved.

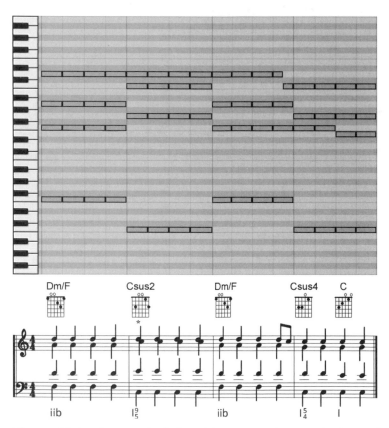

Figure 15.4 Suspended chord being used as a substitute for a common triad.

Suspended chords represent a great addition to the spectrum of available chords—especially when harmony is mostly dominated by common triads. Their use can bring in a much-needed hard edge to the harmony. "Insomnia" by Faithless offers a fine example of the use of these chords, in which sus2 and sus4 chords are main features of the powerful main trance riff.

Naturally, suspended chords can be used on any degree of the scale required. The best guide as to the suitability of a given suspended chord is what your ears say. If it sounds right, then you should use it. You should spend some time exploring suspended chords and listening to the different types. Figure 15.5 offers an illustration of some of these and how to play them on the keyboard.

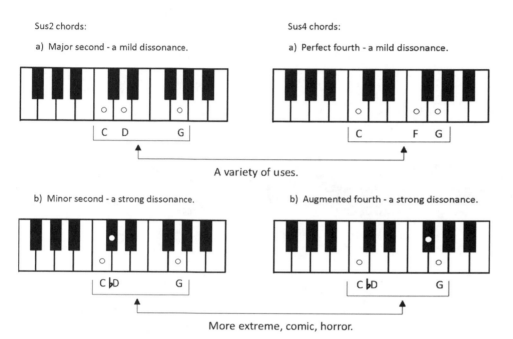

Figure 15.5   Playing suspended chords.

Added Note Extensions

Another important group of extensions are the added note variety. The basic idea of an added note chord is that you take an ordinary triad—say, for example, C major—and add to it other notes in order to give that sonority more punch, spice, color, power, energy, or percussive impact. The notes that are added in this way often resemble other extensions, such as the ninth, eleventh, and thirteenth. However, the characteristic feature of added note chords is that the thirds that lie in between are omitted. This can be understood by examining the main types of added note chords, which are illustrated in Figure 15.6.

a. Chord of the added sixth

b. Chord of the added ninth

c. Another form of appearance of the chord of the added ninth

d. Added sixth and ninth chord

Added Sixth Chords

In terms of classical harmony, a sixth chord is regarded to be any first inversion triad. In popular music, however, a sixth chord refers to what classical musicians call an *added*

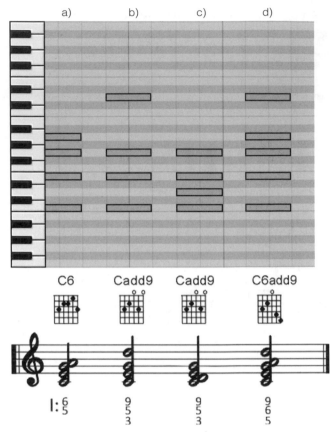

Figure 15.6   Added note chords.

sixth chord, obtained by taking any root position common triad and adding to it another note a sixth above the root. Figure 15.7 illustrates this.

a) Select a common triad.

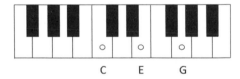

b) Add another note a major sixth above the root:

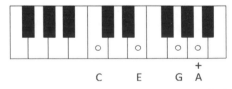

Figure 15.7   How to create and play an added sixth chord.

When this process is applied using major and minor common triads and also using minor sixth intervals, this leads to a number of different types of generic added sixth chords. Figure 15.8 shows these.

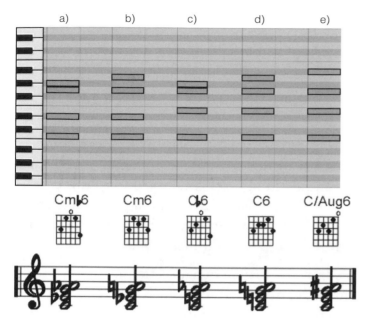

Figure 15.8   Different types of added sixth chords.

a. Minor triad with minor sixth

b. Minor triad with major sixth

c. Major triad with minor sixth

d. Major triad with major sixth

e. Major triad with augmented sixth

Probably the most commonly used forms of sixth chord are common triads to which have been added a major sixth. This results in a four-note sonority that modern musicians often tend to use as an alternative to a common major triad. While using this type of added sixth chord is fairly straightforward, explaining it can be more problematic. This is because a C6 chord uses exactly the same notes as an A minor seventh chord in first inversion. For all intents and purposes, therefore, they are the same chord. Yet this analysis of the sixth chord does not really do justice to its practical musical use. In jazz, bebop, and popular music, generally, the sixth of the chord has always been used simply to spice up the triad. This means that the root is still perceived as being the same as the root of the triad to which the sixth is attached. Therefore, to call C6 an A minor triad in first inversion is just not logical. Another way of looking at an added sixth chord is as a thirteenth chord with the seventh, ninth, and eleventh omitted, as you can see in Figure 15.9.

Yet even this interpretation seems to be a very complex way of looking at what is really a very simple chord—a triad that is simply being spiced up through the addition of a dissonant embellishment!

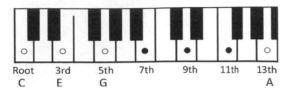

Figure 15.9   Added sixth as a type of thirteenth chord.

The attractiveness of the added sixth chord is that it has a rich, warm, and complex sound that blends in well with musical textures that are full of dissonant extensions. A plain, unadorned common triad would stand out like a sore thumb amidst this type of texture. With the sixth added, the chord has a more complex dissonant profile, but there is not enough dissonance there to make the harmony sound unstable. So in these contexts, the sixth chord makes a great substitute for a straight tonic triad.

That being said, a sixth chord can be used on any degree of either major or minor scale where we find a common triad. The added major sixth tends to have a brighter and more open sound than the more dissonant minor sixth. For this reason, the added major sixth chord is probably more frequently used as an addition to both the major and the minor common triads. Here it is recommended that you spend some time exploring sixth chords in different types of spacing and as they occur on different degrees of the scale. Exploration of this sort helps you know and understand a particular chord and get a feel for what goes with it.

The most common forms of sixth are probably those on the tonic degree, as illustrated in Figure 15.10(a), and the subdominant. Here it is noteworthy that the latter progresses particularly well to the tonic chord as a variation on the plagal cadence: IV6-I (see Figure 15.10(b)).

Added Ninth Chords

Another popular way of spicing up a common triad is to add a major ninth. Triads to which a major ninth have been added are appropriately termed *added ninth chords*. With the major chord, this makes for a nice, rich harmony, while to the minor chord the ninth adds a bit of sharpness and sting. Figure 15.11 illustrates these two forms of added ninth chord in a variety of forms.

a. A major chord of the added ninth in closed position voiced in four parts. To create this chord, a major second is inserted between the root and the third of a major triad.

b. A major chord of the added ninth in four parts, where the ninth is placed above the triad.

c. A major chord of the added ninth in wide-open spacing.

d. A minor chord of the added ninth in closed position, where the ninth is inserted between the root and third of the minor triad.

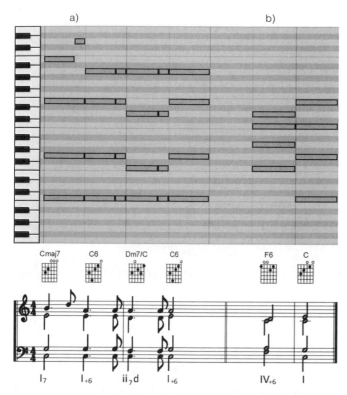

Figure 15.10   Examples of the use of added sixth chords.

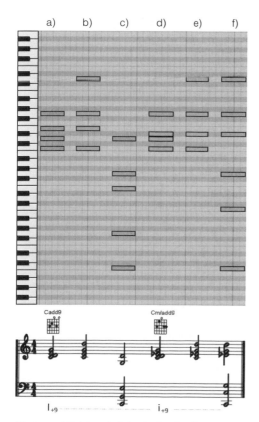

Figure 15.11   Added ninth chords.

e. A minor chord of the added ninth, where the ninth is placed above the triad.

f. A minor chord of the added ninth in wide-open spacing.

Added ninth chords are used in a similar way to chords of the added sixth—that is, they are commonly used as substitutes for ordinary common triads. Due to the mildly dissonant ninth, their use can lead to a warmer, richer sound than is possible with ordinary triadic harmony. And although a ninth can be feasibly added to any triad on any degree of the scale, in practice not all added ninth chords are regarded as having an agreeable sound. Those chords with a minor ninth—on the mediant and leading note of the major scale, for example—tend to be used less frequently owing to their increased level of dissonance. An exception is perhaps the dominant added ninth of the minor scale, where the dissonant minor ninth helps to increase that feeling of dominant tension.

Added Sixth/Ninth Chords

An even richer sound can be obtained by adding both a major sixth and a ninth to an ordinary common triad—a chord that is a firm favorite with jazz musicians. The addition of the sixth and ninth creates a beautifully complex five-note sonority that is very rich in overtones. And this represents the principal attraction of this kind of chord—that warmth of harmony that comes from bringing out the upper harmonics of a common chord. To appreciate this, play an added sixth/ninth chord and listen carefully to its qualities. Figure 15.12 shows how to do this in three simple steps.

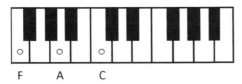

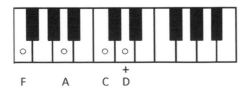

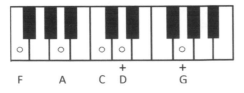

Figure 15.12 Creating and playing an added sixth/ninth chord.

Figure 15.13 illustrates two basic forms of added sixth/ninth chords—the major chord with added major sixth and ninth and the minor chord with added major sixth and ninth. Each chord is presented in a variety of positions.

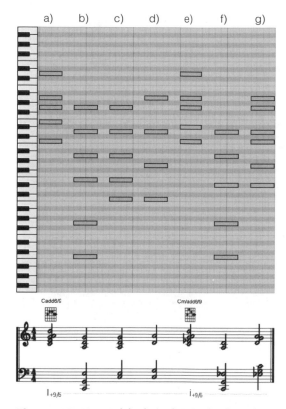

Figure 15.13   Added sixth/ninth chords.

a. A major triad to which has been added the sixth and ninth.

b. An added sixth/ninth chord in wide spacing.

c. An alternative wide spacing.

d. An added sixth/ninth chord voiced for four parts. This produces a chord of equal fifths—also known as a *quintal tetrad*.

e. The minor form of added sixth/ninth.

f. A minor added sixth/ninth chord in wide spacing.

g. A minor added sixth/ninth chord in first inversion.

Added sixth/ninth chords work best when they are presented within a fairly complex chordal texture—that is, a texture full of extensions, such as sevenths, ninths, and so on. Figure 15.14 illustrates a typical use of added sixth/ninth chords in popular music harmony. Observe that every chord has some kind of extension, maintaining the complexity and hard edge of the harmony. The chord in bar 1 is a tonic added ninth chord;

in bar 2 it is a mediant seventh chord in root position. The chord in bar 3 is a subdominant added sixth/ninth chord; in bar 4 it is a dominant seventh with suspended fourth, the suspended fourth resolving down to the third of the dominant seventh in the fourth quarter of bar 4. And the short passage ends with a tonic added ninth chord.

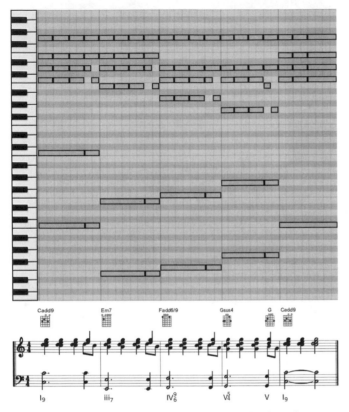

Figure 15.14   Use of added sixth/ninth chord.

Using both suspended and added note chords in your compositions can give your harmonies a very modern and contemporary feel. They can also make your chord progressions sound more original, fresh, and distinctive. Therefore, any time spent studying these chords, playing them through, combining them with other chords, and listening to their particular qualities is always very profitable.

Conclusion

The focus of this chapter was on the study of chords that can be used as dissonant substitutes for ordinary common triads. This included suspended chords and added note chords. We saw that although suspended chords probably have their origin in the use of melodic suspensions, the chord formed at the moment of suspension gave rise to a sonority that can be used as a chord in its own right. Such chords—called *suspended chords*—can be treated in a regular way, where the suspension finds a resolution in the chord that follows. However, suspended chords can also be used as substitutes for the chord of resolution in a very effective way. And by standing in for the regular common triad, such substitutes bring a valued element of hard-edged dissonance into the musical texture.

We then went on to study added note chords, which included chords of the added sixth, added ninth, and added sixth and ninth. We saw that these also provided valuable alternatives to the use of common triads, particularly in musical passages where a certain level of dissonant tension needed to be maintained. Having studied these chords, we now find ourselves in the position where it is possible to productively study those other chordal extensions talked about at the beginning of the chapter—namely chords of the ninth, eleventh, and thirteenth. This subject will provide the topic for the next chapter.

16 Chords of the Ninth

Having considered suspended and added note chords in the previous chapter, it is now time to move on to the study of those extended chords from which both suspended and added note chords ultimately come. These are the full and complete chords of the ninth, eleventh, and thirteenth. As a collective group, ninth, eleventh, and thirteenth chords tend to build upon the foundation that is provided by seventh chords. As such, I suppose these other extensions are like variations of the particular character and color of the seventh chord. This means that although the basic function of the seventh chord remains the same, each extension adds its own particular quality to it.

In practice, this means that although chords of the ninth, eleventh, and thirteenth might be forbidding in their complexity, in essence they are nothing more than further extensions to the dissonant factor that is the seventh. This means that having already learned how to deal with dissonances at the level of seventh chords, these other chordal extensions—such as the ninth, eleventh, and thirteenth—become that much easier to handle.

How to Create an Extended Chord of the Ninth, Eleventh, or Thirteenth

To create an extended chord beyond the seventh at the keyboard is a very simple affair. All you have to do is follow the steps indicated in Figure 16.1.

Under ordinary circumstances, the process of producing extensions tends to stop at the thirteenth. This is because adding another third to the thirteenth would bring us up to the fifteenth, which in fact brings us back to the root note some two octaves higher. So after the thirteenth, there is no point in generating further extensions—at least not within the bounds of the major or minor scale.

Voicing Extensions

When all of the notes of a thirteenth chord are played on the keyboard, the resulting chord can sound quite unusable, coming across as a dense and compact wall of dissonance. And when heard in this way, it is perhaps difficult to conceive of a musical situation in which such a chord could be used. A thirteenth chord, after all, has seven notes—all of the notes of the major or minor scale. Therefore, if we go to the keyboard

203

a) Select any seventh chord.

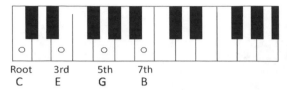

Root   3rd   5th   7th
C   E   G   B

b) Add another note a third higher than the seventh.
This note is taken from whichever major or minor key
you are in. In this way the seventh chord is then turned
into a ninth chord:

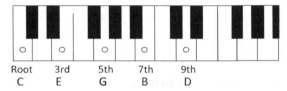

Root   3rd   5th   7th   9th
C   E   G   B   D

c) Add another note a third higher than the ninth.
In this way the ninth chord is then turned into
an eleventh chord:

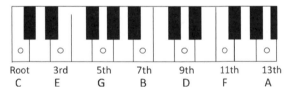

Root   3rd   5th   7th   9th   11th
C   E   G   B   D   F

c) Add another note a third higher than the eleventh.
In this way the eleventh chord is then turned into
a thirteenth chord:

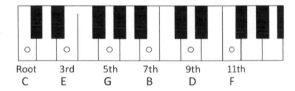

Root   3rd   5th   7th   9th   11th   13th
C   E   G   B   D   F   A

Figure 16.1   Creating chordal extensions beyond the seventh.

and press down with our forearm as many of the white notes as possible at the same time, we are in effect producing a thirteenth chord!

Yet in terms of their practical use, complex chords such as the thirteenth are nearly always thinned out by the omission of certain notes. And they are also often used within a nice open and wide spacing, which makes them sound much more user friendly. Besides, when writing harmony using only four voices, the chord has to be thinned out for the simple reason that the voices are only capable of producing four notes at the same time. What this means for our use and study of complex chords is that they have to be reduced down to their very essence.

So what is the essence of a ninth, eleventh, or thirteenth chord? And which notes are essential for the preservation of that essence? In answer to these questions, we can observe that first of all, the root of a chord is pretty essential, for it is the root that gives the chord an aural foundation. Without the root, in most cases the ear would not be able to discern what the chord is. Or it may discern another note to be the root. So in nearly all cases, the root is essential. Chords of dominant function, such as the diminished and half-diminished seventh, are perhaps the exceptions.

Generally, the third of a complex chord is also considered to be fairly important because it is the third that defines the character of the chord as being major or minor. Without this character, the chord would sound more ambiguous. Under certain circumstances this might be desirable. The use of power chords is a good example, in which the third is deliberately left out. But under ordinary circumstances where we are writing our music in either the major or the minor key, the third is a very important chordal component because it gives the chord its major or minor feel. So given a choice between including the third or the fifth of a chord, the third is very often our first choice.

The seventh is also absolutely essential, because it is the seventh that qualifies a chord as being an extension in the first place. Without the seventh, the ear would therefore construe the chord as being simply an added note chord. If that is what is intended, great. But without the seventh, the chord cannot be considered to be a ninth, eleventh, or thirteenth. It simply becomes a suspended or added note chord.

So far this accounts for three of the voices of our four-voice limit: the root, the third, and the seventh. That leaves us with only one voice. And it is therefore with this remaining voice that we voice either the ninth or the thirteenth. The eleventh is perhaps an exception in that the eleventh is often used as a replacement for the third of a chord. In that case, a more common voicing for the eleventh would be to omit the third and include the fifth. The reasons for this will become clear when we look at eleventh chords in the next chapter.

Viewed in this way, extensions after the seventh are much easier to handle than they at first seem, because it is often a simple matter of adding a ninth, eleventh, or thirteenth over the foundation of a seventh chord. Figure 16.2 offers an illustration of a regular way in which to voice chords of the ninth, eleventh, and thirteenth using only four parts.

Without exception, the use of the ninth, eleventh, or thirteenth of a chord will load a chord with extra dissonance. For example, the ninth is consonant with the seventh but dissonant with the root and the third. The eleventh is exactly the same. The thirteenth is different in that it is consonant with the root and the third but dissonant with the seventh. So whichever way we look at it, the ninth, eleventh, or thirteenth offers a further increase of the dissonance levels already present in an extended chord because of the seventh. As extra dissonant factors, the ninth, eleventh, and thirteenth therefore display a tendency to resolve in customary ways. And as we shall soon see, it is this tendency toward resolution that tends to explain the conventional pathways of progression of these complex chords. I'll refer to this point numerous times in the next few chapters as we proceed to the more detailed study of chords of the ninth, eleventh, and thirteenth.

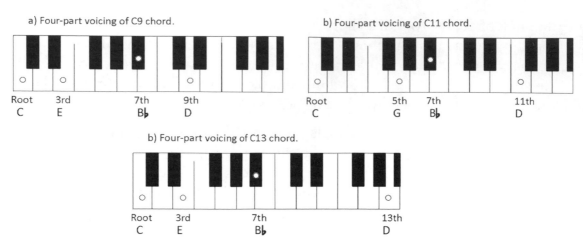

Figure 16.2 Voicing of ninth, eleventh, and thirteenth chords in four parts.

Ninth Chords

A ninth chord consists of five notes arranged in a stack of four thirds. When all five notes are played at the same time, the result is a rich, complex sonority for which musicians and audiences alike have a great appreciation. The harmonic complexity of jazz owes much to the frequent use of ninth chords in every possible position and every possible degree of the scale where their use proves effective. And most popular songs use at least one ninth chord somewhere.

Modern styles of popular electronic music also favor the rich, warm sound of ninth chord harmony. Whether this be a sample of a ninth chord on strings or even just a Rhodes keyboard stab to which delay has been applied, many dance tracks—particular those belonging to the house, deep house, and Detroit techno styles—owe their rich, luxurious sound to the liberal use of ninth chords.

Ninth chord harmony can be freely used on any degree of the scale that it is required. In Figure 16.3, you will see the seven ninth chords of the major key.

Looking at these chords, you can see that there are different types of ninth chords. The most important distinction is between those chords with a major ninth, which are indicated simply by 9, and those with a minor ninth indicated by ♭9. Here you will gain invaluable experience by deliberately playing these chords through and listening carefully to their different qualities. These differences in aural quality will reflect the particular intervallic makeup of a given ninth chord. Within a small book such as this, to individually examine the intervallic makeup and aural quality of every single ninth chord would take up too much space. Besides, this is investigative work that you should now undertake for yourself. Having a firm foundation of experience with chords up to the seventh, it is a relatively simple matter to take each seventh chord and add a ninth to it—bearing in mind that in the minor key there may be numerous options for each seventh.

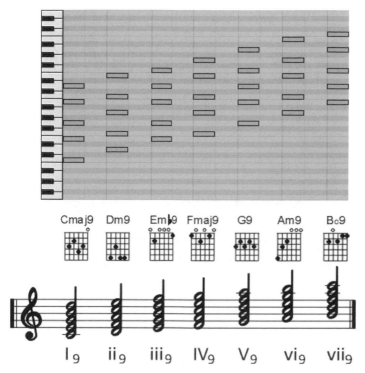

Cmaj9 Dm9 Em♭9 Fmaj9 G9 Am9 B♭9

I_9 ii_9 iii_9 IV_9 V_9 vi_9 vii_9

Figure 16.3 Ninth chords of the major key.

While investigating and examining ninth chords, you will discover that chords with a minor ninth tend to be more dissonant than those with a major key. This dissonant quality may in turn affect the frequency of their use. The dominant ninth of the minor key consists of a dominant seventh chord and a minor ninth interval. This produces a powerful feeling of dominant tension that has been much used by composers. However, the mediant ninth of the major key consists of a minor seventh chord with a minor ninth—a sour-sounding sonority that for some reason is just not appealing to the ear. To overcome this, musicians will often freely raise the ninth to give the sonority a more appealing sound. This involves introducing into the scale a note that does not ordinarily belong to it—namely an F sharp, as you can see in Figure 16.4.

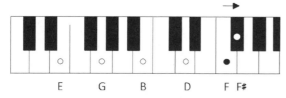

E   G   B   D   F F♯

Figure 16.4 Chromatically altering the mediant ninth.

This practice of introducing notes that are foreign to the key is called *chromatic alteration,* a subject we will consider in more detail in Chapters 19, 20, and 21. The use of chromatic alteration can have a significant effect upon our perception of the function of a given chord, although it all depends upon how and why chromatic alteration is being used. In some cases, chromatic alterations made to chordal extensions do alter the color of a given chord, but they do not adversely affect our appreciation of its function. This is because the functional notes of a chord tend to be the root, third, fifth, and seventh. This means that an alteration made to, say, the ninth, eleventh, or thirteenth can often be used to great advantage to improve the color and quality of a chord without interfering with its function in the harmony.

Voicing a Ninth Chord in Four Parts

Because a ninth chord has five notes, when writing for four parts, one of the five notes must be omitted. The logic behind the decision to omit certain notes from a complex extended chord was discussed earlier in this chapter with reference to ninth, eleventh, and thirteenth chords. Having already discussed this issue, let us now consider the various options available to us when voicing a ninth chord in four parts—in the light of those observations made earlier. Figure 16.5 presents these options.

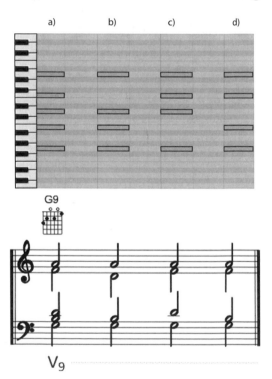

Figure 16.5   Options for voicing a ninth chord in four parts.

In (a), you can see the complete dominant ninth chord of the key of C major in closed position—which means that it appears as a stack of four thirds piled upon the root note G. In (b), you can see that a note has been omitted to reduce the chord down to four parts. But here we have omitted the seventh. By all rights, therefore, this chord is simply a triad to which has been added a free ranging ninth. As such, it counts as an added ninth chord rather than a ninth chord proper.

In (c) the third has been omitted. This counts as a ninth chord, although without a third it is difficult to know what kind of ninth chord it is—whether it is a major or a minor ninth chord. Nevertheless, this does count as a valid option for voicing a ninth chord in four parts. As an option, it is valuable when the part writing prevents inclusion of the third. Finally, in (d) you can see that the fifth has been omitted. This voicing is ideal, because it includes the third, which enables us to know what kind of ninth chord it is; the seventh, which qualifies it as an extension; and the ninth, which tells us what kind of extension it is.

Regular Pathways of Progression of Ninth Chords

You can discern the regular pathways of resolution of the ninth by looking at the way in which ninth chords originally arose through the use of melodic embellishments within the context of triadic harmony. Have a look at Figure 16.6, which shows the use of such an embellishment in the form of a pair of accented passing notes in the upper two voices that fill in the third between C and E belonging to the C major chord in bar 1 and the A and C belonging to the F major chord in bar 2.

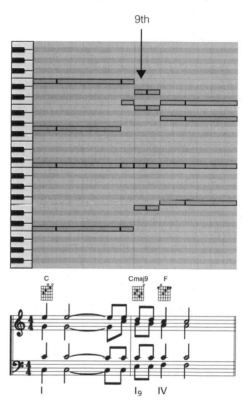

Figure 16.6   Ninth chord arising from use of a pair of accented passing notes.

At the point where the passing notes occur, we can see an appearance of the tonic ninth chord, which is indicated as I_9. The characteristic feature of this chord is that both the ninth and the seventh are forming a dissonance with the root note C. Observe that both of these dissonances then resolve to consonant harmony notes in the chord that follows. This felt need for the resolution of the dissonances present within a ninth chord has tended to dictate the regular pathways of progression of ninth chords in music.

The most commonly occurring example of this is the dominant ninth chord. Dominant chords have always been a first choice of chords to add dissonant extensions to. This is because the moment where the dominant progresses to the tonic is a great place to build up dominant tension. One of the most popular methods of generating dominant tension is to add loads of dissonant notes to the dominant—which include the seventh, ninth, eleventh, and thirteenth. These dissonances then help to elaborate and enhance the dominant to tonic close or cadence. In the case of the dominant ninth chord, the ninth represents an extra loading of dissonance on top of the seventh. Being a third apart—in other words, consonant with one another—the ninth and seventh show a tendency to resolve down to the third and root of the tonic triad (as you can see in Figure 16.7(a)). An alternative to this is that the ninth resolves before the seventh, so leaving the dominant seventh chord (see Figure 16.7(b)).

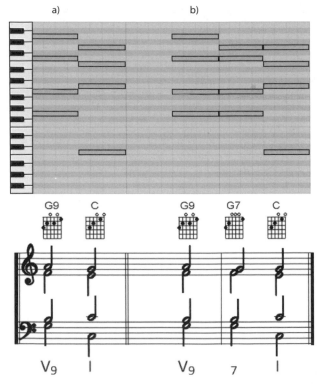

Figure 16.7   Regular pathway of progression of dominant ninth chord.

This drive toward some kind of resolution also appears within secondary chords of the ninth—in other words, occurring upon other degrees of the scale. But of course there is nothing to stop us progressing from one ninth chord to another in order to perpetuate the feeling of tension in the music. In Figure 16.8(a), you can see an example of this in which the chord of Am9 progresses to Fmaj9. First observe that the ninth has been prepared as a result of its presence as a harmony note in the previous chord. Second, observe that the dissonant ninth of the Am9 then resolves to the third of the following Fmaj9 chord. This Fmaj9 chord then delays the resolution of the seventh of the Am9 chord until the progression hits the dominant eleventh chord—indicated as V_{11}. In this way the feeling of tension in the chord progression is maintained.

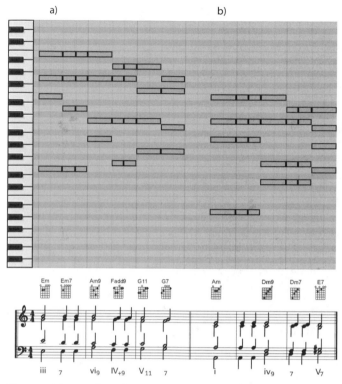

Figure 16.8   Chord progressions involving ninth chords.

In Figure 16.8(b), you can see an example of the use of a ninth chord in the minor key in which Dm9 progresses to the dominant seventh chord of A minor. It does this through a characteristic pattern of dissonance resolution in which the ninth and seventh resolve stepwise to the notes below them in the scale.

As seen in both of these progressions, common approaches to a chord of the ninth will often involve some kind of preparation in the preceding chord. And the chord will often be left through regular resolution of the dissonant ninth.

Inversions of Ninth Chords

Inversions of ninth chords need to be examined and used on their own merits. These merits are assessed by the sound of the chord to the ear. However, bear in mind that when all of the notes of a complex inverted chord, such as a ninth, are crowded together, the chord can often sound quite dismal. Each inversion therefore needs to be spaced in an appropriate way—in other words, in such a way that it sounds effective to the ear. A certain degree of experimentation with a variety of different kinds of spacing is always productive here. Often a very wide and openly spaced voicing of a complex chord works best. You can see examples of this type of spacing in Figure 16.9.

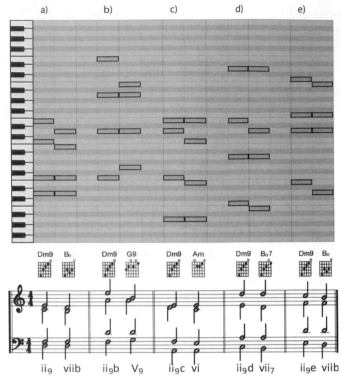

Figure 16.9   Treatment of inversions of the supertonic ninth chord.

When an effective method of spacing a given chord using four voices has been found, this chord then needs to be examined individually for its own voice leading tendencies toward resolution and progression. Here you must bear in mind that although we have been focusing primarily on regular pathways of progression of the ninth chord, it is also worthwhile to explore irregular pathways of progression in which the dissonances are not prepared or resolved. Again, the most useful guide here is your own ear. Does this progression sound right?

In Figure 16.9, you can see this process of methodical investigation applied to all of the inversions of the supertonic ninth of the major key.

a.   Root position supertonic ninth with regular resolution to leading note triad in first inversion. By regular resolution, I mean that the seventh and ninth have resolved stepwise down to the next notes in the scale.

b.   First inversion supertonic ninth with irregular resolution to dominant ninth chord. This resolution is irregular because the ninth does not resolve downward by step. Instead, it skips to the third of the dominant ninth chord.

c.   Second inversion supertonic ninth with regular resolution to the submediant triad.

d.   Third inversion supertonic ninth with regular resolution to the leading note seventh chord.

e. Fourth inversion supertonic ninth—where the ninth provides the bass note—with regular resolution to the leading note triad.

Investigating a particular ninth chord in this way can be very productive in that it trains the ear to discern what works and what does not work when it comes to the use of complex harmonies, such as the ninth.

Having knowledge of ninth chords gives us more options in terms of our harmony. Here we need to bear in mind that although ultimately ninth chords originally arose through the process of embellishment, using ninth chords freely as independent chords in their own right leads to the possibility of creating rich, warm, and complex textures that are a far cry from simple triadic harmony. Naturally, the first step toward the creation of such textures lies in studying the qualities of the ninth chords on particular degrees of the scale and investigating with your ear how other chords lead up to them and what kinds of chords are best used to follow them.

Conclusion

We began this chapter by taking a look at chordal extensions beyond the seventh. These included those extensions of the ninth, eleventh, and thirteenth. We then looked at how to create a ninth, eleventh, or thirteenth chord from a given seventh chord. We also considered the issue of voicing and how the way in which we voice a complex extended chord actually makes it usable in the first place. Otherwise, the extended chord could come across as a compact mass of dissonance. To be able to do this, we observed, each extension has to be reduced down to its very essence—in other words, that which are considered to be the most essential elements of a given extended chord. We observed these essential elements to be the root, third and/or fifth, the seventh, and then the extension—whether this be the ninth, eleventh, or thirteenth. We saw the fact that these extensions are all dissonant with some other component of the chord as an important consideration in terms of the regular pathways of progression of such chords.

Having introduced the idea of the extensions of the ninth, eleventh, and thirteenth, we then went on to look specifically at chords of the ninth. This included how to voice a ninth chord effectively, the regular pathways of progression of ninth chords, and finally the various inversions of ninth chords. In looking at these issues, I mentioned the importance of personal investigation and experimentation with ninth chord harmony. In any study of harmony, this is always an essential element because harmony cannot be learned simply by reading about it. The theory and ideas need to be put into practice in actual musical situations. This means that the chords being discussed need to be played, listened to, and studied closely.

Having considered the extension of the ninth, in the next chapter we will move on to the study of the next extension, which is the extension of the eleventh.

17 Chords of the Eleventh

Eleventh chords represent the next notch up from ninths on the scale of chordal extensions. Therefore, as shown in the previous chapter, to obtain an eleventh chord we simply add another third on top of any ninth chord. Doing this produces a complex sonority of six notes consisting of five thirds superimposed over the root note. So it comes as no surprise to learn that when all of the notes of an eleventh chord are played simultaneously, the result is a very dissonant chord. And the chord is dissonant for the simple reason that an eleventh chord literally consists of one triad superimposed upon another. We can appreciate this with reference to the dominant eleventh of the major key, which is illustrated on the keyboard in Figure 17.1.

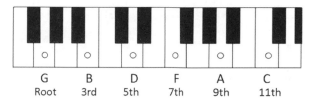

G   B   D   F   A   C
Root   3rd   5th   7th   9th   11th

Figure 17.1   Dominant eleventh of the key of C major.

Looking at this impressive chord, we can see that it embraces two discrete triads. There is the dominant triad of G major at the bottom, over which has been superimposed the subdominant triad of F major. So no wonder there is a sense of intense conflict about this chord. It embraces within itself the two primary chords of the key! This sense of conflict is intensified in the minor key because of the increased levels of dissonance. This comes from the minor ninth intervals between the root and ninth and the third and eleventh. These are illustrated in Figure 17.2 with reference to the dominant eleventh chord of C minor. Observe that there is a dissonant minor ninth between notes G and A♭ and another minor ninth between notes B and C. Their presence in this chord leads to a sonority that is literally fraught with a feeling of tension and conflict.

Uses of Eleventh Chord Harmony

Despite the complexity of the eleventh chord, it is a chord that is used with great frequency in modern music. Generally, however, this use remains unrecognized because musicians and songwriters have found their own way of categorizing and notating their

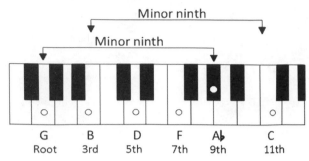

Figure 17.2 Dominant eleventh chord of the minor key.

use of eleventh chord harmony in general. A good example of this is sus4 chords, which we considered in the previous chapter. Observe that the characteristic feature of both the chords Gsus4 and G7sus4 is the eleventh above the root note G—note C. Both of these chords may therefore be viewed as being a very thinned-out way of using the resources of eleventh chord harmony. You can see these chords illustrated in Figure 17.3. Those notes marked with a black spot are the ones omitted from the eleventh chord to give rise to the suspended chord.

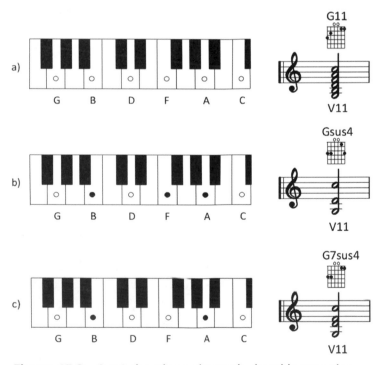

Figure 17.3 Sus4 chords as eleventh chord harmonies.

In (a) you can see the complete eleventh chord, while (b) shows that Gsus4 is the same eleventh chord with the third, seventh, and ninth omitted. Similarly, (c) shows that G7sus4 is also an eleventh chord with the third and ninth missing.

Eleventh Chord Harmony in Split Chords

Eleventh chord harmony also finds a great deal of unrecognized use in the form of split chords. Split chords are where a chord is being used over a bass that seemingly is not a part of the chord itself. To notate split chords, the symbol for the chord comes first, followed by a slash, after which the note to be used in the bass is indicated. Therefore, example Fm/G indicates that you should play an F minor chord over a G bass note. Looking at the chord G11 in Figure 17.4 , you can see that it embraces numerous possible split chords.

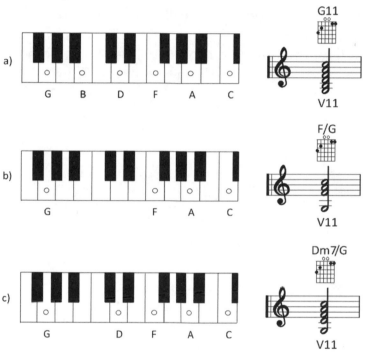

Figure 17.4   Split chords as uses of eleventh chord harmony.

In (a) you can again see the complete eleventh chord, while in (b) you can see the same eleventh chord showing itself as a chord of F major played over a note G in the bass. In (c) the eleventh chord shows itself as a D minor seventh chord being played over a note G in the bass.

When studying eleventh chord harmony, therefore, you must be prepared for the fact that although a chord of the eleventh is not always indicated, through the use of split chords, eleventh chord harmony might in fact be being used. The use of such split chords is very common in both jazz and popular music. A glance at any songbook will often reveal numerous examples. For an example of the use of both of the split chords just discussed, listen to Carly Simon's "In the Wee Small Hours of the Morning."

Voicing an Eleventh Chord

The most common eleventh chord used in music is the dominant eleventh. Like the ninth, it represents a brilliant way of loading the dominant seventh with even more pent-up tension. For practical use in a piece of music, however, this dominant eleventh chord will almost always be thinned out in some way. This means that we can be selective about our use of those elements of conflict inherent to the dominant eleventh. This applies especially if we are writing the eleventh chord in four parts. As an eleventh chord consists of six notes and we only have four parts with which to write the chord, two of the notes belonging to the eleventh chord must be omitted. We would not normally omit the seventh because the seventh qualifies the chord as being an extension. Therefore, including the seventh, we have the options that are illustrated in Figure 17.5.

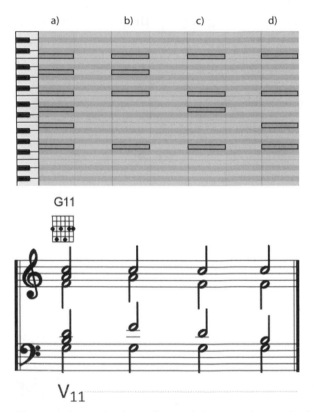

Figure 17.5   Options for voicing an eleventh chord in four parts.

In (a) you can see the complete dominant eleventh chord G11. In (b) the third and fifth have been omitted. This is a very effective voicing because it removes the minor ninth clash between the third and the eleventh. This voicing appears as the split chord F/G just discussed. In (c) the third and the ninth have been omitted. This again makes for an effective voicing, and superficially it appears to be a D minor seventh heard over a G bass line—in other words, a split chord. In (c) the ninth has been omitted from the chord, and the result is a very dissonant eleventh chord that brings out the potential clash between the third and the eleventh. It is perhaps not surprising that this voicing is probably the least used among the three just described. And when it is used, you will often find, particularly in jazz, that musicians soften it by sharpening the eleventh.

Use of Other Eleventh Chords

Like the chord of the ninth, eleventh chords can feasibly be used on any degree of the scale where they are required. And again like the chord of the ninth, there are different types of eleventh chord depending upon which degree of the scale it occurs. Each type of eleventh has its own particular quality and color. For the purposes of becoming acquainted with these qualities, an eleventh chord should be built upon all degrees of the major and minor scale, and their particular aural colors and qualities should be closely studied.

When you do this, you will discover that some eleventh chords have a more pleasing sound than others. This is mostly determined by the placement of the minor ninth. In certain eleventh chords, the minor ninth produces a quality that is just not pleasing to the ear. A good example is the tonic eleventh chord of the major key, in which there is a minor ninth clash between the third and the eleventh—see Figure 17.6(a) for an illustration of this. This can make the tonic eleventh a dour-sounding sonority.

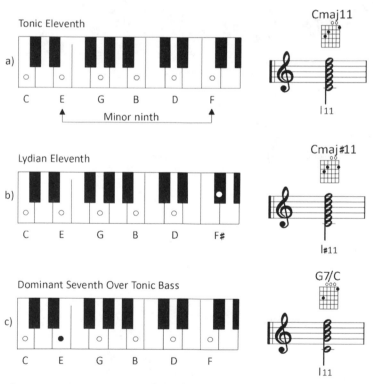

Figure 17.6   Features of the tonic eleventh chord of the major key.

Over the years musicians have learned to improve this chord by sharpening the eleventh. This gives rise to a chord known as the *Lydian eleventh,* which, using an augmented fourth, has a much more attractive sound (see Figure 17.6(b)). Yet this practice of altering eleventh chords should never be taken as a rule. This is because the unaltered tonic eleventh of the major key can also be used in such a way as to give the impression of dominant harmony being used over a tonic bass note. This works well, especially because it avoids the third of the tonic eleventh and therefore the inevitable minor ninth clash between the third and ninth. In both major and minor keys, this dominant over tonic effect represents a time-honored way of producing a certain tension in the harmony (see Figure 17.6(c)).

As you investigate eleventh chords on different degrees of the scale, you will discover that the mediant eleventh of the minor key can also produce problems in its unaltered form because it sounds like the dominant seventh of the relative major key being played over its own tonic. This means that if you are not careful, it can sound like you are modulating. See Figure 17.7(a) for an illustration of this. To avoid this, you can sharpen the eleventh to make good use of the Lydian eleventh effect (see Figure 17.7(b)). Similarly, the eleventh on the mediant of the major key has a dour sound due to the

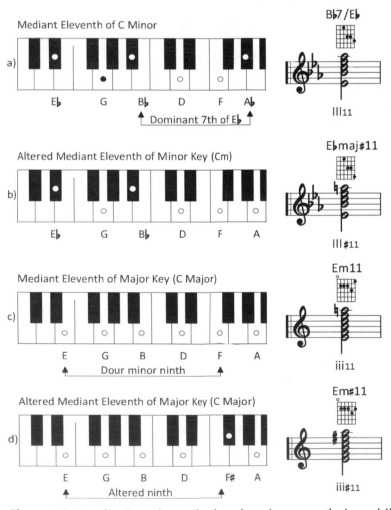

Figure 17.7   Altering eleventh chords to improve their usability.

minor ninth present in it (see Figure 17.7(c)). You can remove this dour quality by leaving out or sharpening the ninth (see Figure 17.7(d)). The eleventh on the dominant degrees of the major key is also often sharpened in the same way to remove this dour-sounding minor ninth.

In making these observations, you will appreciate that they are intended only as a guide toward those salient features that warrant further investigation. And a guide is given for the simple reason that eleventh chords are so complex, that to discuss all of the features of every eleventh chord would probably fill an encyclopedia. Here it is your ear that needs to do the work, listening carefully to each chord and looking at different ways of voicing the chord, altering certain notes, until you get a sound that sounds right for your ear. And as you study the individual qualities of these eleventh chords, you will soon realize why musicians have chromatically altered certain chords or deliberately omitted certain notes to try to get a better sound from them. Eleventh chords are absolutely brilliant for the sense of conflict that they can introduce to the harmony, but it is a sense that needs to be carefully handled.

Treatment of Eleventh Chords

Eleventh chords always produce a feeling of tension. This is because basically, an eleventh chord is a glorified suspended chord that is forever awaiting resolution. The way in which the dissonances in eleventh chords do tend to resolve is exactly the same in principle to ninth and seventh chords. The dissonant notes usually resolve stepwise to the harmony notes of other chords. This means that eleventh chords progress best to those chords whose harmony notes offer resolution to the dissonant elements of the eleventh chord.

We can illustrate this through reference to a typical dominant eleventh resolution in which the dominant eleventh progresses to the dominant seventh chord—a very common pathway of progression for the dominant eleventh. See Figure 17.8(a) for an illustration of this. In Figure 17.8(b), you can see the same essential progression, except that it has been voiced differently. Including the ninth along with the eleventh, the ninth is shown resolving stepwise to the root of the dominant seventh chord that follows. In Figure 17.8(c), you can see numerous eleventh chords on degrees of the scale other than the dominant being used: a submediant eleventh (vi_{11}), in which the eleventh resolves to the third of the A minor seventh chord that follows, and a subdominant eleventh (IV_{11}) in which the eleventh is held over irregularly into the dominant seventh chord that follows. These examples of the use of eleventh chords show that as long as the chord that follows carries the appropriate notes of resolution of the eleventh chord, it is often a viable progression.

It does need to be stressed, though, that whatever observations are being made here, these need to be supplemented by a person's own investigations into eleventh chord harmony. This is because harmony that uses ninths, elevenths, and thirteenths lies at the

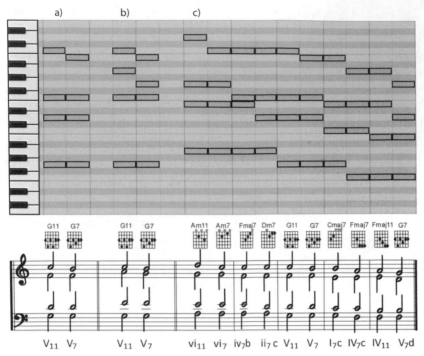

Figure 17.8 Uses of eleventh chords.

very cutting edge of harmony as it is used in today's music. And a fresh approach to this type of harmony could potentially work wonders.

Initially, I recommend that you take a particular eleventh chord in a particular voicing and experiment with different ways of progressing both to and from that chord. Some of these progressions will be regular progressions—in other words, progressions in which the dissonant elements are prepared and/or resolved. Others will be irregular progressions—in other words, the dissonant elements will not be prepared or resolved. Both types of progression—regular and irregular—have a place and an expressive value. It is only through this kind of investigation and experimentation that it is possible to find your own preferences and values so far as the use of harmony in your music is concerned.

Inversions of Eleventh Chords

Eleventh chords contain so many notes—a full six out of the seven notes of the scale—that it becomes almost pointless to speak of inversions of eleventh chords. This is because each inversion will either closely resemble or be identical to another chord. Therefore, it is best simply to assume that an eleventh chord will always be used in root position.

Conclusion

In this chapter we investigated eleventh chord harmony from a number of different standpoints. First, we looked at the impressive levels of dissonance in an eleventh chord and how that dissonance is a result of the presence of two triads that conflict with one another. Due to this apparent presence of separate triads within the one chord, we saw how so-called split chords are often simply a form of appearance of eleventh chord harmony. From there, we went on to study the best ways to voice an eleventh chord and observed that through the way in which we voice an eleventh chord, we can be selective about those conflicting and dissonant elements that we actually use. I stressed the importance of personally investigating the different qualities of eleventh chords, because it is only though this detailed personal aural study of each chord that you can understand why and how musicians have tended to chromatically alter eleventh chords. Finally, we looked at treatment of eleventh chords from a conventional standpoint that dictates that the dissonant elements should be prepared and/or resolved. Here it must be stressed that this traditional approach to eleventh chord harmony is only one approach, and I hope that as you try to use eleventh chords in your own music, you will find a number of different approaches to them that work for you.

18 Thirteenth Chords

The final extension we are about to consider is the thirteenth. The thirteenth takes the chord of the eleventh and adds yet another third to it. You can see how this works by taking a look at Figure 18.1, which illustrates the tonic thirteenth of the C major key. To produce the tonic thirteenth chord, I have simply added a third above the eleventh—note F—to produce note A.

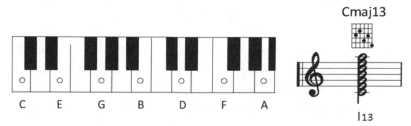

Figure 18.1 The tonic thirteenth of the C major key.

The result of this is a seven-note chord that contains every single note of the scale. Containing every single note, the thirteenth chord could not be more dissonant.

Traditional Uses of Thirteenth Chords

Probably the best place to begin a study of the use of thirteenth chords is with the regular treatment of the most commonly used thirteenth chord of all—the dominant thirteenth. To create a dominant thirteenth chord, we take the chord of the dominant eleventh and add a thirteenth to it. This interval of the thirteenth is universally used to enhance the inherent tension of the dominant seventh chord. It does this by adding in yet another dissonant note—the thirteenth itself. In effect, this means that it is therefore possible to reduce the dominant thirteenth down to an extremely simple three-note chord formula in which the third, fifth, ninth, and eleventh have been omitted. You will find this greatly reduced and thinned-out thirteenth chord illustrated in Figure 18.2.

When conceived of in this fashion, understanding the implications of using a thirteenth chord are so much easier. You can appreciate these implications by analyzing the interval characteristics present in this three-note thirteenth chord formula. First, observe that the thirteenth itself is consonant with the root note, with which it forms an interval of a compound major sixth. As such, the relationship of the thirteenth to the

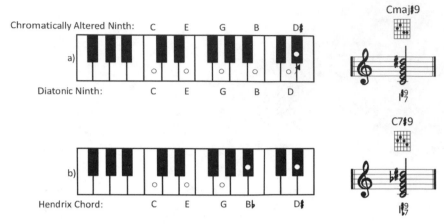

Figure 18.2 Three-part dominant thirteenth chord.

root note is not the source of tension present in this three-note chord. The tension stems from the fact that the thirteenth forms a dissonant interval of a major seventh with the seventh of the dominant—note F.

Through these observations, we can now understand how the interval of the thirteenth loads the dominant harmony with an increase of tension. The seventh of the dominant forms a dissonance with the root note, while the thirteenth forms a dissonance with the seventh. The result is a significant increase in the feeling of dominant tension. Naturally, it is the way in which this tension is dispelled that explains the regular treatment of this chord. For in a regular sense, where dissonant chordal components are usually resolved by step, the dissonant major seventh tends to fall down to the fifth of the dominant chord. See Figure 18.3(a) and (b) for an illustration of this. However, there is an alternative to this in which the thirteenth is treated as an appoggiatura. In this sense, the thirteenth acts as a substitute for the fifth of the dominant—note D. In this case, the thirteenth then leaps down in appoggiatura fashion to the tonic degree (see Figure 18.3(c)).

In the minor scale, the dynamics of the three-note thirteenth chord are virtually identical, as you can see from the minor versions of the same types of decorated V to I cadence in Figure 18.4. Figure 18.4(a) shows a dominant thirteenth resolving to a dominant seventh, which then deceptively cadences to a submediant triad. In Figure 18.4(b), the thirteenth is treated as an appoggiatura, which leaps down to the tonic of the minor key.

Reducing the thirteenth chord down to its bare essence in this way accelerates an understanding of its function. This is because more involved ways of voicing the dominant thirteenth chord tend to build upon this basic essence—in other words, including the third for a four-part voicing, and so on. This means that if you are going to use a dominant thirteenth chord, you would get the root, seventh, and thirteenth in as a matter of priority. Other notes would then be chosen on their own merits for the sonority.

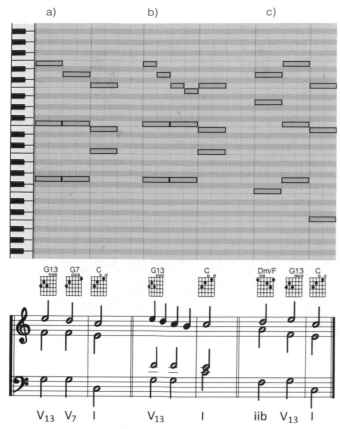

Figure 18.3   Treatment of three-part dominant thirteenth chord.

The Thirteenth and Drone Music

Although the overt use of thirteenth chords other than the dominant thirteenth is perhaps rare, we need to be prepared for the fact that thirteenth chord harmony can often manifest in more subtle ways in which it is not immediately apparent. The reason for this is that the chord of the thirteenth has a particular logic to it, and this logic is not always very clearly understood. And neither are the musical and harmonic effects that arise from it.

Take, for example, the idea of inversions. In theory, the first inversion of the tonic thirteenth is where the third—note E—is in the bass. However, the chord that results from this is at the same time as the mediant thirteenth, as you can see in Figure 18.5.

The thirteenth chord has thus led us to the strange point where the theory of inversions begins to break down. Every thirteenth chord that can be built upon each degree of the scale is at the same time an inversion of the tonic thirteenth. If the mediant thirteenth is the same as the first inversion of the tonic thirteenth, this means that every thirteenth chord is really a subset of the one tonic thirteenth chord. The implications of this for musical harmony are very important, because it means that at the level of the thirteenth

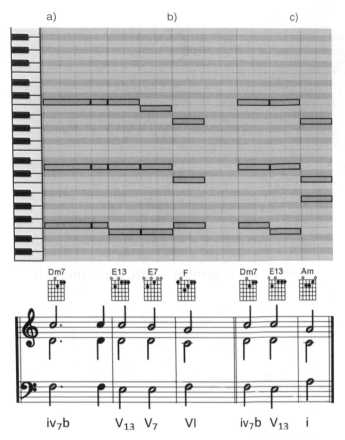

Figure 18.4   Three-part treatment of the dominant thirteenth in the minor key.

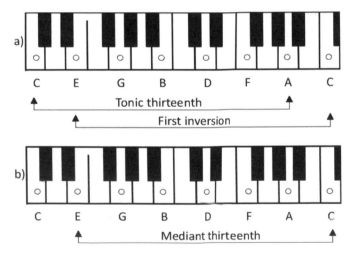

Figure 18.5   Equivalence of first inversion tonic thirteenth to mediant thirteenth chord.

chord, there is really only one chord, one root, and one ultimate harmony. All other chords are simply the facets of that one chordal mass.

This observation in turn implies a certain type of musical value—a value in which there is only one pervading harmony underlying the music. Practically speaking, this value manifests in numerous ways. One such value lies in the characteristic use of a drone or drones, which continually underpin the harmony of the music. Drones of this sort have been used in music for a very long time now. And as I mentioned at the beginning of this book, drone-based harmony represents one of the earliest and simplest types of harmony there is. So it is rather strange that when we now get to the most complex chord of all, the thirteenth, a resurgence of values for drone-based music tends to emerge.

The basic idea of a drone is that it forms a continuous reference point amidst the ever-changing flux of the harmony. And no matter what happens in the other parts, the unchanging drone serves to anchor the harmony. This means that, in effect, the functional distinction between the different triads tends to disappear, and the emphasis instead shifts to the sheer beauty, color, and ambience of the musical texture.

Although drone-based music has been around for hundreds of years, a value for it has grown considerably over the last 50 years. Probably beginning with the minimalist movement of the 1960s, this value has had a profound influence upon the development of much modern popular and electronic music, especially within the spheres of ambient, chill-out, spiritual, and New Age music. Affecting the music of the Beatles, Velvet Underground, Brian Eno, Kraftwerk, and many others, the whole idea of drone-based music has developed an impetus and momentum that has established itself as a musical movement in its own right.

This topic, however, unfortunately leads us to the very edge of the limits of functional harmony within the major and the minor scales. To go beyond this point is to enter into the sphere of advanced harmony, in which the paradox of the complete thirteenth chord is directly involved in many modern developments in musical harmony. These include:

- Advanced modal harmony.

- Chord-scale theory. (The chord is the scale, and the scale is the chord.)

- Jazz harmony.

- Pandiatonic harmony.

- Use of compound chords and split chordal streams.

- Bitonality and polytonality.

- Use of different types of chord shapes, such as quartal (built up from fourths) and quintal (built up from fifths) harmony.

- Use of tone clusters.

- Alternative intonation models.

- And so on...

Unfortunately, to cover these topics would require more books, because they really belong to the domain of advanced musical harmony. In this book I am simply laying a foundation for the study of advanced harmony. This foundation necessarily focuses upon the functional harmony associated with the major and the minor scales. Once you have grasped functional harmony, those more advanced areas of harmony just mentioned will become much easier to approach, understand, and use—should your interests develop in those more specialized directions.

Conclusion

This chapter focused on the most advanced and complex chord possible within the range of the major and minor scales—the chord of the thirteenth. Consisting of all seven notes of the scale, the potential complexities of thirteenth chord harmony are enormous—especially for those types of harmony that go beyond the traditions of functional harmony as it is generally understood. We found a way to cut through that complexity by focusing upon traditional use of the thirteenth chord, which mostly revolves around use of the dominant thirteenth. Here, we found it convenient to reduce a thirteenth chord down to its very essence—a simple chord of three notes—which revealed itself to be yet another extension of dominant harmony.

Having considered the thirteenth chord, it is now time to go on to the topic of chromatic harmony. By the term *chromatic harmony,* I mean the use of chordal tones that lie outside of the range of a given major and/or minor scale. The use of chromatic harmony is common in virtually all types of modern and popular music. For this reason, chromatic harmony represents a very important topic for this book on musical harmony.

19 Modal Interchange

Over the last few chapter of this book, we are going to explore chromatic harmony. Chromatic harmony is an absolutely brilliant way to bring a sense of new color, expression, and direction to our chord progressions. And its proper use liberates us from ever having to use the same formulaic chord progressions over and over again. Through chromatic harmony, we can create original-sounding, fresh, colorful, and atmospheric chord progressions. We can create chord progressions that automatically suggest the vast expanse of outer space or the lushness of a tropical forest. In fact, chromatic harmony opens up a whole world of atmosphere, color, and suggestion, which can both stimulate our creativity and increase the emotional power and range of expression of our music.

To use chromatic harmony, it is necessary to employ what are termed *chromatic chords*. So what is a chromatic chord? It draws from those notes of the chromatic scale that lie outside of the major or minor scale belonging to that key. The use of such chords is common in all styles of music that use major and minor scales. This is for the simple reason that the use of chromatic chords leads to a great enhancement and expansion of chordal and modal color, resources, and options that are available to us.

A simple example of the use of a chromatic chord would be the use of a D major triad in the key of C major. If we use this triad, we need to use the note F♯, which does not belong to the major scale of the key of C. Accordingly, this chord of D major is categorized as being a chromatic chord for that key. If we compare two chord progressions in the key of C major that go from chord I to ii to IV to V, and in the second chord progression we substitute what is ordinarily the D minor triad for a D major triad, we can not only hear the difference in the two chord progressions, but we can also listen to the effect that the chord change has.

For my ear at least, the second progression involving the use of the chromatic chord not only is brighter, but it is a stronger chord progression as well. Naturally, when using a chord that does not belong to the key, there is always the risk of weakening tonality—in other words, the sense of the key itself. For this reason there is literally a whole art and science surrounding the use of chromatic chords generally.

Note from Figure 19.1 that chromatic chords are fairly easy to spot in written music. They are betrayed by the accidentals—that is, sharps, flats, or natural signs needed to

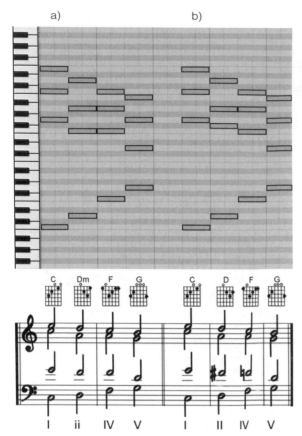

Figure 19.1   Use of D major chromatic chord.

both indicate and cancel chromatic notes. This means we can easily spot the chromatic chord in bar 4 because of the sharp needed to raise the note F up to F♯. And this sharp sign is then cancelled in the following chord because we need an F natural for the F major chord.

Chromatic Chords from Modal Interchange

All chromatic chords have their own particular origins—that is, they tend to come from somewhere. One important source of chromatic chords is *modal interchange*. At the first level, this is simply the borrowing of chords from the parallel minor mode to be used in the major mode and the borrowing of chords from the parallel major mode to be used in the minor mode. This type of chromatic chord has been popular for hundreds of years, and it still is very popular because it leads to refreshing changes of color within the major or minor terrain of a piece of music.

The seeds of modal interchange probably lie in the minor key itself. As already shown in Chapter 6, the natural minor key has no major dominant triad. So we sharpen the seventh degree, which gives us the third necessary to create a major dominant triad. Where does that triad come from? This major dominant triad comes from the parallel major key. It borrows from that key in order to improve the effect of a V-I chord progression. The harmonic minor mode therefore already has a built-in tendency toward chromatic harmony—that is, the use of chromatic notes and chords. Yet for the minor key, this process does not stop there.

To get rid of that awkward augmented second between the sixth and seventh degree of the harmonic minor scale, we often sharpen the sixth. This procedure leads to the melodic minor scale. Where does this sharp sixth come from? It is borrowed from the parallel major key. As a result of that borrowing, we can see that the melodic minor scale in its ascending form not only is a product of modal interchange, but that this process of modal interchange has led to the creation of a scale that is virtually identical to the parallel major scale except for one note—the third degree. See Figure 19.2 for a clear illustration of this.

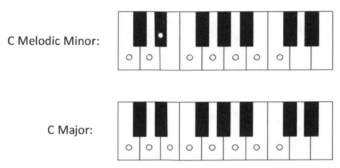

Figure 19.2   Differences between the melodic minor scale and the parallel major scale.

Looking at this closeness between the two scales causes us to ask the question: What is the essential difference between the major and the minor key? The melodic minor mode clearly shows us the answer, because although it is virtually identical to the major mode, music written within it still has a strong minor character. The answer, therefore, is that it is the modality of the tonic triad. When the tonic triad is minor, even though all of the other notes might belong to the major scale, the tonality itself is minor. And by the same token, when the tonic triad is major, then no matter what other notes might be used in the scale, the tonality itself comes across as being major.

This is a very important point, because it shows us that in the same way that elements of the major key can be borrowed to enrich and supplement the minor key, the process can also be reversed. It is possible to borrow elements from the minor key to enrich and supplement the major key. As long as the character of the tonic triad is preserved, the key of the music—major or minor—will be self-evident. This process, in the total range of its effects and possibilities, is called *modal interchange*.

Let us now consider some examples of modal interchange. In Figure 19.3, you can see three classic examples of modal interchange. In (a), a Neapolitan sixth chord is acting as a substitute for the expected supertonic pre-dominant harmony. Built upon the flat second degree of either major or minor scale, the Neapolitan sixth chord is probably a remnant of the old Phrygian mode, which is identical to the natural minor scale except for the flat second degree. Accordingly, for the key of C major the Neapolitan sixth represents a chromatic chord, the chromatic notes being D♭ and A♭. In (b) you can see an Fm chord borrowed from the parallel minor mode in order to harmonize the chromatic passing note A♭. Finally, in (c) is an example of a Tierce de Picardie—a final cadence to the tonic major chord when in the minor key. The chromatic note for this chord is therefore note E, which is foreign to the scale of C minor.

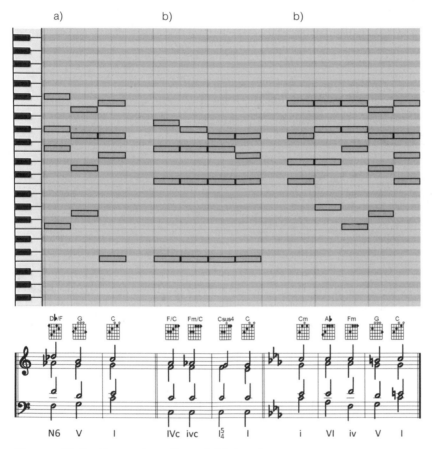

Figure 19.3   Examples of modal interchange.

Through modal interchange, chords from the minor key are in effect available in the parallel major key and vice versa. This leads to an expansion in the number of chords that can be used in either major or minor key. Figure 19.4, for example, shows the chords theoretically available in the C major key through the process of modal interchange. The chromatic chords—that is, those that use chromatic notes for the key—are easy to spot because the chromatic notes have been filled in black.

Instead of seven chords, observe that we now have 17 chords. And this just includes triads. Every chord in Figure 19.4 can also be extended into a seventh, ninth, eleventh, or thirteenth.

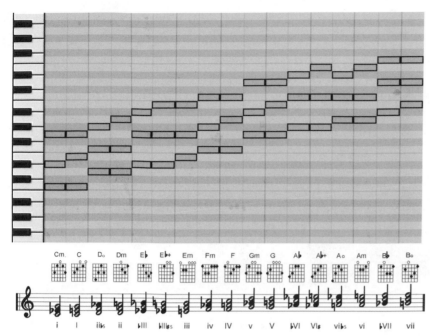

Figure 19.4   Chromatic chords resulting from modal interchange.

This great expansion of the resources available in either major or minor key leads to the possibility of really fresh and interesting chord progressions, with major/minor exchange being just one possibility. This is where a major chord progresses to its minor equivalent, or the opposite. Figure 19.5 shows some of the possibilities.

In example (a), the tonic major seventh chord exchanges for a tonic minor seventh, followed by a subdominant major seventh exchanging with a subdominant minor seventh. The result is a nice swaying between the major and minor tonality. Example (b) shows the use of a chromatic sixth chord—Fm6—borrowed from the parallel minor mode to harmonize the chromatic passing note A♭. And finally, example (b) shows the minor seventh of the subdominant being used as an auxiliary chord with the major seventh.

This type of chord change is very popular for the simple reason that it can be very atmospheric. Major turning to minor offers a darkening of color, while minor to major offers a distinct brightening of color. Whichever option is used, both are highly effective ways of achieving variety and contrast in a chord progression.

Another common instance where modal interchange is used is where a chromatic melodic line is being harmonized. A chromatic line is where the melodic part moves up or down the chromatic scale, rather than the diatonic scale. Melodic lines that move chromatically have been popular since time immemorial. Commonly found either in the lead or the bass, the descending chromatic bass line in particular has always been a firm favorite with composers. In Figure 19.6 you will see a falling chromatic bass line harmonized with chords that are freely borrowed from the parallel minor mode.

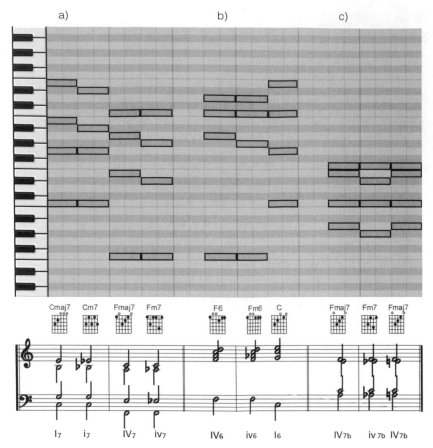

Figure 19.5   Examples of major/minor exchange.

The chromatic chords here are the Cm chord used to begin the chord progression, the Gm chord providing the harmony over the chromatic note B♭ in bar 2, and the Fm chord providing a harmony over the note A♭ in bar 3. Note that through use of these chromatic chords, we are able to put a satisfactory harmony to all of the chromatic notes involved in the descending chromatic bass line.

Composers and songwriters have been using modal interchange for a very long time now. And this free borrowing and exchange between the major and minor keys has led to a gradual blurring in the distinction between the major and minor keys. It has also led to the existence of a common pot of chords available within a key that everybody draws upon to create their chord progressions. This pot contains all of the chords from both the major and the minor keys. And what dictates the chords used is nothing more than what sounds right.

Naturally, this gives rise to chord progressions that, although sounding great, are difficult to classify as being in the major or the minor key. The most important thing, I suppose, is the tonic triad—if the tonic triad is major, then the music will sound like it is being written in the major key; whereas if it is minor, it will sound like it is being written in the minor key. This is irrespective of what other chords are being used.

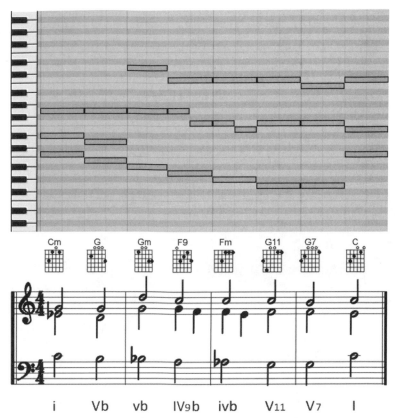

Figure 19.6   Chromatic bass line harmonized with chords using modal interchange.

A good example of this is the chord progression used in Figure 19.7, which consists of four root position major triads. There is no doubt that this chord progression is in the major key, although it uses an equal balance of chords from both the major and the minor key: C and F major from the C major key and E♭ and A♭ major from the minor key. Note that this type of chord progression implicates some kind of cross-relation. A cross-relation is where you get a note in one part and its chromatic alteration in another part within close proximity to one another.

In Figure 19.7, you can see two examples of this type of chord movement. The first is that note E belonging to the C major triad in bar 1 forms a cross-relation with note E♭ in the bass in the second half of bar 1. The second is where note A in the part below the lead in bar 2 forms a cross-relation with the note A♭ in the bass.

This type of chord progression has a great freshness and vivid sense of color about it. And it comes from a totally free borrowing of chords from either tonality. As a result of that free borrowing, the conventions that have traditionally surrounded the major and minor keys begin to break down. What is the difference between them if they use the same basic set of chords? The only difference is the character of the tonic triad. This means that the only requirement when writing in the major key is to use a major tonic triad. And the only requirement when writing in the minor key is to use a minor tonic triad. Apart from that, the choice of other chords to use is totally free.

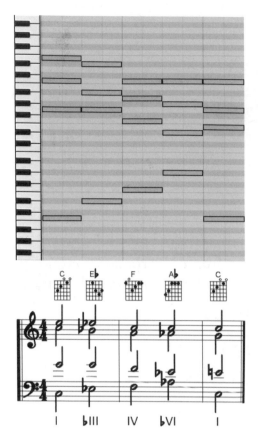

Figure 19.7   Four-chord major chord progression.

Conclusion

We began this chapter by introducing the topic of chromatic harmony, and we observed that a chromatic chord is one that uses notes that are foreign to the major or minor scale of the key in question. I gave an example of a D major common triad being used in the key of C major. This chord is a chromatic chord because it uses the note F♯, which does not belong with the key of C major.

From there we went on to consider one of the most common sources of chromatic chords—the process of modal interchange. Looking first at the minor scale complex, we saw how the different versions of the minor scale were obtained through the process of modal interchange. This means that chromatic harmony is naturally endemic to the minor scale complex itself. But we also saw how this process could be reversed. Elements and chords from the minor scale could equally be used and borrowed in order to enrich the major scale. The result of this process—called modal interchange—is a great expansion in the range of chords available within the major or the minor scale. This expansion in turn opens up new possibilities for chord progressions in the major or the minor key.

Modal interchange, however, is only one potential source of chromatic harmony. Another source, which we will consider in the next chapter, is secondary dominant harmony.

20 Secondary Dominant Chords

In the previous chapter, we observed how chord progressions could be enriched by borrowing chords from the parallel major or minor key. Involving the use of alterations of particular scale degrees, these borrowed chords were accordingly described as being chromatic for the key. Another source of chromatic harmony, also obtained by borrowing from other keys, is secondary dominant harmony. The idea of secondary dominant harmony is that a chord other than the tonic is preceded by its own dominant seventh, ninth, eleventh, and so on. This has the effect of temporarily tonicizing that particular chord. However, this process of tonicization is so fleeting and temporary that it is not regarded as being a proper modulation.

This type of chord is called a *secondary dominant*. To use a secondary dominant, it is generally necessary to chromatically alter certain degrees of the major or the minor scale. To illustrate this, Figure 20.1 provides an example of the use of secondary dominant harmony.

The occurrence of the secondary dominant is easy to spot because it uses a chromatic alteration, which is note C♯—a chromatic note for the key of C major. This note C♯ is in fact the leading note of the supertonic key, which is D minor. And this note occurs as a part of a leading note triad of the supertonic key. Here you might recall that the leading note triad is commonly used as an agent of dominant function. So in effect, what we have here is basically a dominant to tonic cadence in the supertonic key. Superficially, this might be seen to be a chromatic modulation. Yet the movement to the new key is so brief that we can see that really it represents nothing more than a way of chromatically decorating a classic ii-V-I progression in the home key. The dominant of the supertonic key is accordingly represented as a V over ii.

The consequences of using secondary dominant harmony are an expansion in the range of chordal colors available within a given key and an enrichment of the key through the use of numerous chromatic notes that in a conventional sense are considered to be foreign to it. This enrichment comes at a price, however. If we use too much secondary dominant harmony, there is the risk that the key will become confused, ambiguous, or unsettled. If that is the intention, of course, then absolutely fine. But it is necessary to be aware of the risks.

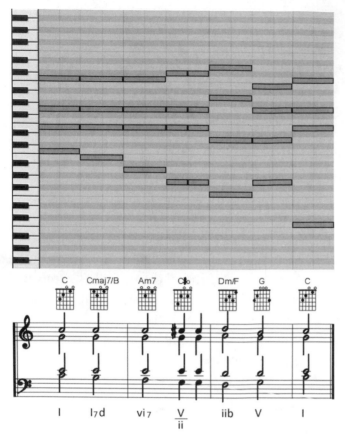

Figure 20.1   Example of use of secondary dominant harmony.

Once we have become aware of the possibility for secondary dominant harmony, the next task is to take a reconnaissance of where and how it can be applied within a particular key. For example, in the major key, any of the common triads other than the tonic can be effectively preceded by their own dominant.

Let us quickly go through these secondary dominants.

   a. The third of the submediant triad has been sharpened in order to create the dominant chord of the supertonic key: D minor.

   b. The third and fifth of the leading note triad have been chromatically sharpened in order to produce the dominant chord of the mediant key: E minor.

   c. The third and seventh of the tonic seventh chord have been chromatically flattened to produce the dominant seventh chord of the subdominant key: F major.

   d. The third of the supertonic seventh chord has been chromatically raised to produce the dominant seventh chord of the dominant key.

   e. The third of the mediant seventh has been chromatically raised in order to produce the dominant seventh chord of the submediant key: A minor.

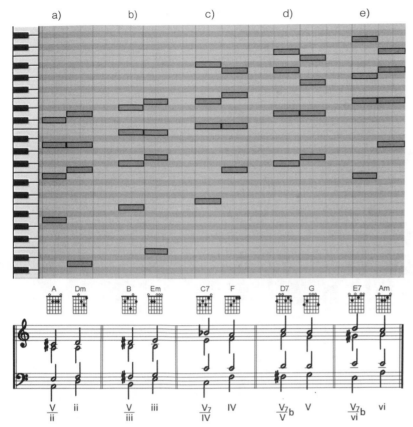

Figure 20.2   Secondary dominants within the major key.

Looking at these progressions, we can see that they all have something in common. They all involve the process of temporarily tonicizing one of the common triads in the key other than the tonic. Generally, therefore, the principle of secondary dominant harmony does not apply to the seventh degree of the major scale. This is because the leading note triad cannot act as a tonic chord. This means that it therefore cannot be tonicized through use of a secondary dominant.

Within the minor key there are also numerous opportunities for the use of secondary dominant harmony. Here a secondary dominant can be used wherever there is stable triad that can be tonicized. In Figure 20.3, you can see the most common options for secondary dominant harmony in the minor key.

The first example, (a), is perhaps unusual because it uses the dominant of the Neapolitan seventh chord, which itself is a chromatic chord for the key of C minor—in other words, it uses the chromatically flattened second degree. This works well, however, because Neapolitan harmonies are mostly used as pre-dominant chords. So to tonicize the pre-dominant in this way tends to enhance its effect. The next example, (b), shows use of the dominant seventh chord of the mediant key for which, in the natural minor mode, no chromatic alterations are actually required. In (c) you can see the tonic seventh of the minor key being chromatically altered to produce the dominant seventh of

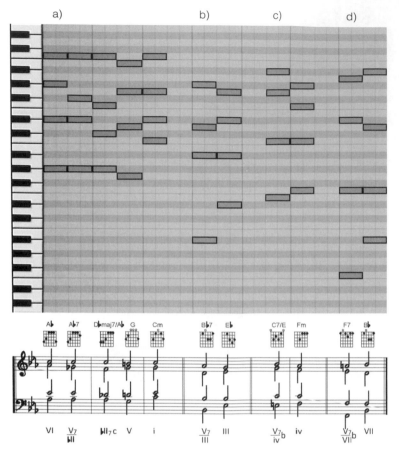

Figure 20.3 Secondary dominant harmony in the minor key.

the subdominant key. Finally, in (d) the subdominant seventh of the minor key is being chromatically altered to produce the dominant seventh of the subtonic key: B♭ major.

Approaching a Secondary Dominant Chord

Any chord that performs a dominant function can be feasibly used as a secondary dominant. This includes the dominant triad, leading note triad, diminished seventh, half-diminished seventh chord, and so on. To become familiar with secondary dominant harmony, you should examine each option on its own merits and find successful methods of approach and resolution of the chord. In terms of approaching a secondary dominant chord, the most common approach is by way of a chromatic passing note or notes. Each diatonic chord is susceptible to chromatic alteration in particular characteristic ways. You need to study and explore all of these.

For example, if we flatten the seventh of a major seventh chord, we get a dominant seventh chord (see Figure 20.4(a)). If we flatten the seventh and at the same time raise the root, we get a diminished seventh chord (see Figure 20.4(b)). In terms of minor seventh chords, it is only necessary to raise the third, and the dominant seventh chord is

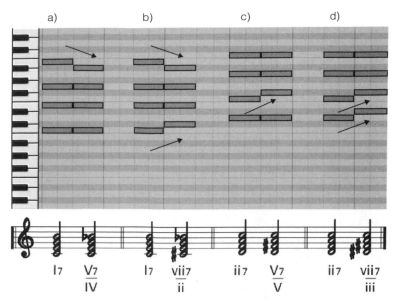

Figure 20.4   Chromatic alterations of common seventh chords.

obtained (see Figure 20.4(c)); whereas if we raise both the root and the third, we get a diminished seventh chord (see Figure 20.4(d)).

Each of these implies resolution in particular ways and to particular chords. Example (a) produces the dominant seventh of the subdominant key, example (b) the diminished seventh chord of the supertonic key, (c) the dominant seventh of the dominant key, and finally (d) the diminished seventh of the mediant key. Through use of chromatic alteration, therefore, there is plenty of opportunity to use secondary dominant harmony. This in effect is simply a way of chromatically decorating and enhancing regular chord progressions within the key.

Irregular Resolution of Secondary Dominants

Ordinarily, a secondary dominant would progress to its implied tonic chord. However, there is always the possibility of employing a deceptive resolution—that is, proceeding to a chord other than the implied tonic. Figure 20.5 shows two examples of this. In (a), the root and third of the supertonic seventh are raised to create what appears to be the dominant ninth of the mediant key—in other words, the diminished seventh chord. Instead, it progresses to a C major chord in first inversion. In (b), the third of the mediant seventh is raised to give the dominant seventh of the submediant key, which is A minor. However, instead of progressing to the anticipated A minor chord, a chord of F major follows.

Another technique that has been commonly used is to progress from a dominant or secondary dominant chord to another secondary dominant—rather than progressing to the intended tonic. This technique has been used at least since the Classical era, and it is a brilliant way of prolonging the feeling of dominant tension in the music. Representing

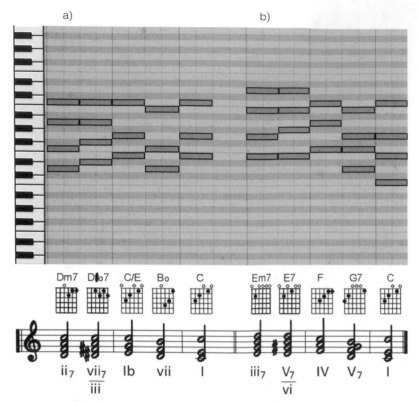

Figure 20.5 Irregular progressions of secondary dominant chords.

one of the major features of the harmonic language of jazz, blues, rock, funk, soul, and so on, this provides a great way to produce music that literally revels in the feeling of unresolved dominant tension. Let us look at some examples of this.

In Figure 20.6(a), the submediant seventh of the minor key is flattened to give the dominant seventh of the flat supertonic key, which is D♭ major. However, instead of progressing to the flat supertonic chord, the dominant seventh simply shifts down by a semitone to go to the dominant seventh chord of the home key. Example (b) shows a similar example in the major key in which the secondary dominant C7, instead of progressing to the subdominant chord that represents its tonic, instead passes on to the secondary dominant F7, which in turn then passes on to the regular dominant of the key, which then cadences to the tonic chord.

In this way it is possible to set up an entire chain of secondary dominants. The effect of this is to maintain a continual feeling of dominant tension during which the sense of tonality is often suspended.

A favorite technique with jazz musicians is to use secondary dominant chords as substitutes for regular chords. Minor sevenths are particularly useful for this type of treatment because only the third needs to be raised to turn the chord into a dominant seventh chord. The results of doing this are often very fresh and colorful-sounding chord progressions. Compare for example the progressions (a) and (b) in Figure 20.7. The first is a

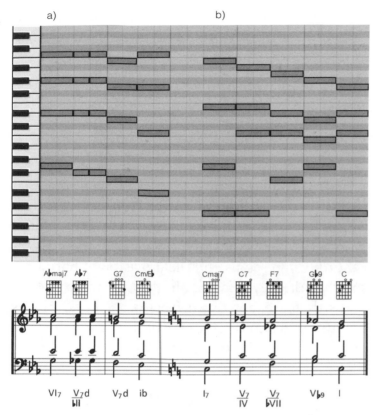

Figure 20.6   Secondary dominant chain progressions.

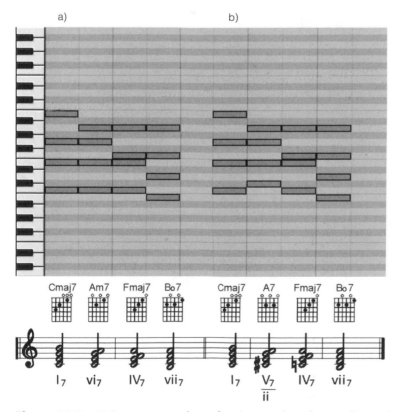

Figure 20.7   Using a secondary dominant chord as a diatonic chord substitute.

straight diatonic Cmaj7-Am7-Fmaj7-Bo7 progression, whereas in the second progression a dominant seventh chord has been used as a substitute for the Am7 chord. The result is a stronger and much more colorful chord progression.

Being aware of this practice, it is useful to experiment with using dominant chords as substitutes for ordinary chords. When used appropriately and effectively, they can lift a chord progression from the banal to the extraordinary.

Conclusion

In this chapter we focused upon a type of chromatic chord that, like the chords used through modal interchange, can be construed as being borrowed from another key. Therefore, to use the chord of D7 in the key of C major is to borrow the dominant seventh chord from the supertonic minor key. The results of doing this are the possibility for the creation of more colorful chord progressions and the provision of harmonic support for various chromatic notes within the key. Having, in the last two chapters, considered sources of chromatic chords that are borrowed from other keys, in this next chapter it is time to look at an unusual group of chords that, although they are also classified as being chromatic, cannot actually be interpreted as belonging to any other key.

21 True Chromatic Chords

In our study of chromatic harmony, so far we have seen that many of the chromatic chords that can be used within a particular key can be interpreted as having been borrowed from other keys. This includes chords obtained through the process of modal interchange and the use of secondary dominants. There is, however, a large group of chromatic chords that do not originate in this way. They are chords that occupy a purely chromatic world. Musicians, composers, and songwriters have been experimenting with this type of chromatic chord for centuries. This is because true chromatic chords are an absolutely brilliant source of new chordal color, mood, and possibility. When used effectively, they can lift a chord progression from the banal to the brilliant. They can also offer new ways of thinking about harmony and new directions in which chord progressions might be taken. They can also lead to the creation of unique scalar environments that offer new opportunities for musical composition. So whichever way we approach this topic, it is one that is full of exciting and intriguing possibilities.

Augmented Sixth Chords

To obtain a chromatic chord, one or more of the notes of a diatonic chord needs to be chromatically raised or lowered. When this is done in such a way as to create a chord that belongs to no other key, the result is a true chromatic chord. A good example of such chords is chords of the augmented sixth, which in one form or another have been used by musicians and composers to decorate their chord progressions for hundreds of years. Like any other chromatic chord, augmented sixth chords arise when we chromatically alter particular degrees of the major or minor scale. Let us now see how by looking at some examples.

In Figure 21.1(a), you can see a regular diatonic pre-dominant to dominant progression in the minor key. This occurs in the form of the first inversion of the subdominant triad progressing to the dominant triad in root position by way of a suspended chord. Now notice that the sixth formed by the upper and lower voice of the subdominant triad (A♭ up to F) opens out to the octave of the dominant triad that follows, the top note F rising up to G and the bottom note A♭ falling to G.

In (b) you can see the same essential chord progression, except that this progression has been chromatically decorated and enhanced through use of an augmented sixth chord.

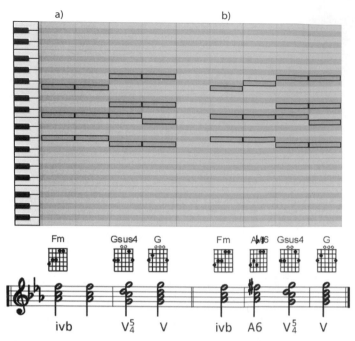

Figure 21.1 Use of chord of the augmented sixth.

This chord is labeled as A6. Notice that to create this chord, we have simply sharpened the upper note F of chord iv. By sharpening the F in this way, we have set up a tendency tone—rather like a secondary leading note—which then smoothly rises up to the dominant note G. It does this in the fashion of a chromatic passing note.

Augmented sixth chords are so named because of this unique interval that occurs when this passing note is introduced. For it is a major sixth (Ab to F) that has been chromatically augmented by a semitone (Ab to F♯).

The profile of this particular chord is unique on account of the presence of the interval of the augmented sixth. This interval does not occur anywhere within the major or minor scale. As such, augmented sixth chords, therefore, cannot be construed as being borrowed from any other key.

The Italian, French, and German Forms of the Augmented Sixth

Chords of the augmented sixth come in three well-known traditional forms. The chord used in Figure 21.1 is the simplest form, having only three notes. It is called the *Italian sixth*. If we add a perfect fifth above the Ab to create a four-note chord, we get a German sixth chord. If we replace that fifth with an augmented fourth, we get a French sixth chord. Figure 21.2 shows the intervallic makeup of all three of these traditional forms of augmented sixth chord.

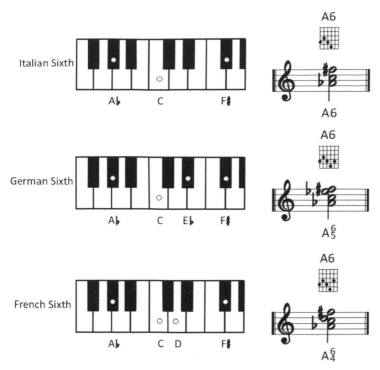

Figure 21.2 The three traditional types of augmented sixth chords.

All three types of augmented sixth chords perform an identical function. They function as chromatically enhanced pre-dominant chords, the augmented sixth interval opening out to the dominant root and its octave. As such, apart from minor differences in voice leading, the example given in Figure 21.1 offers a general indication of the use of an augmented sixth chord. That is to say that augmented sixth chords most commonly occur on the submediant degree of the minor scale and the flattened submediant degree of the major scale.

Augmented Sixth Chords as Chromatically Altered Dominants

Although the chromatic profile of augmented sixth chords is quite unique, in terms of function, they tend to perform a secondary dominant role. And this is the general key that enables us to appreciate what augmented sixth chords actually do. We can understand this more clearly if we compare French and German forms of augmented sixth chord with dominant seventh and/or ninth chords. Take a look at Figure 21.3. On the left is the French sixth chord, and in (a) we can see this chord as we represented it in Figure 21.2. In (b) we have placed the same chord but in a different inversion with note D in the bass. If you look at the profile of this chord, it is easy to see that it is simply a dominant seventh chord with a flattened fifth.

On the right of the figure, you can see the German sixth chord in the position in which it was represented in the previous figure. In (b), you can see the same chord in a different

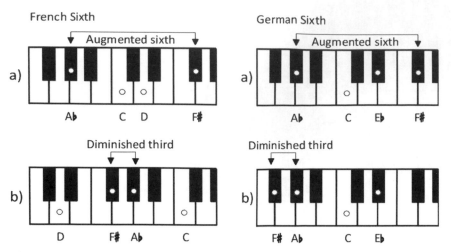

Figure 21.3   Augmented sixth chords as chromatically altered dominants.

position with the note F♯ in the bass. Looking at the German sixth chord in this position, it is easy to see that it is simply a diminished seventh, the third of which has been chromatically flattened. Notice that the augmented sixth interval appears in its inverted form when the chords are viewed from these positions—in other words, as a diminished third.

Viewed from this perspective, augmented sixth chords are simply chromatically altered dominant or secondary dominant chords. As such, augmented sixth chords really belong in the same category as chromatically altered dominants. The proof of this lies in the fact that musicians use a great many altered dominant chords that have that characteristic interval of the augmented sixth (or diminished third). In Figure 21.4, you can see a list of augmented sixth chords—in other words, chromatically altered dominant chords that use the interval of the augmented sixth. The list stops with chromatic variants of the dominant triad, dominant seventh, half-diminished seventh, and diminished seventh. This is because to bring in dominant chords of the ninth, eleventh, and thirteenth would generate an absolutely huge number of chromatic variants.

All of these chords have been used at some time or another by musicians—especially jazz musicians, for whom this list is an improviser's delight. The dominant seventh with flattened or sharpened fifth provides but two good examples. Another is the diminished seventh chord with sharpened fifth, often nicknamed the *Tristan chord* on account of its prodigious use by Wagner in the prelude to his opera *Tristan und Isolde* (1865).

Looking at this list of chords, we can see that every single one has at least one augmented sixth interval. So let us now think about what these chords have to offer us as musicians and composers of our own music. First and foremost, each chromatic variant of the dominant seventh or ninth as seen earlier in this chapter offers its own particular

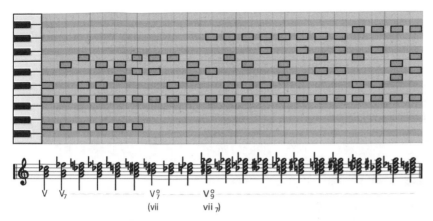

Figure 21.4   Chromatically altered dominant chords using the augmented sixth.

shade of dominant or secondary dominant color. And while some of these chords are enharmonically equivalent to regular diatonic chords, they are distinguished from them by their alterations. Therefore, the second chord on the list is enharmonically equivalent to an E minor triad in first inversion. The difference lies only in the way the two chords are spelled. An E minor chord in first inversion would be spelled as G, B, and E, while this chord is spelled as G, B, and F♭. Although seemingly insignificant, this makes a huge difference between the two chords. For a start, there is a functional difference between them. The E minor chord is diatonic, while this chromatically altered dominant seventh chord can perform a dominant or secondary dominant function.

Then there is the alteration to take into account. Chromatic alterations within this kind of chord are usually treated as tendency tones, which then influence and determine the pathways of resolution/progression of the chord. Therefore, sharp alterations tend to rise upward, rather like secondary leading notes, while flat alterations tend to fall downward, like declining or falling tones. So immediately, any comparison of the chord G B F♭ with a chord of E minor disappears when we realize that the note F♭ of the chromatically altered dominant indicates a tendency to fall to the note E♭—in other words, the third of the tonic minor triad in a regular V7-i cadence.

You can see this chromatic V7-i progression in Figure 21.5(a). Notice that the color, mood, and atmosphere of the V7-i progression is totally different than the regular diatonic V7-i progression. As a result of one alteration, the harmony now has an ethereal and mysterious quality. Notice as well that the chromatically altered chord progression has automatically generated its own unique scalar environment—a six-tone musical scale that clearly offers further opportunities for melodic invention and general composition (see Figure 21.5(b)). It is in this sense that chromatically altered chords are very useful, because they can break the old, tired patterns of chord construction and lead to new, fresh-sounding chords, chord progressions, and even new musical scales.

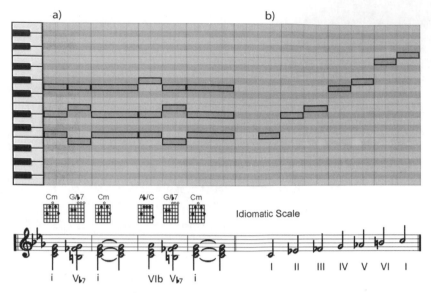

Figure 21.5   Chord progression involving chromatically altered dominant sonority.

Tritone Substitution

The ability to generate unique harmonic colors and scalar environments is only one feature of these chromatically altered dominant chords. They can also be used to create links between distant keys, and these links can then be used to create chord progressions of great color and variety. A good example of this is the technique known as *tritone substitution*, used in jazz harmony. To understand the principle behind this, take a look at Figure 21.6.

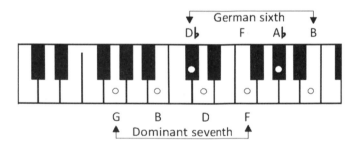

Figure 21.6   Enharmonic equivalence of dominant seventh and German sixth chords.

This diagram compares and contrasts two chords—a chord of the dominant seventh and a chord of the augmented sixth. The first point to consider is that both the dominant seventh chord and the German sixth chord are enharmonically equivalent. This means that if they both used the same bass note, they would both use the same notes on the keyboard. Therefore, for a dominant seventh on G, we would use the notes G, B, D, and F. For the German sixth chord on G, we would use the notes G, B, D, and E♯.

The next point to consider is that the dominant seventh chord on G shares the same tritone as the German sixth chord on the note D♭. This tritone—between notes F and

B—resolves in the same way in both chords, in that it tends to open outwards to the C and E of an implied C major triad. Because the tritone in both of these chords shows the same tendencies, one chord can be opportunistically swapped for the other. In practice, this means that instead of progressing to a regular diatonic seventh chord, we can instead progress to a chromatic chord whose root is a tritone up from that. The result is a fresh influx of new chromatic color into a chord progression as a result of the tritone switch.

Once you understand this principle, you can then apply it flexibly to lift chord progressions out of the ordinary. A good example of this—so that you can see tritone substitution in action—is the Louis Armstrong song "What a Wonderful World" (the music and lyrics of which were written by George David Weiss and Bob Thiele). You can see the chords for the verse section in Figure 21.7(a).

Tritone Substitution
↓

a)	F	Am	Bb	Am	Gm7	A7	Dm	Db	C7	C7	F	F
b)	F	Am	Bb	Am	Gm7	A7	Dm	Gm	C7	C7	F	F
	I	iii	IV	iii	ii7	V7	vi	ii	V7		I	

Figure 21.7 Chord progression in Louis Armstrong's "What a Wonderful World."

Looking at this chord progression, you can see that it is a regular diatonic chord progression in the key of F major except for the use of two chromatic chords. There is the secondary dominant of the submediant A7, which is used to temporarily tonicize the succeeding D minor triad. And then there is the chromatic chord of Db major. This is such an unusual chord to use in the key of F major that we are prompted to look for the reasoning behind its use. The reasoning lies in the technique of tritone substitution. We can see this by comparing the chord progression used in the song to the chord progression shown in (b). This chord progression shows a standard ii-V7-I cadence. However, instead of the usual chord ii—in other words, Gm—a substitute chord has been used whose root is a tritone above the chord of Gm. This represents a very obvious and notable use of tritone substitution. And it is notable because the use of this chromatic chord of Db major not only lifts the entire chord progression, but it also makes the final cadence very distinctive.

Suffice it to say, if you are ever struggling to create a fresh-sounding chord progression, tritone substitution can provide an effective way of generating alternative possibilities.

A Wealth of Chromatically Altered Chords

Chromatic alteration is clearly a rich and fruitful way of varying the sound and color of ordinary chords. Generally, dominant and secondary dominant chords are commonly used for this purpose. Naturally, the more notes in a chord, the more possibilities that the chord will offer for chromatic alteration. Therefore, complex chords, such as dominant ninths, elevenths, and thirteenths, can be altered in a great variety of ways. When we looked at these chords in earlier chapters, we noticed how eleventh and thirteenth chords in particular have a compound nature, consisting of one chord superimposed over another. The upper chord can thus be construed as being one layer and the lower chord—the foundation—another.

This upper layer offers great possibilities for chromatic alteration for the simple reason that the function of a complex six- or seven-note chord is determined by the lower layer. So feasibly, you can introduce chromatic alterations to change the color of the upper layer without interfering with or altering the function of the chord. And these can sometimes give the impression that the lower layer is in one key, the upper layer in another. When this happens, it is called *bitonality* (or *polytonality* if it is more than two keys). In an approach to this type of harmony, it is well worth spending some time taking a dominant eleventh or thirteenth chord and experimenting with chromatically raising and lowering the notes of the chord, especially the notes belonging to the upper layers. Although this can bring the levels of dissonance in a chord up to the hyper levels, these experiments can often result in the creation of some really interesting, complex, and beautiful sonorities.

Non-Dominant Chromatic Alterations

You can also chromatically alter other chords than dominants. Learning how is a matter of taking an ordinary diatonic chord and seeing how it can be chromatically altered and then testing out the result—in other words, experimenting with how the dissonant elements might resolve, chords to which the chromatically altered chord can progress, and so on. A good example of this is the major augmented ninth chord. To create this chord, you simply take a major ninth chord and chromatically raise the ninth. You can see the method of doing this in Figure 21.8(a).

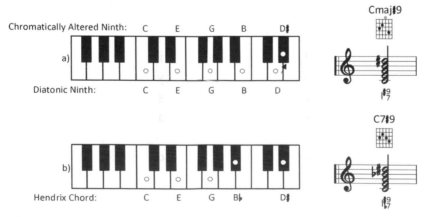

Figure 21.8 Chromatically altered tonic ninth chord.

This particular chord has a very distinctive sound. And it can easily be used as a substitute for the ordinary tonic ninth. A notable feature of this chord of the raised ninth is that when the seventh—note B—is omitted, the result is a compound chord that sounds just like a minor chord being played over a major chord. This compound chord has always been very popular in blues and jazz, especially in closed positions where the simultaneous sounding of a major and minor third give an impression of a "blue" third. Another popular variant of this chord is where the seventh is also flattened, as you can see in Figure 21.8(b). This chord is popularly called the *Hendrix chord* due to its use by Jimi Hendrix in songs such as "Purple Haze."

Experiment with Chromatic Alteration

A complete survey of the practice of chromatic alteration would be impossible in this small volume, as would an investigation of every single chord and its possibilities. Chromatic alteration of ordinary diatonic chords is such an extensive and popular practice, and it produces so many variations and extends into so many areas of advanced harmony, that we simply do not have room for it here. However, as these developments all took place in the first place by musicians and composers experimenting with chromatic alteration, the best approach to learning more about chromatic alteration is to spend time experimenting and investigating its possibilities. Take any chord and apply as many alterations as you can to it. Having done so, then look to see how those alterations affect the color of the chord and its tendencies to progress to other chords. You never know, but through this type of experimenting, you might just come out with a completely new sound.

Conclusion

The main focus of this chapter was on the study and investigation of true chromatic chords. In simple terms, this means that they are ordinary diatonic chords that, through the process of chromatic alteration, are then turned into chords that occupy a purely chromatic world. The first type of chromatic chord we looked at was the chords of the augmented sixth. Beginning with the study of three traditional forms of augmented sixth chords, we then went on to see how augmented sixth chords are really chromatically altered dominant chords. To support this, I showed you a list of many such augmented sixth chords, each of which represented a particular way to alter a dominant triad, diminished triad, diminished seventh chord, or half-diminished seventh chord—all chords of dominant function. I chose one particular chord as an example of the treatment of such chromatic chords, and we saw how just this one chord led to the total transformation of a V7-i cadence, as well as giving rise to its own idiomatic scalar environment.

From there, we then went on to look at the technique of tritone substitution—a technique that depends upon the enharmonic equivalence of the dominant seventh chord to a chromatically altered chord of the augmented sixth. We also looked at some of the possibilities for chromatically altering non-dominant chords and observed that any diatonic chord could feasibly be altered by chromatically raising or lowering certain notes. Finally, we observed that because chromatic alteration yields so many possibilities, it is not possible to study the subject with any hope of completion within a small volume. So, I recommended that you experiment with chromatic alteration and see what you can come up with. This type of experiment, using your own ears, can often lead to more exciting results than any amount of research on a topic.

Having studied chromatic harmony over the last few chapters, it is now time to consider the final topic of this book. That is the topic of modal harmony. Strictly speaking, modal harmony is not the same as functional harmony. Functional harmony has grown up from the use of the major and minor scales. Modal harmony, however, looks beyond the major and minor scales and uses scales that are not strictly a part of the system of functional harmony. Yet there is a strong connection between the two systems, and if you have a grounding in functional harmony, modal harmony will give you no problems whatsoever, provided that you understand what that connection is.

22 Modal Harmony

I n a nutshell, modal harmony is basically the use of harmony within scales other than the major or minor scale. It therefore embraces the harmonic practices used very much in folk, ethnic, and other such popular music that commonly uses modal scales. Examples of these scales are the Dorian, the Mixolydian, or the Hungarian minor that I talked about in *Music Theory for Computer Musicians* (Course Technology PTR, 2008). This subject of modal harmony is a vast topic, and to study all of its features would easily require a separate volume. Therefore, in this chapter all that we can really do is to offer an introduction to modal harmony. If you have followed this book so far, that means you now have a good appreciation at least of functional harmony and some of its various offshoots. This appreciation will bear you in good stead as you approach modal harmony—and hopefully, using the indications given here, coupled with your experience and practice of functional harmony, you should have all of the ingredients necessary to master the arts of modal harmony.

In some measure, modal harmony in the modern sense arose out of the practice of modal interchange. As I have already shown, modal interchange enables an expansion of the number of chords that are available within a given key. This expansion in turn enables us to create chord progressions that cleverly mix the colors of the major and minor keys together. One of the important offshoots of this is that when we do mix chords from the major and minor scales, we find that we are gradually brought into the orbit of harmony that is based on modes other than the major and minor scales.

This applies in two senses. It applies to the seven diatonic modes so commonly used in modern popular music and also to other modes, often called *artificial scales,* many of which are also used in modern popular music—particularly rock music, which has always been known for its liberal approach to musical scales. But let us first consider the seven diatonic modes.

Diatonic Modal Harmony

The seven diatonic modes have always been immensely popular with musicians and composers on account of the wealth of melodic and chordal color that these modes can evoke. Indeed, I have never met a musician or composer who has not admitted to a fascination with these old modal scales. Each scale tends to generate its own particular mood or color, from the dark and often Spanish feel of the Phrygian mode, to the bright humor and playfulness of the Lydian mode.

Ordinarily the seven diatonic modes are studied in a sequence of changing tonics that rises up the seven white notes of the keyboard. As a part of this sequence the Ionian mode is on note C, the Dorian mode on note D, the Phrygian mode on note E, and so on. However, to learn modal harmony, you need to think of the modes in a different way. You must think of them as emanating from the same tonic note. That is the Ionian mode on C, the Phrygian mode on C, and so on. This is because modal harmony uses a common pot of chords based on the harmonic form of the chromatic scale of a given key. Each mode is thereby viewed as a particular selection of notes from that chromatic scale. And the chords to be used in the modal harmony are selected accordingly. So our first job is to transpose the seven modes onto a common keynote. In Figure 22.1, you can see all seven of these modes that use the common tonic note of C.

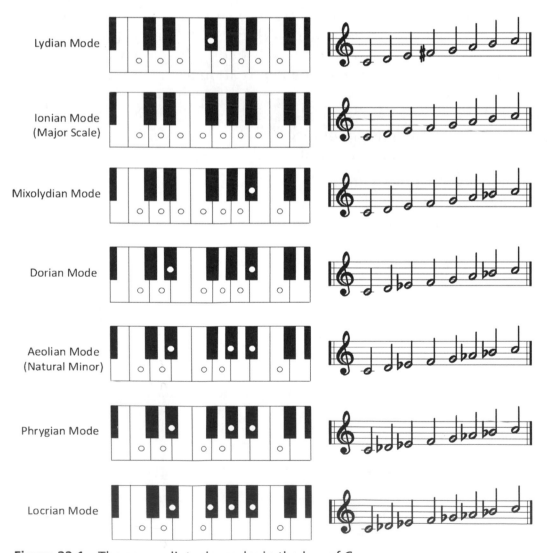

Figure 22.1 The seven diatonic modes in the key of C.

Modal Colors

As emanating from a common keynote, each mode is viewed as being a sum of intervals generated from that common keynote. Therefore, the Lydian mode at the very top, in addition to the common tonic, uses a major second, major third, augmented fourth, perfect fifth, major sixth, and major seventh. Representing a sum of bright intervals (major and augmented), the Lydian mode is accordingly the brightest mode of the group. As the list goes down, the number of bright major and augmented intervals decreases one at a time, and the number of dark, minor, or diminished intervals increases one at a time. The scale therefore ends at the bottom with the darkest mode of all—the Locrian mode, with its minor second, minor third, perfect fourth, diminished fifth, minor sixth, and minor seventh. As such, the seven modes represent a nice graduation of color—rather like the colors of the rainbow—with the Lydian mode being the brightest mode at the top, and the Locrian mode being the darkest mode at the bottom.

The Harmonic Form of Chromatic Scale

When the modes are all viewed as emanating from a common tonic, to be able to obtain all seven modes from a given tonic note, we need a complete chromatic scale. Therefore, for the Phrygian mode we need a flat supertonic degree; for the Lydian, Ionian, Mixolydian, Dorian, and Aeolian modes, we need a major supertonic degree. Table 22.1 presents this complete chromatic scale whose tonic note is C. It is called the harmonic form of the chromatic scale because each degree of the scale represents a relationship with the central tonic note. This relationship is represented as an interval with the tonic.

Table 22.1 Harmonic Form of Chromatic Scale

Degree	Note	Interval with Tonic	Mode
I	C	Tonic	All
bII	Db	Minor second	Locrian, Phrygian
II	D	Major second	All except Phrygian and Locrian
bIII	Eb	Minor third	Locrian, Phrygian, Aeolian, Dorian
III	E	Major third	Mixolydian, Ionian, Lydian
IV	F	Perfect fourth	All except for Locrian and Lydian
#IV	F#	Augmented fourth	Lydian
bV	Gb	Diminished fifth	Locrian
V	G	Perfect fifth	All except for Locrian and Lydian
bVI	Ab	Minor sixth	Dorian, Aeolian, Phrygian, Locrian
VI	A	Major sixth	Dorian, Mixolydian, Ionian, Lydian
bVII	Bb	Minor seventh	All except for Ionian and Lydian
VII	B	Major seventh	Lydian, Ionian

Therefore, the second degree of the Phrygian mode is the flat supertonic degree of the harmonic form of chromatic scale—forming with the tonic note an interval of a minor second. The second degree of the Ionian mode is the regular supertonic degree of the harmonic form of the chromatic scale. This degree forms an interval of a major second with the tonic note. In this way, each mode represents a sum of particular interval relations to the common tonic note. So let us now see how this applies to the practice of modal harmony.

A Common Chromatic Pot of Chords

Looking at the harmonic form of the chromatic scale, it becomes easy to see how the practice of modal interchange between the major and minor modes leads us to the very edges of the territory of modal harmony. This is because modal interchange leads to the existence of a common pot of chords whose roots cover virtually every degree of this chromatic scale. On the first degree, we have the tonic major or minor triad. On the flat supertonic degree, there is the Neapolitan triad. On the supertonic there is a minor triad, and so on. In other words, the process of modal interchange leads to the use of a range of chords that is suitable for use not just in terms of the major and minor scales, but also in terms of this larger group of diatonic modes. Take a look at Table 22.2. This

Table 22.2 Range of Common Chords (Major Scale = Ionian, Minor Scale = Aeolian)

Chord			Symbols	Mode/Modes of Origin
C	E	G	C	Lydian, Ionian, Mixolydian
C	Eb	G	Cm	Dorian, Aeolian, Phrygian
Db	F	Ab	Db	Phrygian
D	F	A	Dm	Ionian, Mixolydian, Dorian, Aeolian
D	F#	A	D	Lydian
Eb	G	Bb	Eb	Dorian, Aeolian, Phrygian
E	G	B	Em	Lydian, Ionian
F	Ab	C	Fm	Aeolian, Phrygian
F	A	C	F	Ionian, Mixolydian, Dorian
G	Bb	D	Gm	Mixolydian, Dorian, Aeolian
G	B	D	G	Lydian, Ionian
Ab	C	Eb	Ab	Aeolian, Phrygian
A	C	E	Am	Lydian, Ionian, Mixolydian
Bb	D	F	Bb	Mixolydian, Dorian, Aeolian
B	D	F#	Bm	Lydian

sets out the range of common triads available through modal interchange and the modes that use those triads.

The only exception to this is the Locrian mode, which is not included on this list. This is because the Locrian mode has a diminished triad on the tonic degree. A diminished triad cannot be established as a tonic chord because a diminished triad is an agent of dominant function. Therefore, harmony, as far as the Locrian mode is concerned, is a matter of perpetuating and emphasizing the feeling of dominant tension inherent to the chord on the first degree of the scale. And this is the only real possibility the Locrian mode offers for harmony. Yet this does not mean that the Locrian mode is unusable. It is a matter of recognizing and working with the forces it generates rather than trying to force it to obey traditional rules.

For harmony in all of the other modes, it is a simple matter of selecting from the common pot of chords on the chromatic scale the chords that are needed. Therefore, in Figure 22.2(a), I have selected the chords of B♭, F, and C major to produce a characteristically Mixolydian chord progression. In Figure 22.2(b), I have selected the chords of C minor, E♭, and F major to create a characteristically Dorian three-chord progression.

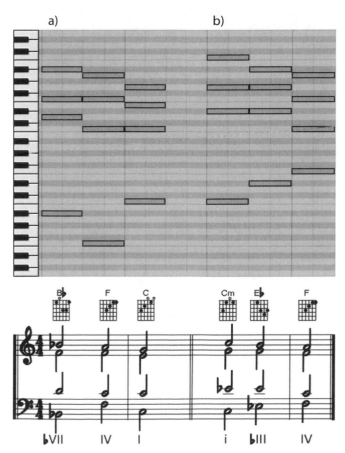

Figure 22.2 Modal chord progressions.

Suppressing the Tonicizing Influence of the Dominant Seventh

If you have learned the principles of functional harmony up to this point, selecting the common chords appropriate for your modal progression or melody will be a very easy thing to do. Arranging those chords in a logical chord progression and voicing each chord appropriately will also be easy for you. The salient issue as far as modal harmony is concerned is suppressing the tonicizing influence of the dominant seventh chord. This is because whenever we hear a dominant seventh chord, our ear expects a tonic chord to follow. With the Ionian mode this is fortuitous because the dominant seventh chord is on the fifth degree. But with the other modes, the dominant seventh chord is on other scale degrees. As far as the Lydian mode is concerned, we find the dominant seventh chord on the second degree of the scale. This means that if we are not careful about our use of this chord, there will be a tonicizing effect toward chord V of the Lydian mode. And once this takes place, the whole effect of the mode is destroyed. The chord progression will sound like it is being written in the major scale on the fifth degree (the scale of G major if the tonic of the Lydian mode is note C). So when handling the chords of a given mode, you need to learn to suppress, avoid, or subvert the tendencies of the dominant seventh chord. The exception to this practice is perhaps the Mixolydian mode, where the tonic seventh is a complete dominant seventh chord. This makes the dominant seventh chord really hard to avoid. So the answer here, as found in countless rock and popular music songs in the Mixolydian mode, is to work with it rather than against it and simply revel in that feeling of unresolved dominant tension!

Expanding the Range of Modes

There is another reason for viewing the modes as emanating from a common tonic. This again has to do with the process of modal interchange. The general effect of modal interchange is that it leads to a subtle blurring of the distinctions between the major and minor scale systems to the point that the only recognizable feature that really identifies the key is the character of the tonic triad. When the tonic triad is major, the chord progression automatically speaks of the major key; and when the tonic triad is minor, the chord progression will automatically speak to us of the minor key. In this respect, the other modes that we have just looked at are simply either variations of the major tonality due to their major tonic triad (Lydian, Ionian, and Mixolydian) or else variations of the minor tonality due to their minor tonic triad (Dorian, Aeolian, and Phrygian).

Looking at modes in this way—as particular variations of a major or minor tonality—leads in turn to the point where an expansion of modal scales becomes possible. A simple example of this that is easy to appreciate is the harmonic major mode, which is identical to the regular major scale except for its flat sixth degree. This scale is created where a minor subdominant triad is used as a substitute for the regular major subdominant triad. Another example is the double harmonic mode, which again is identical to the major scale except for its flat second and sixth degrees. This scale arises when a Neapolitan triad (Db, F, and Ab) is used as a substitute for the customary minor supertonic triad (D, F, and A). Like the regular diatonic modes we have just considered, therefore, these other modes tend to be generated when we select certain chords from the common pot of chords present in the chromatic scale of that key (as shown in Table 22.1). In Table 22.3, you will find a list of the most common modal variations that are or have been used.

Table 22.3 Expanded Range of Seven Note Modes

I	II	III	IV	V	VI	VII	VIII	Common Name
C	Db	Eb	F	G	Ab	Bb	C	Phrygian
C	Db	Eb	F	G	Ab	B	C	Harmonic Phrygian
C	Db	Eb	F	G	A	Bb	C	Phrygian Sharp Six
C	Db	Eb	F	G	A	B	C	Leading Whole Tone
C	D	Eb	F	G	Ab	Bb	C	Aeolian/Natural Minor
C	D	Eb	F	G	Ab	B	C	Harmonic Minor
C	D	Eb	F	G	A	B	C	Melodic Minor/Jazz Scale
C	D	Eb	F	G	A	Bb	C	Dorian
C	D	Eb	F#	G	Ab	B	C	Hungarian Minor
C	Db	E	F	G	Ab	Bb	C	Phrygian Sharp Three
C	Db	E	F	G	Ab	B	C	Double Harmonic
C	Db	E	F	G	A	B	C	Neapolitan Major
C	Db	E	F	G	A	Bb	C	Neapolitan Mixolydian
C	D	E	F#	G	A	B	C	Lydian
C	D	E	F#	G	A	Bb	C	Harmonic Scale
C	D	E	F	G	Ab	Bb	C	Major/Minor
C	D	E	F	G	Ab	B	C	Harmonic Major
C	D	E	F	G	A	B	C	Ionian/Major
C	D	E	F	G	A	Bb	C	Mixolydian

The third degree of each scale determines whether a given mode belongs to the major or minor side of tonality. Where the mode has a major third degree, it is regarded as being a bright, major color; whereas when a mode has a minor third degree, it is regarded as being a darker minor color. Therefore, the double harmonic mode is a major modal color, while the leading whole tone mode is a minor modal color.

Each mode represents a fascinating mix of colors in its own right. And interest in the mode lies in discovering what these are and bringing them out in the music that uses them. Bear in mind that when you're trying to use these scales, not all of them sit very well with the principles of traditional functional-type harmony. This is because they often represent a curious mixture of regular diatonic chords and chromatic chords. So their suitability for functional-type harmony is often determined by how many common triads they have. Therefore, when using a given mode, first find out the chords available to it. In Figure 22.3, you can see the chords available within the double harmonic scale.

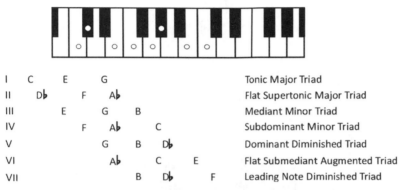

I	C	E	G		Tonic Major Triad
II	Db	F	Ab		Flat Supertonic Major Triad
III	E	G	B		Mediant Minor Triad
IV	F	Ab	C		Subdominant Minor Triad
V	G	B	Db		Dominant Diminished Triad
VI	Ab	C	E		Flat Submediant Augmented Triad
VII	B	Db	F		Leading Note Diminished Triad

Figure 22.3 Analyzing the chords within a modal scale (the double harmonic scale).

Looking at these, you can see that we have a common triad on degrees I, II, III, and IV; a diminished triad on degrees V and VII; and an augmented triad on degree VI. What an amazing concoction of triads! Once you have taken note of the chords, you can then home in on the common triads—in this case, those on degrees I, II, III, and IV—and build your chord progression around those. Each mode offers its own set of characteristic colors. The chromatic progression from Db major to E minor, for example, is a very strong characteristic color in this particular modal scale. Having discovered this through careful listening, we can then bring that into our improvisations.

Breakdown of the Principles of Functional Harmony

In some of these modes, the principles of functional harmony clearly begin to break down and are just not applicable. A good example is the leading whole tone scale, which offers only one usable common triad— the minor triad on degree I. So at least in this case we have a good tonic triad that we can use. All of the other triads are either augmented or diminished. The way to approach these is to look for chords that can represent functional triads by proxy. The augmented triad on degree III is a good example because when in first inversion (using the notes G, B, and Eb), it has the profile of a dominant thirteenth chord with the fifth, seventh, ninth, and eleventh missing. So in this case, we can use this augmented triad as a dominant substitute. And the augmented triad on degree II of the scale also offers a usable pre-dominant chord—in other words, a good substitute for the subdominant. In this way, we can build a chord progression in such a way that we work with the chords available in the mode. A good example is Figure 22.4, in which only three chords are used: the tonic minor triad and the two augmented triads on degrees II and III.

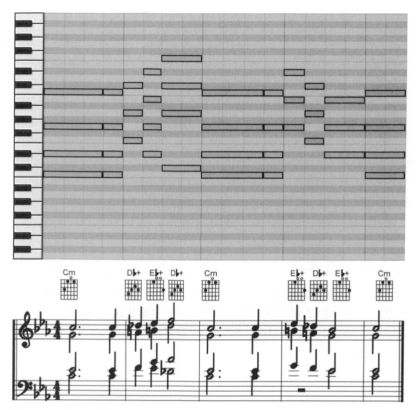

Figure 22.4   Chord progression using the leading whole tone scale.

Immerse Yourself in a World of Modal Color

If the idea of these alternative modes interests you, you can make great progress with them by learning a particular mode—say, at the keyboard—and then totally immersing yourself in the particular world of sound that it tends to generate. Having already learned the principles of functional harmony, matters of melody, harmony, and chords to use will all automatically emerge as a result of that immersion process. Perhaps the most useful thing to bear in mind with these major and minor modal variants is that they are modes that definitely suit an improvisational approach in order to discover those harmonies and modal colors that attract and please your own ear. Once you have found these, you can build from there. And above all, have fun with them!

Conclusion

In this chapter we looked at the idea of modal harmony as a basic byproduct of modal interchange. The reasoning for this is based on the logic that modal interchange led to an expansion of the chords that could be used in a given key. This expansion in turn led to the possibility of homing in upon selections of chords that suggested and corresponded to certain traditional modes. We approached the seven diatonic modes and emphasized the importance of viewing these modes as all emanating from a central tonic note. This led to the recognition of each mode as a basic modal color that derived from the particular selection of intervals from the chromatic scale of that key.

We saw the basic issue of modal harmony to be a relatively simple one when it is approached after a study of functional harmony. And in particular, a study of functional harmony can help one to understand and then suppress the tonicizing influence of the dominant seventh and its derivatives. In addition to the seven diatonic modes, we looked at other modes as the common products of the process of modal interchange. Like modal chord progressions, these other modes also emerge from the use of particular selections of chords from the common pot of the chromatic scale. We analyzed one such mode in terms of its chordal constituents, while we looked at another mode in terms of the way it implied a basic breakdown of the principles of functional harmony. We also discussed methods of both adapting to and taking advantage of that eventuality.

Although in this chapter it was only possible to briefly introduce the idea of modal harmony, I hope that this introduction will offer you a sound platform on which to study and explore modal harmony further. Modal harmony is undoubtedly a fascinating topic of investigation, and it is something that has generated (and continues to generate) new and exciting musical possibilities.

23 | Conclusion

I n a book of this sort, whose main concern has been the practical materials of harmony, it has unfortunately been impossible to go into lengthy analyses of the use of these materials in a wide body of music—either classical or modern. Aside from passing and cursory references, this book has been more interested in defining what those basic materials are and discussing various general features that have surrounded their use. The reason for this is that in the end, people who learn the practical principles of harmony probably do so in order to improve their ability to produce their own music. In doing so, it is then hoped that they will also develop their own unique approach to the use of the basic materials and concepts of musical harmony. This is because the principles of musical harmony are not and can never be written in stone. They are always flexible, adaptable, and forever subject to further innovation and development.

In studying the subject, though, there are certain basic principles that cannot be dismissed. Each chapter in this book considered these basic principles. After a brief introduction to the subject of musical harmony, we went on to see how the interval represents the basic building block of musical harmony and how, ultimately, all chords are nothing more than a combination of musical intervals. I stressed the importance of knowing these intervals—knowledge that covers an appreciation of their aural qualities, how intervals are both named and represented, and the difference between simple and compound intervals. This knowledge of course needs to be built upon a proper foundation of understanding of intervals that already includes knowledge of interval inversions and enharmonic equivalence among intervals.

From there, we went on to consider the different types of harmony that composers can use and how the functional harmony of the classical era of music still has a great relevance for today's music. Associated with the major and minor scales of the classical key system, we saw the importance of functional harmony as providing us with a good foundation from which to approach the study of harmony generally.

We then considered the principles of part writing, based on the idea that although harmony is ultimately concerned with the simultaneous combination of different notes, the melodic lines that serve to connect those harmonies together are of equal importance. For harmony to work, in other words, the various melodic parts that make up the harmony need to have their own logical melodic progression. It is here that we first meet some of the traditional rules of musical harmony, such as the prohibition of consecutive octaves and fifths, hidden fifths and octaves, and trying to avoid overlapping between voices. Although I do not wish to lay down any rules in this book, I pointed out that behind the rules there was often a certain logic, and that rather than trying to simply blindly obey any rules of harmony, we should certainly take into account the logic behind them—especially when studying the principles of harmony that ultimately stem from the classical tradition.

From there we went on to consider how to voice a common triad. Involving principles such as spacing, doubling, and chordal inversion, we discussed the importance of voicing a chord in a well-rounded and balanced way. Harmony, after all, concerns itself with the progression of chords, but unless we can voice a single chord effectively in the first place, we are not going to do a very good job of voicing an entire chord progression.

I devoted a whole chapter to the subject of tonic and dominant harmony because these represent the two most important chordal functions underlying the functional system of harmony. By learning about tonic and dominant harmony, therefore, we put ourselves in a good position to develop a working knowledge of other chordal functions broached over the chapters that followed, such as the subdominant, mediant, or submediant.

Everything from the eighth chapter onward basically amounted to a study of the way in which the basic triadic harmonies represented by the seven triads of the scale can be decorated and embellished—either melodically, through the use of embellishments such as the passing note and auxiliary, or harmonically, through the incorporation of embellishing extensions, such as the seventh, ninth, eleventh, and thirteenth. All of this amounts to various ways and means of handling dissonance as a constructive force in musical harmony.

When we went on to study the first level of extension—the seventh—the study was made more complex because of differences in attitude toward the seventh in general. In a classical sense, the seventh is a dissonance and is therefore treated in a formulaic way involving both preparation and resolution. In a more modern sense, the seventh is an integral part of the chord and therefore does not necessarily need to be either prepared or resolved. Therefore, although in classical times consecutive dissonances such as seconds and sevenths tended to be avoided, in modern music this practice is all rather normal. So, we discussed the importance of appreciating both viewpoints. In one musical context, unprepared and unresolved sevenths might sound out of place, while in another context they can sound absolutely great.

This difference between traditional and modern practice was seen to be further widened with chords of the ninth, eleventh, and thirteenth. Although such chords can be treated in conventional ways, they can also be treated in more modern and unconventional ways. In fact, we saw thirteenth-chord harmony, potentially involving all seven notes of the scale within a chord, to be such a complex issue that it became clear that even today, not all of the implications of the chord of the thirteenth are fully understood. As such, free use of the thirteenth chord brings us to the very cutting edge of musical harmony.

The last few chapters went on to consider the important topic of chromatic harmony on three levels. First we saw how, through the process of modal interchange, chord progressions can be composed within a much wider and broader territory that feasibly covers every note of the chromatic scale. Then we saw how, through the use of secondary dominant harmony, chord progressions can also be given more color, tonal definition, and an expanded range that touches upon the keys embraced by all of the common triads of a key. Finally, we went on to consider the use of true chromatic chords—that is, chords that, not belonging to or being borrowed from any other particular key, occupy a purely chromatic world in their own right. These, too, were seen as an important source of enrichment of chord progressions and the expansion of their range beyond the limits of the major and minor scales. Finally, we touched upon the subject of modal harmony and saw how the practice of modal interchange leads to the very fringes of modal harmony, as well as the point at which harmony in a functional sense begins to break down and become less applicable. We considered various modes, together with various methods for approaching and using these modes in our music.

Discussing these various features of harmony is one thing; putting them into practice is another. They can only really be grasped through the completion of practical exercises—both exercises of the kind presented within this book and exercises devised by you. Ideally, you should be able to harmonize any melodic lead that you compose and add a suitable harmony above any given bass line. And you should be able to find the chords that are suitable for the job. What kind of harmonization would best suit a given lead? Triadic harmony that has a traditional sound or harmony that uses extensions and has more of a hard dissonant edge? Such are the some of the questions that you need to answer when adding a harmony either above or below a given melodic line. Ideally, you should also be able to put together chord progressions that can often provide a great stimulus from which to create new music. But to be able to do this, you need to understand the logic by which one chord can connect with another. I hope this book has helped you with your ability to do this in an effective way that you find useful for your own music.

References and Recommended Further Reading

Hindemith, Paul. *Traditional Harmony*. Schott Music Intl. Mainz: 1968.

Persichetti, Vincent. *Twentieth-Century Harmony: Creative Aspects and Practice*. Norton. New York: 1961.

Piston, Walter. *Harmony*. Fifth edition. Norton. New York: 1988.

UNIVERSITY OF CHESTER WARRINGTON CAMPUS

Prout, Ebenezer. *Harmony: Its Theory and Practice*. University Press of the Pacific. Honolulu: 2004.

Steblin, Rita. *A History of Key Characteristics in the 18th and Early 19th Centuries*. UMI Research Press. Ann Arbor: 1983.

Steinitz, Paul. *One Hundred Tunes for Harmonization from the Great Masters*. Novello. London: 1998.

Index